Language as a Local Practice

Language as a Local Practice addresses questions of language, locality and practice as a way of moving forward in our understanding of how language operates as an integrated social and spatial activity.

By taking each of these three elements – language, locality and practice – and exploring how they relate to each other, *Language as a Local Practice* opens up new ways of thinking about language. It questions assumptions about languages as systems or as countable entities, and suggests instead that language emerges from the activities it performs. To look at language as a practice is to view language as an activity rather than a structure, as something we do rather than a system we draw on, as a material part of social and cultural life rather than an abstract entity.

Language as a Local Practice draws on a variety of contexts of language use, from bank machines to postcards, Indian newspaper articles to fish-naming in the Philippines, urban graffiti to mission statements, suggesting that rather than thinking in terms of language use in context, we need to consider how language, space and place are related, how language creates the contexts where it is used, how languages are the products of socially located activities and how they are part of the action.

Language as a Local Practice will be of interest to students on advanced undergraduate and postgraduate courses in Applied Linguistics, Language Education, TESOL, Literacy and Cultural Studies.

Alastair Pennycook is Professor of Language Studies at the University of Technology, Sydney. Publications include *English and the discourses of colonialism* (Routledge, 1998), *Critical applied linguistics: A critical introduction* (Lawrence Erlbaum, 2001) and *Global Englishes and transcultural flows* (Routledge, 2007), which won the BAAL Book award in 2008.

Language as a Local Practice

Alastair Pennycook

Routledge
Taylor & Francis Group

LONDON AND NEW YORK

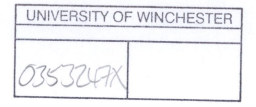
First edition published 2010 by Routledge
2 Park Square, Milton Park, Abingdon, OX14 4RN

Simultaneously published in the USA and Canada by Routledge
711 Third Avenue, New York, NY 10017

Routledge is an imprint of the Taylor & Francis Group, an informa business

© 2010 Alastair Pennycook

Typeset in Times New Roman by Taylor & Francis Books
Printed and bound in Great Britain by CPI Antony Rowe, Chippenham

British Library Cataloguing in Publication Data
A catalogue record for this book is available from the British Library

Library of Congress Cataloging in Publication Data
Pennycook, Alastair, 1957-
Language as a local practice / Alastair Pennycook. – 1st ed.
p. cm.
Includes bibliographical references and index.
1. Sociolinguistics. 2. Language and languages – Variation. I. Title.
P40.P4115 2010
306.44 – dc22
2009037317

ISBN10: 0-415-54750-4 (hbk)
ISBN10: 0-415-54751-2 (pbk)
ISBN10: 0-203-84622-2 (ebk)

ISBN13: 978-0-415-54750-5 (hbk)
ISBN13: 978-0-415-54751-2 (pbk)
ISBN13: 978-0-203-84622-3 (ebk)

Contents

Acknowledgements

My particular interest in the term *practice* grew out of a series of seminars and workshops run by my colleagues in the Centre for Research on Learning and Change at the University of Technology Sydney (UTS). I am particularly grateful for the various conversations, discussions, readings and debates with Paul Hager, Alison Lee, Roger Dunston, Donna Rooney, Ann Reich, Hermine Scheeres, Nicky Solomon, Keiko Yasukawa and others, as well as invited speakers such as Bill Green and Steven Kemmis, who were more than generous with their time and ideas. I am fortunate too that the Language Studies Academic Group formed in 2008 has been able to maintain a strong intellectual focus on language matters, and I am grateful to all members of that group for their sustenance. Theo van Leeuwen, a member of that group as well as being Dean of the Faculty of Arts and Social Sciences at UTS, has been magnanimous with his ideas and support. I have been lucky in my colleagues. Meanwhile a new generation of doctoral students has continued to push my thinking in different directions: Julie Choi, Takako Yoshida, Maria Harissi, Marianne Grey, Bong Jeong Lee, Breda O'Hara Davies. And it is a great pleasure to be able to continue to work with former students, now colleagues and co-authors, such as Celia Thompson, Ros Appleby and Emi Otsuji.

As ever, I am greatly indebted to that wonderful worldwide community of scholars with whom I am privileged to be able to talk through my ideas, and from whom I learn so much, including Lynn Mario Menezes de Souza, Elana Shohamy, Bonny Norton, Vaidehi Ramanathan, Tim McNamara, Stephen May, Brian Morgan, Radhakrishnan, Sinfree Makoni, Suresh Canagarajah, Jan Blommaert, Chris Stroud, Samy Alim, Awad Ibrahim, Ryuko Kubota, Claire Kramsch, Ruanni Tupas, Beatriz Lorente, Angel Lin, Adrian Blackledge, Monica Heller, David Block, Ingrid Piller, Kimie Takahashi, Cynthia Nelson, Brian Paltridge, Martin Nakata, and many others. Thanks as ever to Dominique Estival, flight instructor and real linguist, for attempts to keep my ideas on the straight and level, and for supporting them nonetheless.

A number of parts of this book have been given a public airing elsewhere. Thanks for the chance to talk about the idea of language practices in various forums, amongst which: *Popular cultures and the making of new multilingualisms*, invited talk at the Multilingual citizenship and cities in transition symposium, University of the Western Cape, Cape Town, South Africa, July 2008; *Spatial narrations: Graffscapes and city souls*, plenary address at the Applied Linguistics Association of Australia, July 2008; *Language as local practice*, 24th Annual Singapore Association of Applied Linguistics Distinguished Speaker Lecture, Singapore, April 2008; *Changing Practices in Global ELT*, plenary address to the IATEFL Conference, Exeter, UK, April 2008; *Practice as the new discourse*, plenary address to the Discourse and Cultural Practices Conference, Sydney, December 2007. Thanks to all those – Lionel Wee, Chng Huang Hoon, Ruanni Tupas, Beatriz Lorente, Ruth Wodak, Chris Candlin, Claire Kramsch, Ryuko Kubota, Ahmar Maboob, Chris Stroud and many others – who have given me feedback on these and other talks.

Thanks to Oxford University Press for permission to use Chapter 3, 'The *Reverend on Ice* again: similarity, difference and relocalisation' – a revised version of A. Pennycook, (2007) 'The rotation gets thick, the constraints get thin: creativity, recontextualization and difference', *Applied Linguistics*, 28(4) 579–96. Thanks too to the editors of that special edition of *Applied Linguistics*, Janet Maybin and Joan Swann, and to Guy Cook and Ronald Carter for further comments on earlier versions of the paper. Permission to reuse parts of earlier papers for Chapter 4, 'Talking in the city: the linguistic landscaping of locality', has been kindly granted by Routledge for a revised version of Pennycook (2009) 'Linguistic landscapes and the transgressive semiotics of graffiti', in E Shohamy and D Gorter (eds) *Linguistic Landscape: Expanding the scenery*; and by Continuum for a different version of that paper: 'Spatial narrations: Graffscapes and city souls', in A Jaworski and C Thurlow (eds) *Semiotic landscapes: language, image, space*. I am indebted to Dirk Gorter and Elana Shohamy for feedback on that first paper and to Crispin Thurlow's and Adam Jaworski's insightful comments on the second paper. Chapter 5 'Kerala tuskers: language as already local', is a revised version of Pennycook (2010) 'Rethinking origins and localization in global Englishes', in T. Omoniyi and M. Saxena (eds) *Contending with world Englishes in globalization*. My thanks to Mutlilingual Matters for permission to publish a revised version of that paper. I am grateful to Springer for permission to use a greatly revised version of Pennycook (2004) 'Language policy and the ecological turn', *Language Policy*, 3 (213–39) in Chapter 6, '*Alibangbang* and ecologies of local language practices'. Anonymous reviewers have also of course played an important role in the development of these papers.

1   Introduction

Language as a local practice

This book is about language, place and doing, about language as a form of action in a specific place and time. In talking of language as a local practice, I am seeking to address far wider concerns than a first reading of these terms might suggest. To talk of language as local practice might appear to invoke nothing more than the sociolinguistic truism that people use languages in particular contexts. This book, by contrast, approaches the issue from a different perspective: the idea that languages are systems of communication that are used by people in different contexts is challenged in favour of a view of language as a local practice whereby languages are a product of the deeply social and cultural activities in which people engage. The focus here is not therefore on language use in context, or the relations between language and particular places. Rather, this book questions the meanings of all these terms – language, local and practice – in conjunction: language is examined here in ways that go against some common assumptions about language systems; locality is explored in its complex manifestations as place; and practice is viewed in terms of mediated social activity. This opens up a range of ways of thinking about the interrelationships among language, place and doing.

The notion of the local has become an increasingly significant focus across the social sciences, to a large extent as a reaction to what has been seen as broad, ungrounded theorizing throughout much of the 20th century. Rather than talk about human nature, universal cognition, or language structure, the focus has shifted towards the local, the grounded, the particular. To talk of practices has also become common. We add the term to words such as language, literacy and discourse to turn these into things we do, rather than abstract entities: scholars of literacy are interested in literacy practices; research across fields of language studies asks what language practices people are engaged in. More broadly, there is a growing interest in the practices of everyday life. This is a move, similar to the orientation towards the local, to capture what actually happens in particular places and at particular times. It is a shift away from broad abstractions about language, discourse and society towards local activity as part of everyday life. To talk of language as a local practice, then, is about much more than language use (practice) in context (locality). To take the notion of locality seriously, rather than merely juxtaposing it with the global, the universal or the abstract is to engage with ideas of place and space that in turn require us to examine time, movement and interaction. To think in terms of practices is to make social activity central, to ask how it is we do things as we do, how activities are established, regulated and changed. Practices are not just things we do, but rather bundles of activities that are the central organization of social life.

Once we bring language into the picture, and consider language to be a local practice, and therefore a central organizing activity of social life that is acted out in specific places, a number of common assumptions about language can no longer hold. The notion of language as a system is challenged in favour of a view of language as doing. A discussion of language in place will open up an understanding of the interactive nature of our physical environments, suggesting not so much that language happens in particular places, but rather that language use is part of a multifaceted interplay between humans and the world. What we do with language in a particular place is a result of our interpretation of that place; and the language practices we engage in reinforce that reading of place. What we do with language within different institutions – churches, schools, hospitals – for example, depends on our reading of these physical, institutional, social and cultural spaces. We may kneel and pray, stand and sing, direct classroom activity, write on the margins of a textbook, translate between patient and doctor, ask when a cut hand might get seen to, or spray-paint the back wall; and as we do so, we remake the language, and the space in which this happens.

Viewing language as action and as part of how places are interpreted, how the meaning of places is reinforced or changed, suggests that thinking about language and locality can no longer be contained with a notion of language in context.[1] The notion of language as practice takes us away from a notion of language as a pre-given entity that may be used in a location and looks, by contrast, at language as part of diverse social activity. Social life is "policed by a range of such practices as negotiation practices, political practices, cooking practices, banking practices, recreation practices, religious practices, and educational practices" (Schatzki, 2002, p. 70). Practices are the key way in which everyday social activity is organized, and language practices, as one such set of practices, are a central part of daily social organization. This exploration of language as local practice takes us in a different direction from studies of the variability brought about in a pre-given language system through its contextual deployment, since it questions not only what we mean by language but also what we mean by context. To look at language as a practice is to view language as an activity rather than a structure, as something we do rather than a system we draw on, as a material part of social and cultural life rather than an abstract entity. As Bourdieu (1977) reminds us, practices are actions with a history, suggesting that when we think in terms of language practices, we need to account for both time and space, history and location.

In this book, therefore, I will address the questions of language, locality and practice as a way of moving forward in our understanding of how language operates as an integrated social and spatial activity. I will deal in depth with each term – language, locality and practice – and in doing so will draw on different perspectives and domains, from practice theory to spatial theory, from graffiti to language ecology. The notions of time, place and locality will come under scrutiny here from a number of different directions. The idea of language spread, for example, will be questioned from a position that considers the possibility of multiple origins: language may not have spread and taken on local characteristics so much as being already local. The notion of creativity will be explored as a way of asking how it is that a particular version of language with a central core and divergent edges has come to hold sway. I will look at how language is related to time and space, and the doing of the everyday, and ask how we can understand repetition as the key to understanding difference. Questions of how we can understand human agency in relation to repeated language acts will be a key concern here, as will be the question as to how we can grasp the very locality of language. Issues of language diversity will be crucial, especially if we attempt to step away from a view of diversity in terms of enumerating languages, and instead focus on diversity of meaning. The ways in which languages can be understood multimodally, as working in different modes in different domains, will also be significant. All these themes come together when we take the notion of language as a local practice seriously.

Let us take a simple example: writing a postcard (to which I shall return in Chapter 7). When I sit down to write a postcard – a practice that in a world of text messages, Facebook, Twitter and Skype may already be located both in temporal and in spatial ways – I engage in a particular local language practice. It is a practice because it is a set of bundled activities that are repeated over time: I have done this before; I will likely do this again; I draw on the memories of postcards written and received, and on other textual threads linked to the place I am writing in and the people I am writing to. It is a language practice because language is central to the activity I am engaged in: it is about linking a place, a feeling, a connection through text that will travel and recreate places, feelings, connections differently elsewhere. And it is local because it is deeply connected to where I am writing, the surrounds, and the ways I may invoke those surrounds in these texts. A choice between languages does not necessarily make it more or less local: if I am in Paris and start one card 'Chère Dominique' and another 'Yo Osc', the first is not more local than the other. Locality has to do with space and place, the use of text on one side of a card (with probable links to an image on the other), sitting at this table, on this street, drinking this beer (*un demi pression de Kanterbräu*). It is a local language practice because of all of this, the sedimented use of language, the activity of writing, the multifaceted relations to place.

Understanding the locality of language

While language is an obviously key term in this book, the idea of the local is also a concept that needs extensive exploration. One use of the term is in juxtaposition with concepts such as 'global', as the opposite of whatever the global is taken to mean. To the extent that globalization is seen in terms of the homogenizing effects of capital expansion, environmental destruction, cultural demolition or economic exploitation, for example, the local becomes the site of resistance, of tradition, of authenticity, of all that needs to be preserved. At the same time, the local can also carry less positive aspects in terms of being parochial, limited, constrained, unsophisticated. Studies of globalization that seek to go beyond a critique of large-scale global change always need to take into account local processes, hence of course the use of terms such as glocalization to deal with local relations to a global language such as English (Lin, Wang, Akamatsu and Riazi, 2002). In order to understand the effects of globalization – whether we deal with this in terms of economics, the environment, political organization or media influence – we need to look locally at what happens: what are the effects of global trade tariffs on these particular garment workers in Thailand? How does the changing climate affect these millet farmers in Ethiopia? What benefits can these women in Bolivia derive from this human rights legislation? How do these listeners to Jamaican reggae music in Finland interpret these sounds, rhythms and lyrics? How do these construction-site workers in Vanuatu interpret the speech given by Nelson Mandela on his 90th birthday and broadcast around the world?

This, then, gives us one sense of the local, as the grounded and the particular. The relation here may not only be in such local reactions to wider happenings but also in the broader mobilizations of local movements. Globalization needs to be understood not only in terms of reactions to global movements from above, made possible by new media, institutions and technologies, but also in terms of local movements being made global: what new mobilizations are made possible through international indigenous peoples' conferences? How can we start to understand the ways in which Australian Aboriginal art has become a global commodity? How does the local practice of blogging participate in the global blogosphere? Is the relocalization of beer production (the move away from large companies towards micro-breweries) a local reclamation of a globalized industry or a global trend towards local manufacture? The ways in which we think about the local, therefore, should not be considered only in terms of embeddedness in time and place, but also in relational terms: The local is always defined in relation to something else regional, national, global, universal, modern, new, from elsewhere.

In Chapter 5 I shall link the understanding of language as a local practice to the idea of worldliness. This understanding of worldliness emphasizes that whatever aspect of language and the world we are trying to grasp, this can only be done while also acknowledging the perspectival heterogeneity of locality. When we speak of language as a local practice, then, this refers not only to the ways in which language use must always be related to place, must always be understood in terms of its embeddedness in locality, but also to the ways in which any understanding of the locality of language must also encompass an appreciation of the locality of perspective, of the different ways in which language, locality and practice are conceived in different contexts. As we shall see further in Chapter 5, this perspective questions the sweeping epistemologies of imperialism, language rights, mother tongues, lingua francas or World Englishes that inform much of the debate on language and globalization. Looking at language as a local practice urges us to think differently about language.

From the perspective of linguistic anthropology, with a particular interest in the notion of language ideologies, or regimes of language (Kroskrity, 2000), the question becomes one of asking how it is that languages are understood locally. As Woolard (2004) notes, such work has shown that "linguistic ideologies are never just about language, but rather also concern such fundamental social notions as community, nation, and humanity itself" (p. 58). For linguistic anthropologists, the problem was that the "surgical removal of language from context produced an amputated 'language' that was the preferred object of the language sciences for most of the twentieth century" (Kroskrity, 2000, p. 5). By studying language ideologies as contextual sets of belief about languages, or as Irvine (1989, p. 255) puts it, "the cultural system of ideas about social and linguistic relationships, together with their loading of moral and political interests", this line of work has shown the significance of local knowledge about language. At the very least, this sheds light on Mühlhäusler's (2000) point that the notion of a 'language' "is a recent culture-specific notion associated with the rise of European nation states and the Enlightenment. The notion of 'a language' makes little sense in most traditional societies" (p. 358).

The point in suggesting that we need to take local understandings of language seriously is not to say that anyone may have as much (or as little) to say about language as a linguist, and that therefore all local perspectives are somehow equally valid. This would be to fall into a hopeless relativism that simply tries to give credit to everyone's different views. We need far more rigour in our thinking about localism than this; and this applies, to be sure, to the broader project of localization: this cannot only be about valuing local perspectives on the world. What we need is to understand that all views on language are located in certain histories and articulated from certain perspectives. Here we encounter the problem, as Croft (2001) notes, that "Just as traditional grammarians tried – unsuccessfully – to fit modern European languages into the mold of Classical Latin and Greek, modern linguists are trying to fit languages of the world into the mold of 'Standard Average European'" (p. xiii). European perspectivalism underpins understandings of other languages. It is such problems that Sinfree Makoni and I (Makoni and Pennycook, 2005, 2007) have tried to address in our call for the need to *disinvent* and reconstitute languages, to question the ways in which languages have been constructed and to look for alternative ways of thinking about language.

We need to seek therefore the ways in which language practices are local, are linked to local perspectives, insights and worldviews. This is not to suggest that a speaker of Tok Pisin in Papua New Guinea, Krio in Northern Australia or Jamaican patwa in London, or a French farmer, a Quebec language activist, a hip-hop artist from Gabon or a speaker of Haitian Creole necessarily has a view on language, on English or French, on creoles and other languages, that should be considered as valid as anybody else's; but it is to suggest that unless we can grasp the locatedness of those languages and their speakers, the ways in which language use is part of everyday activity and the meanings given to those activities, we will not be able to grasp what those languages are and how they mean. For Branson and Miller (2000) we "must not only revel in linguistic difference but cope with that difference analytically. Let us recognize the culturally specific nature of our own schemes and search for new modes of analysis that do not fit other languages into a mould but celebrate and build on their epistemological differences" (p. 32).

In order to construct itself as a respectable discipline, linguistics had to make an extensive series of exclusions, relegating people, history, society, culture and politics to a role external to languages: "If the history of a language and its users is not factored into the theory as a primary standpoint", argues (Nakata, 2007, p. 37), "then any knowledge generated about that language is flawed." This is not, as Nakata points out, to reject the whole body of work carried out by linguists – this would be foolish in the extreme – but it is to point to the problem that a linguistic focus on formal aspects of a language "fundamentally separates the language from the people; it falsely separates the act of speaking from what is being spoken". Understanding the locality of language, therefore, is not merely about accurate descriptions of language systems – "as if languages were floating in a vacuum, 'ready-made' within a system of phonetic, grammatical and lexical forms and divorced from the social context in which the speech is being uttered" (Nakata, 2007, p. 37), but about people and place. The ways in which languages are described, legislated for and against, policed and taught have major effects on many people. In trying to develop a perspective on languages as local practices, therefore, we need to appreciate that language cannot be dealt with separately from speakers, histories, cultures, places, ideologies. Language questions are too important to be left to linguistics or applied linguistics if we cannot grasp their locatedness.

To talk of locality is not just to indicate the obvious point that all language use happens somewhere, or simply to start with a 'bottom-up' as opposed to a 'top-down' version of language. The local is too often equated with the 'micro' rather than the 'macro', with smallness, with embeddedness. In this sense, although my orientation shares many features with that of Blommaert (2005, 2008), my focus on the local is different in important ways from his focus on 'grassroots literacy'. Blommaert (2008) takes the term 'grassroots literacy' from Fabian's (1990) *History from Below*, a book that examines a locally written and produced book from Lubumbashi in the Democratic Republic of the Congo. For Blommaert, who also looks at texts, particularly handwritten, from the same region, grassroots literacy refers to "a wide variety of 'non-elite' forms of writing … It is writing performed by people who are not fully inserted into elite economies of information, language and literacy" (2008, p. 7). Blommaert's work provides many useful insights into what I am looking at in this book, and I similarly find Fabian's (2007) injunction to 'think small' by looking at practices a central part of what this is about. But by using the term language as a *local* practice, I am not focusing only on non-elite practices. Rather, I am suggesting that all language practices are local. Grassroots literacy practices such as writing local histories in 'longhand' are local language practices, but so too is signing a presidential decree, an email memo to all staff from the vice-chancellor of a university or the Queen of England's Christmas Day message.

Likewise, when looking at language ideologies – at the ways in which languages are understood locally – we should not assume that this must necessarily be about languages used only within small areas and understood within narrowly circumscribed domains. It is the perspectival understanding of language that is important. Thus, ideologies of English (Seargeant, 2009) are as important as ideologies of Warlpiri, Arrente or Guguyimidjir. When Chinese people refute claims that Chinese is a cover term for a set of mutually incomprehensible languages, and insist that Cantonese, Hokkien, Hakka, Hunanese and other varieties of Chinese should be considered as dialects of Chinese instead of languages, this is also a local language ideology, as is the counterclaim that these should be seen as separate languages. Language ideologies may concern language empires as vast as English and Chinese, as well as language concerns of small communities. By focusing on all language practices as local, therefore, this book provides the conditions for further exploration of grassroots language practices, but it is also interested in how all understandings of language are firmly located in time and place.

While my focus on language as a local practice emphasizes locality, disparity and a focus on grassroots language use, it is not based on a distinction between the local and the nonlocal. What counts as local requires an understanding in relational terms – something is only local in relation to some other concept of space and place – as well as in perspectival terms – the local is always interpreted in particular ways. Furthermore, the local also needs to be understood in relation to a dynamic interpretation of space (see Chapters 3–5). Soja (1989) has pointed out that space has often been treated as dead, fixed, immobile: time moves, space stands still. Yet space, he argues, needs to be seen in a much more dynamic sense, as much more than a background, or a context, in which we act out our lives: space is organized and given meaning in interaction with humans. Within this more dynamic account of space, place can then be seen not so much in terms of the flatly local but rather as the circumstance of our practice. Our words are produced and understood in places that are themselves constructed and interpreted. Language can therefore be considered as a spatial practice (cf. Lefebvre, 1991). As we shall see in the discussion on talking in the city (Chapter 4), the argument here is that doing things locally cannot rest on a pre-given account of what is local; rather, local practices construct locality.

Understanding language as practice

So far I have made a case for looking long and critically at both language and the local. This is perhaps even more important for the notion of practice, since at times it appears an almost empty term: we talk blithely of language practices or literacy practices without the second part of each phrase seeming to mean much. It appears in some ways to be little more than a word whose function is to render the phrase an activity: instead of just language, discourse or literacy as general terms, each becomes an activity: we do literacy, language and discourse. This may be akin to the growing use of terms such as 'languaging', which renders the noun into a verb, thus also achieving a sense of doing. Yet lurking behind this orientation towards activity lies a host of far broader concerns. We might first of all ask why it is that we are increasingly interested in talking of language in terms of an activity. At the very least, such a move appears to shift attention away from language as a system and towards language as something we do. This is not, it should be noted, a move towards language function, but rather a move towards language activity.

The advantage of talking in terms of systems or notions such as competence was that it made it possible to conceive of languages, and our abilities to use them, in terms of definable and systematic entities and their representation in the brain. To shift the attention to the doing of language, by contrast, leaves us with some hard questions: if languages are social activities rather than pre-ordained systems, how do we account for their regularities? And if knowing a language is better understood in terms of a knowledge of how to participate in certain social activities, rather than a brain-based capacity to use a system, how do we account for the ways in which we are able to draw on different linguistic resources in different times and places? If the notion of practice is to be able to fill this gap, it will have to do far more work than as a mere filler after terms such as language and literacy. The notion of practice as it has developed in the social sciences, particularly in light of what has been termed the 'practices turn' (Schatzki, 2001), does indeed have the potential to do some of this work. Since this is the focus of the next chapter, I will only indicate briefly some of the central concerns.

To talk of practice is not the same as talking about use. In particular, the notion of use suggests a prior object that can be taken up and employed for certain purposes. The notion of language use therefore suggests that languages exist out there in the world and can then be taken up and put to some use. Both the notion of languages and the notion of use implied by such a proposition are challenged by this notion of language practice, which suggests that language is a product of social action, not a tool to be used. Likewise, the notion of context may suggest that the use of pre-given languages varies in different locations. As Bourdieu noted some years ago, "linguists and anthropologists who appeal to 'context' or 'situation' in order, as it were, to 'correct' what strikes them as unreal and abstract in the structuralist model are in fact still trapped in the logic of the theoretical model which they are rightly trying to supersede" (1977, p. 26). The problem here, according to Bourdieu, is that this attempt to account for difference as a form of contextual variation from a core is bound by the same logic that promotes a dichotomous relation between structure and agency. For Bourdieu, the important way forward here was to develop instead a theory of practice.

The notion of local practice I will be developing in this book presents a way of thinking where the local is not so much a context in which language changes but rather a constituent part of language practice. Practices prefigure activities, so it is the ways in which language practices are moulded by social, cultural, discursive and historical precedents and concurrent contexts that become central to any understanding of language. A focus on language practices moves the focus from language as an autonomous system that pre-exists its use, and competence as an internal capacity that accounts for language production, towards an understanding of language as a product of the embodied social practices that bring it about. As Schatzki (2001, p. 1) notes, to speak in terms of language practice is to move away from both the structuralist focus on concrete system or structure and the abstract post-structuralist focus on discourse. To talk of language practices, therefore, is to move away from the attempts to capture language as a system, and instead to investigate the doing of language as social activity, regulated as much by social contexts as by underlying systems.

Van Leeuwen (2008) points out that while practice – a focus on 'what people do' – has been seen as a foundational category in sociology and anthropology, in linguistics by contrast, "things have generally been the other way around, with systems (grammars, paradigms) generating processes (syntagms), rather than processes (practices) generating systems (institutions and objectified forms of knowledge)" (p. 5). As this observation makes clear, the point in looking at language as a local practice is not therefore just to focus on the employment of languages for certain purposes, or to find a happy medium between macro-analyses of social and institutional order and micro-analyses of text, but rather to reverse the ways in which language studies have generally privileged language structure over social activity. To look at language as a practice is to view language structure as deriving from repeated activity. While this may seem a radical departure from common accounts of language, it is not so uncommon, as Van Leeuwen suggests, in other ways of accounting for social life. Canagarajah (2007) makes a similar observation when he suggests that Lingua Franca English "does not exist as a system out there. It is constantly brought into being in each context of communication" (p. 91). Lingua Franca English, or any other language, cannot therefore be understood "outside the realm of practice" (p. 94); language is not so much located in the mind of the speaker as it is "a social process constantly reconstructed in sensitivity to environmental factors" (p. 94).

To emphasize practice as foundational for thinking about language might be interpreted as drawing on materialist traditions of language in the line of Holborow's (1999) view that society, and social and economic relations, must always be considered as foundational in relation to language. The line of thinking I wish to draw on, however, while similarly eschewing the 'abstract objectivism' (as Vološinov (1973) called it) of much language study, does not opt for an account of language as dependent on the primacy of the material, but seeks to understand the ways in which language practices and language localities construct each other. In some ways, this view can be seen as drawing on that tradition of Western thinking that has always been more interested in practical thought, running from Artistotle via Vico and Vološinov to more recent thinkers such as Bourdieu, as opposed to the tradition that has always been more concerned with positing abstract structures, running from Plato via Kant to Saussure, Habermas and Chomsky in more recent times. As will be discussed in later chapters, however – particularly in Chapter 3 – the emphasis on locality also requires thinking outside the tradition of Western philosophy, especially since, as suggested above, to understand language locally is also to understand local meanings of language, which must be grounded in local ways of thinking.

To take such a stance on language is not only about trying to reverse the priority of language and social action common in language studies, but rather, by doing so, to open up for consideration a way of thinking about language that has far more space for people, for diversity, for other modes of language use, for desire and action. Canagarajah (2007) asks how we can "practice a linguistics that treats human agency, contextuality, diversity, indeterminacy, and multimodality as the norm" (p. 98). These questions will all come up in different ways in this book. As we shall see in the next chapter, while a notion of practice may open up very useful ways for thinking about how we do language as an activity in place and time, the idea of repeated social activity presents a concern for how we see our role as humans with desires and intentions. How do we account for human agency in the take-up of language? As already discussed, I will be developing the notion of locality here to take us beyond the idea of language in context. How can we grasp the localness of language? If, as I shall be arguing (see in particular Chapter 6), linguistic diversity is less well captured through the enumeration of languages than through the understanding of diverse language practices, how might we start to rethink local diversity? Given the need to take time as well as place into careful consideration in our understanding of language practices, how then do we grasp the ineffability of language? And if language practices are social practices that are always integrated with other practices, how do we account for the transmodality of local language practices?

Critical resistance and new matterings

For those more used to politics having a grander sweep than the local, than the repeated actions of practice, than the apparent reduction of language to small-scale happenings, some explanation of the politics of language as a local practice is due. Certainly, a focus on local practices of language appears to eschew the broad social and economic analyses that are often the bread and butter of critical studies of language and society. Indeed, it might be said that this book appears to focus on the bread and butter itself, or perhaps, worse still, just talk about bread and butter ('Would you like some butter on your toast?') rather than a broader politics (linguistic imperialism, language and discrimination, language and poverty and so forth). As suggested above, furthermore, by assuming that all practices are local, I have not aligned this book explicitly with the notions of disenfranchisement or inequality more evident in terms such as *grassroots* practice. This is perhaps a risk in what continues to be a broader project of language politics, and yet I wish to argue here that this book is no less political for this focus.

First of all, while a focus on local practices may bring us down to the apparently small, it would surely be an error to assume therefore an equation with the trivial. To dismiss the everyday as trivial is a strategy of the elite, akin to the dismissal of popular culture as low culture or the fodder of the masses. To overlook the significance of what is repeatedly done locally, whether from a leftist or a rightist position, is both to privilege and to ignore one's own locus of enunciation. To view everyday practice as irrelevant to a larger politics, furthermore, is also to forget those lessons of history, and of Marxist-oriented history in particular, that urge us to take the material conditions of life very seriously. To look askance at local practices is also part of the troubled history of theory. Indeed it is the twofold watering down of practice in applied linguistics that is part of what I want to address here. On the one hand, applied linguistics has a tradition of considering practice as the other of theory, and the domain for which applied linguists should give advice. From some perspectives, linguists do the theory, and applied linguists apply this theory to domains of practice. This in itself is a highly problematic version of political and theoretical relations, suggesting the separation of doing and thinking, and establishing a hierarchy of knowledge. Practice, from the perspective I will be using it here, does not carry these pernicious overtones. On the other hand, the pluralized tag 'practices' – language, literacy discourse practices – has become so common as to lose the traces of its political context. It is the politics of practice that I wish to bring back to this debate.

The arguments in this book can also be seen in that tradition of what Hoy (2004) calls *critical resistance*, the term he gives to that line of critical thinking that can be followed back through Derrida and Foucault to Nietzsche. Many forms of resistance to power and domination, he argues, and many "utopian imaginings of freedom may not be aware of the extent to which they presuppose the patterns of oppression that they are resisting" (p. 3). As a few astute critics (Canagarajah, 2007; Rajagopalan, 1999; Sonntag, 2003) of the discussions around the global spread of English have pointed out, the mobilization of discourses of imperialism, language rights or even of language as commonly conceived, prevents us from escaping the very epistemological frameworks that are part of the problem. In effect, the terms in which the arguments are framed reinforce and reproduce, rather than dismantle or depart from, those notions that are themselves indelibly tied to the problems we need to overcome. It is for similar reasons that Sinfree Makoni and I (Makoni and Pennycook, 2005; 2007) have argued that while concepts such as multilingualism appear superficially to overcome blinkered monolingual approaches to language, they all too often operate with little more than a pluralization of monolingualism: discourses of multilingualism reinforce the ways of thinking about language that we need to get beyond.

Rather than the abstract, rationalist and universalist approach of Plato, Kant, Rawls or Habermas, the pathway of critical resistance "wrestles with the emancipatory potential of the concrete social situation" (Hoy, 2004, p. 5) at the same time as seeking a form of freedom that "is tied conceptually to the openness to possibility" (p. 234). Critical resistance, in other words, needs to engage locally and to think differently; it needs to find ways of thinking otherwise, of seeing other possibilities. A focus on language as a local practice, therefore, is by no means a concern only with talk about bread and butter. Aside from pointing out that bread and butter, that casual way of describing the ordinary, is itself deeply perspectival, a description of the ordinary that is not so for much of the world, a focus on language as a local practice draws attention, on the one hand, to the everyday, with all the political associations that entails, and on the other, in its critical rereading of language, locality and practice, to an alternative way of thinking about language and the everyday, with all the political implications of such a move.

Put another way, this is about the "the construction of new matterings" (Thrift, 2007, p. 22). Thrift's (2007) *non-representational theory*, which he glosses as "*the geography of what happens*" (p. 2) focuses, like this book, on space, movement and practices. Indeed this book might be similarly explained as a *geography of linguistic happenings*, drawing attention to locality (a geography of social space) and language practices (what happens through language). For Thrift, such a focus points to "political imperatives" such as "the growing realization that there are landscapes of space, time and experience that have been ceded too readily to powerful naturalizing forces which erase the prospect of political action even before it starts by reproducing *backgrounds*, latent worlds that … make certain aspects of the events we constantly come across not so much hard to question as hard to even think of as containing questions at all" (p. 19). 'Language', 'use' and 'context', I would argue, have similarly become part of the background, and in order to see that there are questions worth asking here, we need to shift the ways in which we consider language, locality and practice.

Like Thrift (2007), therefore, I see the political agenda of this book as "the construction of new counterpublics through the assembling of more performative political ecologies" (p. 22). The critique of the conservationist politics behind some ecological approaches to language, in Chapter 6, as well as the development of a performative account of language in other chapters, is part of this move towards an alternative account of language and its place. By asking questions about what counts as object and what as human (see Latour,

2005; Thrift, 2007) and how these relate to place, this book relocates some of the givens of language studies, where languages are taken to be entities used by humans in particular places. In the view developed in this book, the object and actor – language and language user – are questioned in a way that suggests that language, locality and practice are in a constitutive relation to each other: language, or its intentional user, do not pre-exist the doing in the way often assumed by language studies. This presents us with new matterings through a form of critical resistance.

Book overview

In the next chapter I will develop the notion of practice further. Broadening our understanding of the term practice is a key element of the development of a notion of language as local practice. While applied linguistics has always made a particular notion of practice central to its agenda (indeed its very disciplinary cohesion is arguably maintained by its insistence on relevance to practice), applied linguistic conceptualizations of practice as either the implementation of theory (putting things into practice) or the driver of theory (drawing lessons from practice) remain considerably undertheorized precisely because practice is seen as theory's other. While applied linguistics has long acknowledged the importance of the real world, of a level of accountability, of the need for ideas to be applicable to a domain of activity, the notion of practice has not been given space as a theoretical tool. Recent calls for the development of a 'theory of practice' (Kramsch, 2005) to bridge this gap, particularly in the context of what has been termed the 'practice turn' in the social sciences, suggest the need for a more robust understanding of practices. The observation that not only language teaching but now also language can be seen as a practice points both to the fact that a practices orientation is emerging regardless in applied linguistics and also to the need to think through what it means to talk in terms of practices.

In order to take these ideas further, I reconsider in Chapter 3 some of the ways in which we think about language, particularly in relation to time, place, repetition and relocalization. By looking at language as a practice, as repeated social activity, we can start to conceive of language creativity, indeed of agency, through language acts that look ostensibly the same. Once we consider language and repetition in relation to time, it becomes less clear why creativity in language should be thought of in terms of divergence from a core of similarity. This involves a rethinking of both time and space, so that we can consider language use within a concept of flow. From this point of view we can consider creativity in terms of repeated sameness rather than observable difference. Drawing on insights from both hip-hop and the art of Yinka Shonibare (see book cover), as well as philosophies of difference that make iterability and performativity central, this chapter considers the processes of repetition, re-enactment and relocalization. Taking flow and difference as the norm, while asking sameness to account for itself, we can start to see how language practices, the small, repetitive, everyday uses of language, are a central aspect of human difference.

Chapter 4 explores the notion of locality in greater depth, focusing particularly on the urban language practices of graffiti and 'talking in the city'. The transgressive urban semiotics of graffiti open up important directions for an understanding of transmodal language use and location. By looking at theories of urban space, time and semiotics, this chapter suggests a need to include a dynamic account of space, text and interaction in an understanding of language and locality: readers and writers are part of the fluid, urban semiotic space and produce meaning as they move, write, read and talk. Landscapes are not mere backdrops on which texts and images are drawn but are spaces that are imagined and invented. Urban graffscapes are animated by the movement and interactions of city dwellers, and talking in the city gives meaning to the urban landscape. Viewing language as a practice points to the ways in which locality is a discursive creation. Local landscapes are not blank canvases or spatial contexts but integrative and invented environments. The importance of movement, of interactive spaces, leads us into an understanding of locality as dynamic place. Thus, when we look at language as a local practice from this perspective, we can start to see how locality is much more than being in a location; rather, it is about the becoming of place.

Drawing on claims by hip-hop artists from different parts of the world that this cultural form has always been theirs, as well as a discussion of temple elephants in southern India, Chapter 5 suggests that a rethinking of time and place in relation to language opens up different ways of thinking about localization. Processes of (re)localization are more complex than a notion of languages or cultures spreading and taking on local forms; rather, we have to understand ways in which they are already local. Recent debates over the inapplicability of a World Englishes framework to current conditions of globalization, or concerns that a focus on English as a Lingua Franca presents a new form of homogenization, miss the point that we need to react not only to new conditions of postmodernity but also to the postmodern imperative to rethink language. This suggests the need to articulate a new sense of history and location, avoiding narratives of spread, transition, development and origins, and thinking instead in terms of multiple, heterogeneous and simultaneous histories that the dominant historical narrative has overlooked. If we question the linearity at the heart of modernist narratives about language origins and spread, we can start to see that global Englishes do not have one point but rather multiple, co-present, global origins. Just as hip-hop has always been Aboriginal, so has English. Such an understanding of global Englishes radically reshapes the ways in which we can understand global and local cultural and linguistic formations, and takes us beyond the current debates between monocentric and pluricentric models of English. Once we view language as a local practice from this perspective, we can shed the idea that languages are localized by taking on certain local features in favour of a more dynamic account of localization.

Chapter 6 – an ecology of local language practices – examines in greater detail the relation between language and its environment, particularly through a discussion of language ecology, which has been both popular and productive as a way of understanding languages in relation to each other and in relation to the broader environment. A notion of language ecology draws attention to the ways in which languages are embedded in social, cultural, economic and physical ecologies, and operate in complex relations with each other. Despite these advantages, a critical exploration of the notion of language ecology, with a focus on fish names and reef conservation, points to the need to be very wary of the political consequences of some of the biomorphic metaphors that are used: the enumeration, objectification and biologization of languages render them natural objects rather than cultural artefacts. Thus we need to move beyond a form of linguistic realism that can be mapped in the same way as biological ecologies. This exploration raises some crucial issues about language and locality, suggesting that while linguistic diversity may be crucial to being human, the enumeration of different languages may not be its most important measure. That is to say, we may want to look at the diversity of meanings rather than the diversity of languages. This raises questions about how languages relate to the physical world, suggesting that rather than adapting to the world, languages are part of human endeavours to create new worlds. This in turn implies that we need to understand diversity in terms of local language practices rather than language systems.

A key question that emerges from a discussion of language as practice is how this relates to other possible ways of looking at language use. Can a notion of practice perhaps replace terms such as discourse or genre: is practice, as Schatzki (2001) suggests, the new discourse? Chapter 7 looks at ways in which the term practices is used within language studies, particularly in the notions of literacy practices and discourse as a social practice. If our analysis stops short at the moment of identifying practices – at showing that language is a social activity – we fail to engage with the larger concerns about practices as mediating social activities. A major issue for understanding the social use of language is how to account for regularity: why do we do the same or similar things with language over and over? The concept of genre captures this in part by focusing on textual regularities and emphasizing that these occur because of the social purposes to which we put language. The notion of practices, however, can bring a clearer account of how we do things with language, and we keep doing them over and over, both repeating and changing as we go.

Finally, in Chapter 8, these different themes are pulled together to look at the implications of looking at language as a local practice. Returning to the debates discussed in Chapter 2 concerning the notion of practice, this chapter looks at how notions of practice in applied linguistics start to look very different once we consider language already as a practice. For applied linguists and language teachers, practice can no longer be seen as merely the doing of teaching, while language is left as an inanimate system we draw on. Rather, language itself is a practice, with all the social, cultural and political implications such a description entails. Language and identity are the products rather than the precursors of our language practices. This is not, then, a question of applying language theory to practice, but of understanding applied linguistics from a position in which language, theory and practice are all practices. To deal seriously with 'real-world' problems, applied linguistics needs to shift from theory-practice relations and to engage instead with the implications of understanding language as a local practice as deeply real. This chapter concludes by revisiting the major concerns of this book – language, locality and practice; time, space and place – and discusses the broad implications of thinking about language as a local practice.

2 'Press 1 for English'

Practice as the 'generic social thing'

How, asked the philosopher Austin (1962) almost 50 years ago, do we do things with words? For Austin this question was about how our words can have certain effects, how the efficacy of our language may be judged by what it brings about: the launching of ships or the sentencing of criminals in those particular sorts of speech acts that were the activity itself, or the closing of windows and the opening of doors through those acts that got others to do things. Dominant ways of thinking about language in the twentieth century – speech act theory, pragmatics, semantics, language philosophy – have tended to address this question by asking how it is that language, with its grammar and words, can bring about certain effects on the world when people use it. As I suggested in the previous chapter, however, a focus on language as a local practice inverts this ordering of the question, asking how it is that the things we do with words produce language. As Harris (1988) shows in his comparison of how Saussure and Wittgenstein saw the doing of games with words, on the one hand we have a focus on the internal rules of the game that make language possible, on the other a view that language games are part of social interaction. It is this second view that is a focus of this chapter and book, asking not so much how we do things with words, as if the words instigated the doing, but rather how doing words is in itself doing things.

The d'Arenberg d'Arry's Original McLaren Vale Shiraz Grenache 2007 has, according to the Vintage Cellars (2009) *Cellar Press*, "plummy Shiraz fruit and spicy grenache, with a dash of chocolate typical of the region" (p. 8) while for the Brokenwood Beechworth Shiraz Viognier 2006 "dark chocolate, mocha and spice from the Shiraz dominate with hints of cherry blossoms from Viognier" (p. 8). If, however, you favour a cooler-climate Shiraz from New Zealand, you will find that the Murdoch James Martinborough Saleyards Syrah 2006 gives you more "dark plum and forest fruit aromatics, with savoury complexities of black tea and smoky wood spice" (p .9). "As part of a working day", writes wine critic Malcolm Gluck (2003, p. 110), he may taste "over a hundred wines. I rarely think it wise to venture, critically, over 230 bottles in a single day, not because I find my taste buds flagging but because I dry up – linguistically." The struggle, as Aitchison (2003) has observed, is how to turn the doing of wine drinking and wine tasting into words that also do something.

There are two types of wine writer, Gluck tells us: on the one hand, the 'bottom-enders' who "begin on the lees, amongst the solid bits and bobs of the liquid left over from the winemaking" (p. 109). These are writers interested in the background to the wine, the winemaker, the vineyard, the grape variety. Such writers are "social animals before anything else". On the other hand, there are the writers who start "from the business end of the bottle" (p. 109): "You pour out the wine. You regard its colour. You sniff around it. You agitate the glass to release the esters of the perfume and so better to appreciate the aromas, the nuances of the bouquet. You inhale these odoriferous pleasantries, or unpleasantries, through the chimney of the taste, the nostrils (the only access to the brain open to the air) and then you taste. You swill the liquid around the mouth and breath [*sic*] in air so that this liquid is aerated and experienced by up to ten thousand taste buds" (p. 109). These are wine-tasting practices. They are habitual bundles of activities aimed at enhancing the capacity to taste wine.

Both types of wine critic are in fact engaged in social activities – it's just that the one starts with social relations around vineyards, while the other aims to translate this experience of tasting – this practice – into local language practices (writing tasting notes). As Silverstein (2003) comments, to the extent that *oinoglossia* – his term for the language of wine tasting – "is a widely encountered register, a speaker of English inevitably places him- or herself in relation to this social structure of the wine world by using a word or expression either professionally terminologized in it or, somewhat more potently, penumbrally entextualized according to the tasting-note genre" (p. 226). To talk or write about wine is thus equally a social practice that is related in complex ways to the practices of tasting. Like Silverstein, I am interested in exploring how language and the things we do in the world, which include language, are related. This book is concerned with how these relations among language and practice and locality work, how the ways in which we do language render it a practice. In this chapter, however, a central focus will be on the notion of practice itself, on the doing, the sniffing, the swilling, the sipping, the tasting.

Towards a theory of practice

In order to grasp the implications of thinking seriously about language as a local practice, we need to engage first of all with a notion of practice. Language and locality, we already know, are terms of great complexity, but practice tends at times to be assumed to be more transparent, or to carry less weight. As I have argued in the previous chapter, however, all three terms need to be dealt with very carefully if we are to come to an understanding of the idea of language as a local practice. Practice is a particularly difficult term, meaning many different things to different people. This is made even harder by the problem that applied linguistics has long seen a particular, and rather limited, notion of practice as central to its agenda; indeed its very disciplinary cohesion is arguably maintained by its insistence on relevance to practice: Applied linguistics is that area of language studies that makes language relevant to areas of practice (language in organizations, language learning and teaching, language policy and so on). From this point of view, practice is a domain of language use for which applied linguists render theories of language applicable. The notion of practice is seen in terms either of the implementation of an idea or theory (putting something into practice) or of the domain from which theories should derive (research deriving from practice-based problems). Practice in this account is the domain of applied linguistic confrontation with the real world, that form of accountability that distinguishes applied linguists from their theory-oriented linguistic cousins.

Defined generally in relation to – often in opposition to – theory, and, given the history of applied linguistic interests, referring frequently to the practice of language teaching, practice here is about what people actually do, or more precisely, what practitioners actually do, since a domain of practice is often defined in more particular terms (we shall return to this particular aspect of practice). In general terms, practice is the domain of applied linguistic accountability, the realm of language use for which applied linguists make theory available and by which they judge the relevance of theory. Thus, in a paper on task-based learning, for example, Swan (2005, p. 384) critiques "older methods, which have failed in practice and which are theoretically unsupported". It has been common, too, to use subtitles for books that point to the applied linguistic focus on both 'theory and practice'. Brian Lynch's (1996) book *Language program evaluation*, for example, is subtitled *Theory and practice* while Grabe and Kaplan's (1996) book on writing gives this primary place: *Theory and practice of writing: An applied linguistic perspective.*

The role of applied linguists, particularly from the perspectives of the British tradition that developed in the 1970s, was to mediate between theories of language and the practice of teaching. Thus Widdowson (1984), defining applied linguistics as "an area of inquiry bearing on the techniques of language teaching", was concerned that descriptions of language should be of relevance to the "practices of language teaching" (p. 5). A long-standing debate, often discussed in terms of the linguistics-applied versus applied-linguistics distinction, concerns the directionality of this relation. On the one hand, the role of the applied linguist is to make theory accountable to the real world of (teaching) practice. For Widdowson (1984), "effective practice depends on theory, but … the theory has to be relevant to the purposes of practice and has to yield principles which can be interpreted and tested as practical teaching techniques" (p. 6). From this perspective, all theory needs to stand the test of practice, and therefore "how far a theory is applicable to practice is a good measure of how far the theory is valid as a theory" (Widdowson, cited by de Beaugrande (1997, p. 280)).

Emphasizing the importance not so much of the applicability of theory to practice as the derivation of theory from practice, Davies (1999), on the other hand, uses the subtitle *From practice to theory* for his *Introduction to applied linguistics*, arguing that applied linguistics should always start with, as Brumfit

(1995) put it, "real world problems". Thus, the goal for applied linguistics is to keep "asking the right questions about institutional language problems and then generalising to other contexts where similar problems can be shown after analysis to exist. Such an approach, which theorises practice, will be explanatory and at the same time provide a set of options for action" (Davies, 1999, p. 143). From this perspective, 'real world problems' are questions of practice, and it is in the investigation of such concerns that we develop applied linguistic theories. While this question of directionality – whether theory should inform practice or practice inform theory – has remained a point of contention for some, others have seen this as more easily reconcilable from a point of view "in which theory and practice can finally be united as equals and dialectical partners – the enterprise of guiding the teaching and learning of languages" (de Beaugrande, 1997, p. 310).

To the extent that this view of practice has been central to many debates about the role of applied linguistics, however, a range of other ways of thinking about practice have been obscured. Putting aside the questions of whether theory might be considered a goal in and of itself in a more autonomous version of applied linguistics,[1] or the problem of tying applied linguistics so irrevocably to language teaching, or the rather patronizing nature of a vision of applied linguistics that helps explain theory to those too busy doing things to have time to deal with ideas, the most serious weakness of these views is the maintenance of a relationship between theory and practice that on the one hand cannot account for the fact that theorizing should itself be seen as a practice (Schatzki, 1996), and on the other leaves practice under-theorized as the opposite of theory. As Kramsch (2005) makes clear, this insistence on 'real world problems' does not account for the ways in which problems become problems; it does not have any broader theoretical tools that can account for the process of problematization.

In order for applied linguistics to be able to deal with 'real-world problems', Kramsch (2005) suggests, we need a 'theory of practice', a theory that can account not only for the relations between language and the real conditions of the world but also for the ways in which those realities are constructed and prioritized. A theory of practice, Kramsch (2005, p. 560) explains, "explores not the conditions that make the real world possible, but the conditions that make possible the very exploration of the real world. It is a reflexive form of knowledge on the conditions of possibility of the research itself." But why, we might ask, a theory of *practice*, rather than a theory of knowledge, discourse, ideology, society or culture, if what we are trying to understand are the conditions of possibility for exploring the real world? Why should applied linguistics, which for decades has sought to articulate a relationship *between* theory and practice, also need a theory *of* practice?

Conceptualizations of practice as implementation or driver of theory remain considerably under-theorized precisely because practice is seen as theory's Other. Thus, while applied linguistics has long acknowledged the importance of the real world, of a level of accountability, it has never acknowledged the equality of practice. Recent calls for the development of a 'theory of practice' to bridge this gap, as well as a social scientific shift towards practices as the key way of theorizing the social, suggest that applied linguistics needs to work towards a way of thinking about practice that allows for a fuller confrontation with the real world: a more robust understanding of practices. This chapter explores how a notion of language as local practice has major implications for a rethinking of applied linguistics. We will move away here from a notion that applied linguistics mediates between theory and practice, since, from the point of view I intend to open up, practice is not a mere doing of things, but rather is a combination of thought and action. Critical theories of practice (or of *praxis*) have always problematized the theory/practice divide, insisting that a notion of practice needs to account for practical reasoning, for the thinking that is bound up with the doing. Thrift's (2007) *non-representational theory*, for example, "questions the divide between theoretical and practical work by ceding certain theoretical conundrums to practice" (p. 22). We shall return to this later.

Practice as it occurs within these theory/practice debates is not the only use of the term within applied linguistics, however, so a brief terminological mapping may be useful here.[2] First, there is the sense of practice as repeated action for improvement (things will improve with practice). To the extent that applied linguistics has been concerned with language learning and teaching, practice from this point of view has often been concerned with the role of repetition in the development of language proficiency. In his paper on task-based learning, for example, Swan (2005, p. 382) also notes the "important role of practice in fostering automatization", asserting that "practice aids learning" (p. 383). This sense of practice, which DeKeyser (2007, p. 1) claims, "gets a raw deal in the field of applied linguistics", is contrasted not so much with theory as with presentation and input of language on the one hand, and free production on the other. It refers to "specific activities in the second language, engaged in systematically, deliberately, with the goal of developing knowledge of and skills in the second language" (DeKeyser, 2007, p. 1). While the notion of repetition for improvement will not be of central concern to this chapter, the notion of repeated action does carry with it some of the ideas embedded in a notion of practice that I want to develop here. The 'raw deal' that notions of repeated action have received will also be discussed at greater length in the next chapter.

The idea of practice that I am interested in here has also entered applied linguistic discourse, but to some extent through the back door, as it were. This has more to do with activities we engage in, habits, customs, things we do in a very general sense. This idea is often captured by the addition of the term 'practices' to other words, hence language practices, cultural practices, discursive practices and so forth. Thus, in a paper on undergraduate writing (North, 2005), we find discussion of the "literacy practices of particular disciplines" (p. 431), the "literacy practices of undergraduates" (p. 433) and "the discursive practices of the disciplines in which they have studied" (p. 435). Or as Myers (2005, p. 528) argues, the frequent use of questionnaires, interviews, focus groups, or web page surveys which involve interactions around talking, reading and writing, make "language practices" central to the operation of institutions of opinion. This seemingly casual use of the usually pluralised term 'practices' turns literacy, language and discourse from abstract entities into everyday activities that need to be accounted for, and is not only currently pervasive but also of much greater significance than it might at first appear.

I shall return to a discussion of notions such as literacy practices, as well as concepts such as discourse and genre, at much greater length in Chapter 7. At this point it is worth drawing attention to two main points. On the one hand, the use of a notion of practices has become reasonably common in some domains of applied linguistics, notably those concerned with a social account of language. Most obvious here are literacy studies concerned with an account of literacy as a social rather than a cognitive category. This distinction – the social and the cognitive – is of course also disrupted by a thorough theory of social practices, and I shall return to some of these concerns later. On the other hand, a general trend towards thinking in terms of language as activity rather than system (another division that comes into question) has produced a wider range of uses of the term practices after words such as language and discourse. In this case, it remains generally under-theorized, at times little more than a morpheme that turns language nouns into activities. It is part of the goal of this book to bridge these divides, and to ask not only why language is being considered increasingly as an activity but also how we can extend this language practice by thinking through what practices are.

Practices as 'the primary generic social thing'

To take practice seriously as a domain to be theorized is also to acknowledge a shift in the social sciences. Thus, the growing use of the term practices to describe language use needs to be understood in a far broader context. The observation that not only language teaching but now also language has become a practice is by no means trivial, since it can be seen in relation to what Schatzki (2001) has termed "the practice turn" in contemporary theory. According to Schatzki, social scientists have increasingly started to employ the term practices, rather than the more abstract concepts of systems, structures or discourses, to describe the ways in which human activity is organized around shared practical understanding. The sense of practices in the practices turn becomes a conceptualization of human action as a form of meso-politics,[3] an intermediate level between the micro and the macro. It addresses precisely those questions that constantly emerge and re-emerge in discussions of language, society and the individual: How do we come to use language as we do? What controls, determines or produces our language acts? Is it people that do language or language that does people?

If we are rightly suspicious of both over-voluntaristic accounts of language use (we simply say what we intend, or we make choices from given systems of language) and over-deterministic accounts (what we say is a reflex of social, discursive or ideological structure, or language determines the choices we can make), we need to ask how we can understand the relation between human action and social, cultural and ideological preformations. Many concepts have filled this gap, the most recent and popular being discourse as a way of linking the micro-action of language use to the macro-frame of the social. Yet, as Schatzki (2001) argues, practices are, in a sense, the new discourse, the new way of describing that level of mediating social activity where we do things both because we want to and along lines laid down by habit, propriety, cultural norms or political dictates. It is therefore useful to explore the meso-political space of practice that lies between the local and the global in order to develop a more comprehensive theoretical landscape for thinking about the relation between a real world of human action and an applied linguistic domain aimed at language problem solutions.

While one aim of this chapter is to unsettle uses of the term practice(s) – to make the familiar unfamiliar again, to urge applied linguists to pause when we read and write of communities of *practice*, theory and *practice*, language *practices* – another aim is to explore the significance of a reorientation of our thinking about the role of language in the world. To get a handle on this changing terminological landscape, to think through the implications of practice being seen as central to applied linguistics rather than as its level of accountability, to understand in greater depth how a notion of practice as meso-politics may replace other possible levels of social mediation such as discourse, and to work towards a way of thinking about practice that allows for a fuller confrontation with the real world, we need a more robust understanding of practices. To pursue this further I shall now turn to a discussion of the notion of practice, and the implications of a practices turn in the social sciences.

A central concern has to do with what actually constitutes practice. Rather than everything being a practice, and the term therefore becoming little other than a notion of doing, we need a way of seeing how activities may be grouped together in order to constitute a practice. What activities make up the practice of wine-tasting (sniffing, swirling, swilling spitting) and what the practices of wine-writing (how to do wine-tasting with words)? What is it about particular domains of practice for which applied linguistics may see itself as accountable – language teaching, translation, doctor–patient interactions – that defines what is done here as practice? One, largely tautological, response is that these are domains in which practitioners (doctors, teachers and other professionals) do their work. Here, however, MacIntyre's (2007 [1981]) influential account of practice has generated considerable discussion. His claim, for example, that teaching is not a practice might cause applied linguists who have always considered teaching to be self-evidently so, to sit up and take note.

In order to develop an account of the moral culture of advanced modernity by appeal to a form of Aristotelian practical reasoning, MacIntyre (2007 [1981], p. 187) mobilises a particular understanding of practice as "any coherent and complex form of socially established cooperative human activity" in which whatever is done in that activity is done for a purpose internal to that activity (playing chess according to the rules in order to beat an opponent rather than playing in any possible fashion in order to obtain external goods).[4] MacIntyre goes on to draw distinctions between those activities that therefore should or should not be considered practices: neither tic-tac-toe, nor kicking a football (however skilfully) are practices (since their success is to be measured by external criteria), but a game of football or of chess is (since the satisfaction and achievement may be internal to the activity); bricklaying isn't but architecture is; planting turnips isn't but farming is, and so on. Thus, in MacIntyre's somewhat normative vision, a practice "involves standards of excellence and obedience to rules as well as the achievement of goods. To enter into a practice is to accept the authority of those standards and the inadequacy of my own performance as judged by them" (p. 190).

For MacIntyre, then, practice is seen as "a set of social relations in which and through which people collaborate to achieve a certain dimension of human excellence that is distinctive of their practice" (Nyhan, 2006, p. 138). Since engagement in practice from this point of view must be for its own good rather than for other purposes, he therefore discounts those kinds of activities which only serve as a means towards an external end. Hence, teaching is not a practice, since in MacIntyre's view it has no other purpose than as a means to learning (MacIntyre and Dunne, 2002). Noddings (2003) disputes this claim on the grounds that teachers make pedagogical decisions on the basis of internal criteria of educational excellence rather than external criteria of subject excellence. Teaching is therefore "a relational practice – one that has its own distinctive criteria of internal excellence" (p. 251). Likewise, Hogan (2003, p. 221) argues for an understanding of teaching as a way of life, "a singularly conversational way of being human", engaged in "a struggle between higher forms of human freedom and influences which continually threaten that freedom with overt or more subtle forms of captivity". While there may therefore be good grounds to refute MacIntyre's contention that teaching is not a practice, and interesting discussions to be had here about the nature of teaching as part of a broader set of educational practices or as only serving the purpose of bringing about learning, the point we need to take from this is that not just anything is a practice. Practice is not just activity, and therefore, most importantly for the discussion in this book, language as a local practice should not be taken to mean any and all language use. Practice is a higher-level notion than just doing.

Of further relevance to educational understandings of practice is the considerable literature on learning from practice. Unlike the largely cognitivist notion of learning *by* practice, of achieving automatization by repetition, an understanding of learning in informal settings requires a concept of practice as "a body of knowledge, a capacity to make judgements, a sensitivity to intuition, and an awareness of the purposes of the actions" (Beckett and Hager, 2002, p. 92). The focus of this work is on how we know how to do things, how we develop forms of practical knowledge in the very particular and local contexts of our daily lives at work and at play. From this point of view practice concerns the relationship between the doing of daily life (not reducible to activity or technique) and the knowledge to do so. Thus, as Toulmin (1999) suggests, practice becomes the cornerstone of a theory of knowledge that rejects foundational and acontextual depictions of knowledge, insisting instead on knowledge in relation to doing. For applied linguists, such a focus would no longer suggest the application of theory to practice, nor the derivation of theory from practice, but rather the development of a theory of practice: how is it that language users know how to do what they do in the very specific contexts in which they operate, not as a theory of competence underlying performance, but as a knowledge of everyday practice?

Let us take an example. Schatzki (2002, p. 70) lists 'banking practices' as one of the common social practices many of us engage in. Practices are bundles of activities that are organized into coherent ways of doing things. The larger set of banking practices might involve depositing a cheque, withdrawing money and so forth. Traditionally such practices involved going to a bank, lining up, filling out forms, talking to a cashier and completing the transaction (involving a range of social, spatial, linguistic, literacy and numeracy activities). These might differ from context to context, from rural to urban, from poorer to wealthier countries: different opening times, different queuing practices, seats, separation of transactions and cashiers, the presence of armed guards, open counters or closed grilles, different forms and so on, yet there is often a broad similarity, and many of us soon get the hang of managing the bundle of activities that constitute banking practices in various contexts.

This has changed in many contexts, however, with the increased use of Automatic Teller Machines (ATMs), and more recently phone and online banking. For a younger generation, online banking practices may be easy, transparent and the norm, while for an older generation going to the bank remains the familiar set of practices. While the latter may be more 'social' than the former – in terms of possible interactions with other people – both are nevertheless social practices in that they are part of the broader social life in which we engage. The banking practice of using the ATM is one we get used to through repeated action. We learn to use them usually without instruction but rather by watching others, or simply by doing so ourselves (with a bit of help from the screen). There are various predictable steps (the buttons we press, the PIN we enter, the choices we make) and various literacy and numeracy requirements. ATM (or online) banking is a language practice to the extent that language (reading) is involved as part of the process.

There may also be a question of language choice. My local ATM asks me to choose between languages (Chinese – simplified or traditional characters – Vietnamese, Japanese, Korean, Spanish, Italian and Arabic), and indeed using an ATM in a language with which one is less familiar can be hard work. It also makes clearer the relationship between the practice as repeated action and the role that language plays here in directing this action. The issue of having to choose between languages may for some be a concern in itself: the national director of Minutemen American Defence, a group claiming several thousand members who regularly do night-time patrols of the US–Mexico border, explains how she was won over to the Minutemen cause when, several years ago, she phoned a bank and was told "Press 1 for English": "It insulted me. I have travelled all over the world. I don't know where else people have to press 1 for their native tongue" (cited by Munro, 2008, p. 27). Putting aside the spatial and linguistic borders that are being protected here, or the point that Texans who speak Spanish as a first language presumably have to press 2 to get service in their native tongue (with the obvious hierarchy this implies), or that Vietnamese Texans may not even get the choice, we can see quite clearly that such banking practices are local (banking is done in a particular time and place), involve language (which may include language choice) and are repeated bundles of activity.

For now, without concerning ourselves over the debates around what level of skill is required for something to be a practice, or whether practices should only be counted as such if they have internal standards of excellence and rules, we can consider practices to be bundles of everyday (or not so everyday) activities as we cook, go to school, work, attend religious services, engage in recreational activities and so on. As we have seen, such practices may also involve well-integrated language practices; indeed, many of these practices can only be achieved with accompanying language practices, and some practices, particularly in domains such as schooling, work and religion, may be predominantly language based. Language practices, therefore, are deeply intertwined with other social practices.

Locating practice

All this attention to a notion of practice may be seen as part of the wider 'practice turn' in the social sciences. As Schatzki (2001, p. 1) explains, while social theorists once talked in terms of "'systems', 'meaning', 'life world', 'events,' and 'actions' when naming the primary generic social thing", it is now common to talk in terms of 'practices'. An intellectual tradition drawing on the work of Martin Heidegger, Ludwig Wittgenstein and John Dewey, and more recently Pierre Bourdieu, Charles Taylor and Anthony Giddens, has followed a very different trajectory from the structuralist orientation towards language and the social sciences initiated by Saussure, insisting instead that "the meanings of the entities amid and through which humans coexistently live derive from activity" (Schatzki, 2002, p. 86). From an applied linguistic point of view, then, it is evident that much of what has been taken for granted about language, society and mind has derived from an intellectual tradition that has emphasized structure and system rather than activity and practice.

A comparison of how Saussure – who may be seen as the intellectual pro-genitor of structuralist thinking about language – and Wittgenstein – who amongst other things may be seen as an intellectual precursor to recent thought about practices (Schatzki, 1996) – looked at the notion of language games can shed useful light on this (Harris, 1988). For Saussure the game analogy – particularly the game of chess – was employed to show the importance of focusing on language itself. Linguists, Saussure insisted, needed to distinguish between the underlying rules of the game on the one hand, and, on the other, its origins and history, different strategies employed during a sequence of play, and so on. Only by discarding these 'external' elements (history, context, episodes of play, actual games) and focusing on the rules (structure) of the game could we understand how games such as chess worked. Likewise, it was only by excluding history, society, culture, politics, people and use that we could understand the underlying rules of language.

Wittgenstein, by contrast, saw language games in terms of practices and institutions, as activities repeated by a form of social contract. Wittgenstein shows us "how to avoid the fatal flaw of saying that the rule itself (thought of as an abstract or formal entity) is responsible for those actions or thoughts that are involved in following it – as if some mysterious mental process of 'grasping the rule' had to be accepted as basic" (Bloor, 2001, p. 104). Rather, following Wittgsenstein, "we can give substance and depth to the idea that rules are institutions and rule-following is participation in the relevant institutional practices" (ibid). According to Wittgenstein (1963), it is by looking at human behaviour that we can understand what language is doing. This is a crucial point for understanding what I mean by language as a local practice: Rather than focusing on the supposed rules of language that are deemed to be responsible for the language we produce, we can turn our attention towards an understanding that rule-following is institutional participation: "The very ontology of rules is social and grounded in patterns of interaction" (Bloor, 2001, p. 104).

A key question for Bourdieu, in his *Outline of a theory of practice* (1977), was how to steer a course between the grand and seemingly deterministic theories of critical social science, where human action is a by-product of larger social structures, and the voluntaristic views of humanism, with their focus on the rational actions of individuals. The way forward here for Bourdieu was to think in terms of practice – how people do things – and then to develop ways of thinking about how such practices became sedimented and regulated. His notion of habitus, therefore, became a bridge between large social forces and the doing of the everyday: "Through the habitus, the structure which has produced it governs practice, not by the processes of mechanical determinism, but through the mediation of the orientations and limits it assigns to the habitus's operations of invention" (1977, p. 95). As Bourdieu points out, such a "paradoxical product" is hard to conceive if one remains "locked in the dilemma of determinism and freedom, conditioning and creativity" that led Chomsky to seek "freedom" and "creativity" in the "structure" or "nature" of the human mind in order to avoid the trap of Bloomfieldian behaviourism (p. 95).

While Chomsky and others quite rightly reacted against the limited purview of human activity embedded in behaviourist theory, Bourdieu's point here is that the solution should not be sought in the abstractions of structure, but rather in a much richer theory of social action that focuses on the interaction between the layered histories of social and cultural activity that each person brings to an interaction and the many contextual features of that interaction. For Bourdieu, "the habitus, the product of history, produces individual and collective practices, and hence history, in accordance with the schemes engendered by history" (1977, p. 82). Drawing on the work of Bourdieu and Foucault, De Certeau (1984) argues in *The practice of everyday life* that "everyday practices, 'ways of operating' or doing things" should no longer "appear as merely the obscure background of social activity", but rather, should be seen as a key to understanding social and cultural relations (p. xi). This is not, he insists, a return to the individual, but a focus on how everyday practices such as walking, talking, reading, writing, dwelling or cooking are organized. Similarly, Schatzki (2002, p. 70) points to the key understanding that social life is "plied by a range of such practices as negotiation practices, political practices, cooking practices, banking practices, recreation practices, religious practices, and educational practices".

Practice is not therefore mere behaviour or activity; and neither is it juxtaposed with theory. Rather, this notion of practice attempts to make the observable doings of the everyday central to an understanding of social life, and simultaneously to view such activity in terms of regulated and sedimented social conduct. From this point of view, practices are conceived as "embodied, materially mediated arrays of human activity centrally organized around shared practical understanding" (Schatzki 2001, p. 2). According to Schatzki, a notion of practices in the social sciences has started to take over from alternative ways of understanding the relation between social order and the individual. As Swidler (2001) explains, the notion of practices "moves the level of sociological attention 'down' from conscious ideas and values to the physical and habitual" while at the same time shifting attention "'up' from ideas located in individual consciousness" to the broader domain of repeated social and cultural habits (p. 75). Practices are therefore "trans-personal, imbedded [*sic*] in the routines organizations use to process people and things, in the taken-for-granted criteria that separate one category of person or event from another" (p. 75). As activities we engage in that are socially and culturally produced and regulated, practices bridge the gap between individual behaviour and social and cultural structure, while also drawing attention to the importance of repeated activity.

Practices, then, are reducible neither to individual activity nor to socially, culturally or ideologically determined behaviour. As Kemmis (2009) suggests, following Schatzki (2002), practices "*prefigure* the actions of particular actors". That is to say, these "arrangements of sayings, doings, set-ups and relationships" (p. 32) are not individual attributes but rather a set of organizing and mediating conditions that render activity coherent. Practices come in bundles, or 'blocks' as Reckwitz (2002) puts it. A practice is therefore "a routinized way in which bodies are moved, objects are handled, subjects are treated, things are described and the world is understood" (Reckwitz, 2002, p. 250)

They give meaning – always from different perspectives – to what we do, connect us socially to others, and are part of the achievement of practical outcomes. These mediating preconditions of practice, these "arrangemants of ideas, words, utterances, things and people" (Kemmis 2009, p. 37) make possible and give meaning to the things we do. While the notion of discourse (understood in the broad sense of a worldview, an ideology, an organizing principle of society) has for some time been used as a "nonindividualist order-instituting entity" that seeks to explain how it is that behaviour and thought are produced and regulated in particular ways (Schatzki 2001, p. 5), it is now being usurped by the notion of practices. In this sense, practices may be 'the new discourse'. I shall take up this proposition in greater detail in Chapter 7.

Thinking small: new matterings

These different approaches to practice have a number of things in common: they make central the world of the everyday, eschewing metaphysics or universal theories in favour of an understanding of how people achieve daily life. They take seriously the ways we walk, talk, eat, do our banking, shopping and ironing, or perhaps, depending on class and religion, taste wines. These are repeated social practices that mediate between social structure and individuated action: practices are not an end in themselves but rather part of a broader social world. Practices prefigure activity: they are not reducible to things we do, but rather are the organizing principle behind them. Hence the usefulness of looking at practices as meso-political action to capture the level of activity between the individual and the social. Language, from this perspective, becomes a social practice, as are language teaching, translation and language policy; such practices operate above the level of activity and below the level of social order, as mediators of how things are done. Applied linguistics would no longer try to mediate between theory and practice but would be able to see its own theories as practices and its former practices in need of theory.

Practice has been frequently invoked as the domain that keeps applied linguists honest: we should ensure either that our theories are applicable to practice, or that our theories derive from practice. As I am arguing in this book, however, this account of practice falls short of what we need in order to engage with the world, since it has always failed to theorize practice itself. Hence Kramsch's (2005) call for a theory of practice, a reflexive form of knowledge on the conditions of possibility for our understanding of the real world itself: "applied linguistic research, in its efforts to build a theory of practice, should reflect on its political conditions of possibility and openly discuss with practitioners not only the categorization but also the framing of real-world problems" (p. 547). And here, in engaging with those who do the doing, meaning, as Schatzki (2002, p. 58) argues, "is not a matter of difference, abstract schema, or attributional relativity, but a reality laid down in the regimes of activity and intelligibility called 'practices'".

Having made a case for working with a notion of practice, however, it is important that we also consider some of its limitations. In their discussion of human agency, for example, Emirbayer and Mische (1998) characterize practice theory as the "selective reactivation by actors of past patterns of thought and action, as routinely incorporated in practical activity, thereby giving stability and order to social universes and helping to sustain identities, interactions and institutions over time" (p. 971). At the very least, they suggest, this *iterational element* of agency that emphasizes repeated action and consistency needs to sit alongside both a *projective element* (actors' imagined possible future trajectories) and a *practical-evaluative element* (how actors make practical and normative judgements among alternative possible trajectories). Certainly, from some perspectives, a focus on practice as repeated action does appear to operate with a sense of conservative action while not allowing for a greater sense of possibility or judgement. This sense of practice as always past-oriented, and the notion of iteration as always repeating the same things, is something I shall question in discussions of repetition, difference and performativity in the next chapter.

Another concern is that, like all such moves, taking up a notion of practice as the new answer to everything is invariably part of a pendulum swing too far: once we decide that 'it's all discourse', 'everything is linguistically constructed', or in this case, 'everything is a practice', we run the danger of putting all our eggs in one basket. Language, discourse and practice are always too complex to be all about themselves. This is one reason why I am dealing here with language as a local practice, where each term is intended to carry a lot of weight: this is not only about language, nor only about practice, nor only about locality: it is about all three in relation with each other. As I argue at greater length in subsequent chapters, furthermore, although there are suggestions that practice may be the 'new discourse' or the 'new genre' there is room here for practice, discourse, genre or language to sit alongside each other. The idea that practice theory is a new theory of everything goes against any idea of local practice, which always makes the very thinking about practice contingent on locality.

One further question about the notion of practice is whether, by comparison with seemingly more critical sociological frameworks, a practices view of social life is politically bland. Where do power, inequality, disadvantage, prejudice, ideology, gender, class, race, sexual orientation fit into this? Is this, as I suggested in Chapter 1, too much about bread and butter? Or banking and wine-tasting? It might seem that a view of language as practice, rather like conversation analysis (see Chapter 7), tends to bracket away such broader social concerns in favour of a micro-analysis of language in action. This is a real potential danger of the notion of practice, particularly when it becomes the end point of the analysis. Luke (2004) reminds us, in the context of literacy studies, that we need to see the notion of literacy as a social practice not as an end point – as do various approaches to literacy which are content to rest on the finding that literacy is social – but as the starting point for further analysis. To argue that literacy, or language, or cognition are 'social' or 'socially constructed' is not really to tell us much at all. While these arguments may take us beyond a form of foundationalism that attempts to construct versions of literacy, language or cognition as pure and independent products uncorrupted by social life, to point out that these are in fact social practices cannot be the end point of the argument. It is the material or political or ideological consequences of literacy, language or cognitive practices that we need to focus on. The insight that language is a social practice, therefore, is the starting point, not the end point, of the analysis.[5] This needs to be the basis on which much wider analyses can be constructed that maintain a focus on power, politics and the material consequences of language use.

To this end it is important to keep in mind the intellectual lineage of a notion of practice. Arguments over theory and practice go back in Western philosophy to Plato and Aristotle[6] but take on a very particular dimension in Marxist thought (Lobkowicz, 1967; Flewelling, 2005). As Marx pointed out in his *Theses on Feuerbach* (Marx, 2000 [1845][7]), materialist philosophy had to date viewed the material world in terms of external objects; what was needed, rather, was an understanding of concrete human activity: practice (*Praxis* in German and Greek). The focus on the object in materialism had left the space for theorizing practice to the field of idealism, which meant, from Marx's point of view, that activity could never be theorized as real, concrete activity. The same point might be made about practice in applied linguistics: by leaving the theorization of practice to liberal idealists, critical applied linguistics, critical pedagogy or critical discourse analysis may be developing forms of critical theory without ever engaging seriously with an under-theorized notion of practice. Which brings us back to Kramsch's (2005) call for a theory of practice. Practice should not be thought of in contradistinction to theory: theory and practice are a unity. While there is constant debate over the relation of theory and practice, it is this understanding that they are inseparable that has been a cornerstone of critical thought from Marx, via the Frankfurt School and into current versions of critical theory. An understanding of practice or praxis, "that continuous reflexive integration of thought, desire and action" (Simon, 1992, p. 49), is also inseparable from Marx's injunction for philosophers to *change* the world rather than only interpret it.

It is to attempt such a reclamation that I am also returning to practice in this book, not so much to return to Marxian materialism, but to retrieve a notion of practice as concrete, situated activity from its use in applied linguistics either as the domain to which theories should apply or as just an add-on to language, literacy and discourse (language practices). It is this "view of language as intimately interwoven with social practice, and of meaning as similarly dependent on the interpretative context of practical life" that links Marx and Wittgenstein (Benton, 2002, p. 149) through an interest in the everyday. The tension I have been trying to get at in this chapter is described in another context by the anthropologist Johannes Fabian: "I see a general tension and specific contradiction between 'big thinking' about orders and 'small thinking' about practices, something that is also at issue in the continuing debate in anthropology about culture as a system versus culture as praxis" (2007, p. 34). Or, we might add, the continuing debate between language as a system versus language as practice. This 'thinking small' in terms of practices makes central the language of the everyday, avoiding universal or foundational theories in favour of an understanding of how people achieve daily life through language. Language practices are repeated, social and meso-political practices that mediate between social structure and individuated action. They are not reducible to things we say or write or read; but rather are the organizing principle behind them. And they are always local.

The idea of language as a local practice does not, therefore, eschew social theorizing in order to work only at the micro level, as do some approaches to language as micro-activity: it insists on linking social orders and social actions in a more dynamic way than this. It also cannot become yet another system for analysis that starts by claiming to look at the social through language and ends by chasing its own linguistic tail. The notion of language as a practice is not an end point, but a starting point. The issue is not to endlessly describe language practices as yet another socio/linguistic descriptive endeavour, but to use the idea of language as a local practice to understand the material and political consequences of language use. Nor can we arrive at an understanding of local language practices through external, objective analysis, since local language practices also have to be understood perspectivally. As Radhakrishnan (2007) reminds us, worldliness needs to be understood as deeply perspectival. Language as a local practice is not, as the comparison of Saussure and Wittgenstein above suggests, about the internal rules of language that account for utterances, but about the social activities we engage in that produce language.

At the same time it is equally important to see this focus on language as a local practice in terms of questioning "what is in the world", exposing "a whole new frontier of inhuman endeavour, what might be called the construction of new matterings, along with their typical attachments, their passions, strengths and weaknesses, their differences and indifferences" (Thrift 2007, p. 22). As Foucault (1980) put it, "the problem is not so much one of defining a political 'position' (which is to choose from a pre-existing set of possibilities) but to imagine and to bring into being new schemas of politicisation" (p. 190). The political imperative here is to reclaim understandings of space, time, language and context from their frozen state within much social and linguistic theory. The background of the everyday use of language needs to be opened up for re-examination, turned from background into foreground, and thereby reinvested with a new politics. By relocating some of the background assumptions of language studies, where languages are taken to be entities used by humans in particular places, a focus on language as a local practice presents us with new ways of thinking about language actors.

As Thrift (2007) describes practices, they can be seen as things we do that have gained stability over time through the establishment of routines. We are schooled in practices and they continue to reproduce themselves if only because the general social default is to continue as before. This is not, however, to argue for an idea of static performance, as if things will always continue because they have done so up to now. Practices are "continually being rewritten, as unusual circumstances arise" (p. 8). They are "productive concatenations that have been constructed out of all manner of resources and which provide the basic intelligibility of the world: they are not therefore the properties of actors but of the practices themselves" (p. 8). In the next chapter I shall develop this concern further: the idea of language as governed by internal rules and creativity as the breaking of those rules is one way in which language stability and change can be viewed. From the perspective I have been developing here, however, the stability of language practices is a product of repeated social activity, and yet they are also always being rewritten; they are always under change. This is not a question of difference as straying from the norm but of difference as the norm. How the constant relocalization of language through repetition is part of both stability and change will be the focus of the next chapter.

3   The *Reverend on Ice* again
Similarity, difference and relocalization

Fertile mimesis and relocalization

According to conceptual artist, writer and musician DJ Spooky that Subliminal Kid, "creativity rests in how you recontextualize the previous expression of others, a place where there is no such thing as an 'immaculate
perception'" (Miller, 2004, p. 33). In his book *Rhythm Science*, Miller (aka DJ
Spooky that Subliminal Kid) argues that the DJ can be seen as the archetypal
artist of today, using technology to sample, borrow and reproduce sounds and
music from elsewhere. Hip-hop culture, broadly understood, provides a very
particular cultural and ideological background as transgressive art, as a
challenge to norms of language, identity and ownership (Alim, 2006; Alim,
Ibrahim and Pennycook, 2009; Pennycook, 2007a). Aspects of this broad
cultural formation include "an enthusiastic embracing of new technology and
mass culture, a challenging of modernist notions of aesthetic autonomy and
artistic purity, and an emphasis on the localised and temporal rather than the
putatively universal and eternal" (Shusterman, 2000, p. 61). Of particular
interest here is "recycling appropriation rather than unique originative creation, an eclectic mixing of styles" (ibid.), or what Potter calls "the relentless
sampling of sonic and verbal archives" (1995, p. 53).

DJ Spooky describes sampling as "a new way of doing something that's
been with us for a long time: creating with found objects. The rotation gets
thick. The constraints get thin. The mix breaks free of the old associations"
(Miller, 2004, p. 25). Creativity rests in the recontextualization, or as I shall
argue here, the *relocalization* of others' expressions. Theo van Leeuwen's
(2008) understanding of discourse as "recontextualized social practice" (p. 1)
is important here, since it suggests that language practices are social practices in
which other social practices have been recontextualized. The things we do
socially are recontextualized as discourse when we do them in language, or
more broadly as part of a social semiotics. As we shall see in subsequent
chapters, when a newspaper journalist writes about temple elephants in
Kerala (Chapter 5), or reef conservationists discuss fish they have observed
underwater (Chapter 6), we are observing one set of practices recontextualised
in language.

In this book, however, I shall talk about relocalization rather than recontextualization, for several reasons. As I suggested in Chapter 1, I want to move beyond the notion of 'context' and instead engage with a notion of locality that includes theories of space and movement as part of a new way of thinking about how we relate to place. The notion of recontextualization in social semiotics draws largely from Bernstein's (1990) work on pedagogic discourse (the ways in which knowledge is recontextualized in educational contexts). This has been expanded to a broader notion that links to intertextuality or interdiscursivity – the ways in which texts or discourses reoccur or are echoed in other texts. For Fairclough (2001; 2005), Bernstein's (1990) concept of recontextualization entails both hybridity and transformation: it is part of the process of mixing of discourses as they are taken up in different texts, and of the changes that texts and discourses undergo as a result. Recontextualization therefore has to do with "the principles according to which one social practice selectively appropriates others" (2005, p. 65).

Productive though these ideas of recontextualization, appropriation and hybridity can be, they tend to assume the transparency of similarity and difference: recontextualization describes occurrences of the same things in different contexts, and hybridity describes the mixing of two different elements. In order to develop a more dynamic account of relocalization, by contrast, we need to appreciate that hybridization, as Young (1995, p. 26) makes clear, "makes difference into sameness, and sameness into difference, but in a way that makes the same no longer the same, the different no longer simply different". This is the same logic that Derrida uses in his notion of 'brisure' (breaking) in which "difference and sameness" occur in an "apparently impossible simultaneity" (Young, 1995, p. 26). As we rethink notions of time, place and flow, of the possibility of simultaneous sameness and difference, relocalization rather than recontextualization becomes a more useful concept, since it allows us to think in more dynamic terms about place. Rather than drawing on the undeveloped and overused notion of context, relocalization makes notions of locality central. How we understand the idea of the local in relation to time and space will be a major focus of the next chapter, where I shall discuss linguistic landscaping – talking and writing in the city – as a local practice.

Relocalization also draws attention to a central theme of this chapter: similarity, difference and repetition. While recontextualization tends towards a notion of something happening in different surrounds, I want the term relocalization to carry a broader sense of co-occurrence in time and place. As DJ Spooky says, echoing the ideas of Bakhtin (1981; 1986) and Barthes (1977): "it's all about the changing same, the core of repetition at modern thought. The samples and fragments speak the unspoken, the ascent remains unbroken" (Miller, 2004, p. 28). This vision of cultural production as relocalization rather than new construction presents a noteworthy counterpoint to current perceptions of creativity as newness, difference, divergence from what has gone before. A central premise of many conceptions of difference and creativity is that time, and to some extent place, do not change the practice: in other words, doing something again, or doing it somewhere else, do not constitute difference or creativity. In this chapter, however, I shall explore the implications of a deeper sense of locality in relation to time and place. A focus on relocalization can thus suggest forms of change and renewal through what may appear a paradoxical focus on repetition.

Repetition here does not refer to the echoing of phrases commonly discussed in stylistics (Simpson, 2004), nor the use of repeated phrases in discourse that Tannen (1989) and Carter (2004) both observe to be such a common component of the co-construction of discourse. In these cases, while repeated language – either the more formal repetition of poetry and song or the more spontaneous echoing in dialogue – can be very much part of a creative process, repeated language is generally taken to be a repetition of the same thing. The focus in this chapter, by contrast, is on how repetition does not repeat the same thing, how "Repetition, which we might have thought to be a matter of the Same, turns out to be a matter of the Different, the obscure" (Bearn, 2000, p. 444). This is not therefore a question of repetition for stylistic effect or solidarity, but of repetition as an act of difference, relocalization, renewal.

Since a great deal of academic work over the last few decades has taken up the challenge to understand difference, it is perhaps time, as B Fuchs (2001, p. 4) argues, to "consider also the political and rhetorical valence of *sameness* – identification, mimicry, reproduction. As complementary opposites, sameness and difference cannot truly be divided: the study of fidelity in representation leads necessarily to a consideration of adulteration, while accounts of imposed uniformity must generally consider the existence of subversive mimicry, the troubling same-but-different." This is an important point to grasp in relation to a notion of language as a local practice: if practices are concatenations of social activities, repeated again and again, we may appear to be condemned to an endless pathway of repetition. If, however, we can take on board an understanding of 'the troubling same-but-different' in relation to relocalization, we can start to see how language as a local practice is as much about change as it is about staying the same.

In Chapter 2, while making a case for the serious take-up of a notion of practice, I also identified a number of potential problems. One of the most important is the question of repeated action and agency, or put another way, if practices are the key generic social thing and are understood as repeated activity, what space is there for a sense of human possibility, for choice and change? Can we choose or change the practices we engage in? Similarly, as Thrift (2007) notes, a potential shortcoming with the notion of practices is the absence of a "sense of mutability; of the moments of inspired improvisation, conflicting but still fertile mimesis, rivalrous desires, creative forms of symbiosis, and simple transcription errors which make each moment a new starting point" (p. 21). At one level, then, we are back in the same old questions about structure and agency that recur in so many discussions of the

relationship between humans and the social, cultural and ideological structures we have built for ourselves. In this chapter, and other parts of this book,
however, I shall draw particular attention to these ideas of *fertile mimesis*, of
copying that goes slightly wrong, of repetition that is something else, of
sameness that is difference, as a way of understanding how it is we do things
as humans.

In this chapter, therefore, I shall focus on that difficult domain of practice
that is repetition, on the troubling same-but-different space of mimicry, re-
enactment and relocalization. Inspired by examples from contemporary cultural practices, and focusing particularly on philosophies that have taken
questions of repetition, iterability and mimesis seriously, I try to show here
how common assumptions about language use as newness that diverges from
a core of sameness need to be located within a very particular intellectual
trajectory. An alternative understanding of local language practices in terms
of relocalization sheds new light on a range of applied linguistic topics, from
writing to language variation. The alternative, or at least complementary,
understanding raised by DJ Spooky's contention that creativity rests in how
you relocalize the previous expression of others points not only to a contemporary age made possible by digital sampling, but also to a parallel philosophy of language use which I will explore in greater depth later in the
chapter. A central question here, then, is what happens to our understanding
of language as a local practice if we assume not so much the transparency
and normalcy of sameness and the opacity of difference, but rather take difference to be the norm and sameness as that which needs to justify itself.

The creativity of the copy

A headless yet splendidly dressed vicar skates across a pond (see cover picture).
When British/Nigerian artist Yinka Shonibare MBE (he insists on the repeated and ironic use of his MBE) was challenged as a young art student about
doing 'authentic African art' (although born in Britain, he had been brought
up in Lagos, Nigeria), he reflected that on the one hand his own background
was a mixed, hybrid cosmopolitan one – he grew up in Nigeria watching the
Australian TV series *Skippy the Bush Kangaroo* – and on the other the whole
question of authenticity was in need of much more exploration. In Brixton
(London) Market, he came across a stall selling brightly coloured 'African'
clothing that turned out to have been designed in the Netherlands, copying
Indonesian batik. The original colonial project of mass production of these
batiks for the Dutch East Indies had not been as successful as its designers
had hoped, so the manufacturers had targeted West Africa, where independence movements were emphasizing a return to 'traditional' brightly coloured
African clothing. As the success in this market grew, this Dutch wax cloth
started to be made in Manchester, and sold in London. For Yinka Shonibare
MBE (he insists on the repeated and ironic use of his MBE), the interest
here is in the 'fakeness' of authenticity, the way in which these brightly

coloured clothes often associated with West Africa are in fact Dutch copies of Indonesian art.

Starting with these ironies of colonial cloth manufacture, Yinka Shonibare MBE (he insists on the repeated and ironic use of his MBE) clothes headless mannequins (a reference to the French Revolution, as well as a deracialization of his figures) in flamboyant eighteenth-century clothes made from 'Dutch wax' materials. While in other works, such as *Diary of A Victorian Dandy* (1998) or *Dorian Gray* (2001) he inserts himself in a series of photographs reproducing these stories and images, in his three-dimensional mannequin pieces, he reproduces well-known eighteenth-century images, such as Fragonard's painting *The Swing*, or Gainsborough's *Mr and Mrs Andrews Without Their Heads* (1998). And these figures are always dressed in flamboyant colour, using a reproduction of cheap cloth made for African export. In his *Reverend on Ice* (2005), for example, based on Henry Raeburn's painting The *Rev Robert Walker Skating on Duddingston Loch*, a headless mannequin dressed in brightly coloured clothes made from Dutch wax batik skates elegantly on mock ice. The original picture itself, as Shonibare (2008) explains, puts the reverend in an unusual pose, but he relocates it further to render the reverend irreverent. This is all about relocalization, taking a series of elements – well-known images, Dutch wax cloth, headless mannequins – and placing them in new collocations with each other. Bringing questions of race, class and colonialism to a subversion of notions of authenticity and purity, Yinka Shonibare MBE (he insists on the repeated and ironic use of his MBE) makes ideas of repetition, relocalization and iterability central to his art and politics.

While Shonibare may develop this practice of reference and repetition further than other artists, there is nothing so new about the constant cross-referencing of artistic work. And yet, the cultural and intellectual pathway that has led to a vision of both artistic creativity and language use as a process of originary production, newness and difference, has a powerful and influential lineage. Mapping different eras of creativity, Kearney (1988) shows how early theocentric art, where the image was not so much the creative product of an artist but rather the inspiration of God, was gradually replaced in European culture by the anthropocentric or humanist concept of the artist as individual creator: "The modern movements of Renaissance, Romantic and Existentialist humanism replaced this theocentric paradigm of the mimetic craftsman with the anthropocentric paradigm of the original *inventor*. Whether drawing from the scientific idiom of experimenter, the colonial idiom of explorer or the technological idiom of industrial engineer, the modern aesthetic promotes the idea of the artist as one who not only emulates but actually replaces God" (p. 12).

Of central importance here are the cultural and historical particularity of this orientation towards the individual as inspired creator, as well as the substitution of the idea of the *mimetic* creator by this new vision of anthropocentric creativity. As Shusterman (2000) makes clear, this romantic "cult of genius" insisted on the individual as source and inspiration for creative endeavour, works of art being deemed to be manifestations of unique personalities. This notion of the creative artist simultaneously ignored the fact that "artists have always borrowed from each other's works", positing a "sharp distinction between original creation and derivative borrowing" (p. 64). In the shift from the mimetic to the anthropocentric, therefore, the roles of copying, mimesis and external inspiration were discarded as antithetical to the creative genius.

Although a line is sometimes drawn between art and science, between the creative genius and the technician, the romantic notion of the individual, creative artist cannot be dissociated from other modernist movements of science, colonialism and technology. The iconic image of creativity born from the lonely struggles and tortured soul of the isolated artist should not therefore be juxtaposed with an image of industrial sameness (as romantic artists would have us believe), but rather should be seen as part of a broader cultural and philosophical movement that posited creativity as the product of individual difference, whether as artistic endeavour, scientific discovery, geographical exploration or technological invention. Underlying these different domains is not so much a polarity between art and science, originality and technology, but instead a common cultural orientation towards creativity. Rather than dwelling on that almost parodic figure of the lonely artist as the epitome of modernist images of creativity, it is therefore useful to view such artists as the extreme of a more fundamental conception of what constitutes creativity. It came to lie not only in the creative artist, but more broadly in the distinctively individual efforts of particular genius.

While the new was thus deemed to be the creation of difference by the efforts of the individual, language studies struggled with a central tension between the individual and language as system. The rise of structuralist thinking in linguistics and other social sciences in the twentieth century emphasized structure over agency, drawing attention away from the individuality of performance, towards the individual's internalization of systematicity that makes creativity possible. As it developed as a special kind of colonial encounter (Errington, 2008), linguistics, like other European projects of global scientific endeavour, sought "to scientifically taxonomise all aspects of difference – an idea that had great intellectual currency at the time" (Nakata, 2007, p. 32). By doing so, linguistics rendered difference as epiphenomenal variegation, with language users, culture and history peripheral to the assumed similarity at the heart of humanity. Chomsky's inspired rejection of the narrow confines of behaviourism and structuralism, particularly the work of Bloomfield and Skinner, led to a search for creativity – *creative construction* as Dulay, Burt and Krashen (1982) called it in the context of emergent second language grammars – in the ability to generate grammatical sentences from insufficient data. From Chomsky's point of view, the central goal of linguistics was to discover "the rich systems of invariant structures and principles that underlie the most ordinary and humble of human accomplishments" (Chomsky, 1971, p. 46).

Structuralism focused on structure, competence and internal processing as the cornerstone of language use, while struggling to account for agency and variation (bracketed away as performance, sociolinguistics and pragmatics). This view nevertheless shared a set of assumptions with a humanist conception of creativity. Underlying the human condition and its particular feature, language, is a commonality, whether humanist or universalist, that rests on a shared sameness. The structuralist-humanist position takes a strong stance against mimicry or repetition as significant for learning or creativity, especially through the rejection of what were seen as behaviourism's mimetic obsessions. And yet, as Bourdieu (1977, p. 95) remarked, Chomsky's assumption that "the only escape from Bloomfieldian behaviourism lay in seeking 'freedom' and 'creativity' in the 'structure' – i.e. the 'nature' – of the human mind" remains locked within a very particular formulation of universality as an escape from the particular.

We have been left therefore with an intellectual legacy that renders creativity either the production of language from an internal competence, a rule-governed capacity to create well-formed language, or as divergence of language from a set of linguistic norms, the breaking of rule-governed language to produce difference. As Carter (2004, p. 9) observes, "when the word 'creative' is employed it entails uses which are marked out as striking and innovative. Conventionally, this involves a marked breaking of rules and norms of language, including a deliberate play with its forms and its potential for meaning." Creativity is therefore a form of divergence from a common core, difference from an underlying sameness; repetition, mimicry or recontextualization are given short shrift from this point of view.

A puzzle emerges, however, when we look at studies of actual language use and creativity, or the work of DJ Spooky or Yinka Shonibare MBE. It has not escaped the attention of more socially oriented linguists that, rather than the constant creation of different utterances, language use may, by contrast, be a highly repetitious act: "In real life, most sentences that are uttered are not uttered for the first time. A great deal of discourse is more or less routinized; we tell the same stories and express the same opinions over and over again" (Halliday, 1978, p. 4). While such repetitive discourse might be viewed as the contextually limited uncreative language use of the everyday, Tannen (1989) has argued by contrast that repetition is a central meaning-making resource. Indeed, it has been observed both that repetition in discourse may be the norm rather than the exception, and that far from being the exceptional case, creativity in language is extremely common. And not only is the constant play of repeated language in speech crucial to the construction of shared discourse, but repetition has also been found to be a very significant part of creative language use (Cook, 2000, pp. 28–30; Carter, 2004, pp. 6–8).

While this observation does not necessarily unsettle common assumptions about language – after all, it is not hard to observe that language is constantly repeated and that this may also be quite creative – the idea that creativity is the norm rather than a rarity (Carter, 2004; Cook, 2000; Crystal, 1998) does suggest the need for a reconsideration of what is meant by creativity: where a romantic orientation stresses the lone genius (creativity is rare and special) and structuralism the commonality of creativity (all language use is created from the core of invariant structure), a focus on everyday discourse suggests that whether planned or unplanned, poetry or prose, informal interaction or formal text, joke telling, punning or language play, we're all at it: language creativity is the common stuff of everyday language use. Noting the ubiquity of creativity in his data, Carter suggests that "our systems for describing language may need to be realigned to account for the fact that creative language may be a default condition, a norm of use from which ordinary, routine, 'non-creative' exchanges constitute an abnormal departure" (2004, p. 214).

Now if we accept the apparently paradoxical state of affairs whereby the breaking of language norms may be the norm (which surely undermines the notion of the norm), and if, in addition, we acknowledge that repetition is a substantial part of creative language use (which undermines the notion of creativity as difference), we may need to do more than 'realign' our views of language. We are left with the position that everyday, routine practices of language are abnormal and non-creative departures from a world of language use in which creative rule-breaking and repetition are the norm. What if we turn this on its head in order to try to make some sense of things? What if we suggest that rules are not in fact rules but the convergent effects of rule breaking? That is to say, given that the idea that the norm is the breaking of norms lacks a certain coherence, could it be that what we assume are norms are simply not so? This idea will be pursued further below when we look at issues of emergence and sedimentation, arguing that grammar is not a set of norms that we adhere to or break, but rather, the repeated sedimentation of form as a result of ongoing discourse. We produce language as a result of our local practices.

And could it also be that the apparently non-creative repetition of language is in fact more creative than first thought? It is not so much that we repeat things in different linguistic performances and that these repetitions may be part of creative language use, but rather that local language practices repeat difference, not sameness.[1] Of course, in a range of poetic and everyday language uses there may be creative use of repetition, in the sense that the repetition may be part of a creative process, but if we take this insight further, we arrive at the point that repeating the same thing in any movement through time relocalizes that repetition as something different. This is not a case, then, of merely acknowledging that repetition is common in creative language use, but rather, one of coming to terms with a deep contradiction in language studies: if language users constantly break putative rules and yet are constantly repeating language, then something has to give here.

For Taussig (1993, p. 129), mimesis "plays the trick of dancing between the very same and the very different. An impossible but necessary, indeed an everyday affair, mimesis registers both sameness and difference, of being like, and of being Other." What is at stake here, then, "is not so much staying the same, but maintaining sameness though alterity" (p. 129). We need to work from an alternative starting point, where difference is the norm and repetition of the same may be a form of difference. Thinking about language use in terms of fertile mimesis suggests that it is sameness, not difference, that needs to account for itself. To pursue this way of thinking further, to understand that language as a local practice is a form of language repetition that creates difference, we need to open up some alternative ways of thinking about time, space, difference and repetition.

On stepping and not stepping twice in the same river

According to Shusterman (2000), a postmodern cultural formation such as hip-hop undermines the dichotomy between creativity and copying "by creatively deploying and thematizing its appropriation to show that borrowing and creation are not at all incompatible" (p. 64). Shusterman's invocation of postmodernism points in several directions. If viewed in terms of postmodernity (the material conditions of an age of digital technologies; see Pennycook, 2006), we might be tempted to view the digital sampling of DJ Spooky and the hip-hop world only as a form of copying rendered possible by new technologies, or the redressing of mannequins in Yinka Shonibare MBE's work as merely a playful remaking of the past made possible by the mass production of batik. Viewed through the lenses of postmodernism (the philosophical questioning of the assumptions of modernity and the occidentalization of thought; see Venn, 2000), however, we can start to explore the "postmodern conviction that the very concept of a creative imagination is a passing illusion of Western *humanist* culture" (Kearney, 1998, p. 28).

When DJ Spooky suggests that creativity may be seen as the relocalization of the words of others, or Yinka Shonibare MBE sends a headless vicar in bright Dutch wax clothes skating across a fake Scottish loch, we are invited not only to consider the relationship to pre-modernist concepts of creativity and postmodernist possibilities of sampling, but also to engage an alternative philosophical tradition which, in opposition to the framework of core regularity and peripheral play, emphasizes difference, repetition, intertextuality, flow, mimesis and performativity. In the European tradition, these ideas can be traced back to Heraclitus (540–475 BC), who insisted that change was real and stability only illusory, famously proclaiming that:

> Ποταμοῖς τοῖς αὐτοῖς ἐμβαίνομέν τε καὶ οὐκ ἐμβαίνομεν, εἶμέν τε καὶ οὐκ εἶμεν.
> "We both step and do not step in the same rivers. We are and are not."
> (Kahn, 1979)

Heraclitus' ideas were later to influence that line of thinking that runs from Nietzsche to Heidegger (Heidegger and Fink, 1993; Iyer, 2005) and on to Deleuze. It was Deleuze who pushed further the insights of Heidegger's phenomenological insistence that we cannot rely on a notion of a fixed standpoint to understand the world, but rather must see the flow of changing phenomena by focusing on time and becoming. Deleuze argued that modern thought has emphasized sameness and generalizability over difference: the similarity, even universality, of things is taken as a given or a goal, with difference being something that needs to be accounted for in this general model of sameness (human nature, universal language, common structures of thought) (Deleuze and Guattari, 1987). For Deleuze, by contrast, difference should be taken as the foundation of our thinking, with sameness in need of explanation when it occurs. In his key work, *Difference and Repetition*, Deleuze (2004 [1968]) focuses on the ways in which difference occurs, as events, ideas and language are repeated over time: "To repeat is to behave in a certain manner, but in relation to something unique or singular which has no equal or equivalent. And perhaps this repetition at the level of external conduct echoes, for its own part, a more secret vibration which animates it, a more profound, internal repetition within the singular. This is the apparent paradox of festivals: they repeat an 'unrepeatable'" (pp. 1–2). For Deleuze, then, a central question concerns the ways in which repetition – of festivals, words, events, ideas – produces difference rather than sameness. "Each repetition of a word", explains Colebrook, "is always a different inauguration of that word, transforming the word's history and any context" (2002, p. 120).

Following this line of thinking, repetition always entails difference, since no two moments, events, words can be the same. Once we make an understanding of the flow of time central to an understanding of difference, "any repeated event is necessarily different (even if different only to the extent that it has a predecessor). The power of life is difference and repetition, or the eternal return of difference. Each event of life transforms the whole of life, and does this over and over again" (Colebrook, 2002, p. 121). As Deleuze puts it, "We produce something new only on condition that we repeat – once in the mode which constitutes the past, and once more in the present of metamorphosis. Moreover, what is produced, the absolutely new itself, is in turn nothing but repetition ... " (2004, p. 113). Ultimately, Deleuze argues, "It is repetition itself that is repeated." (2004, p. 367). This presents a very different way of thinking about originality, creativity, difference and repetition. Repetition, even of the 'same thing', always produces something new, so that when we repeat an idea, a word, a phrase or an event, it is always renewed. From this point of view, sameness (language structure, identity, cultural norms) needs to be explained rather than assumed, and when we produce something new, this must always be a case of repetition. Language as a local practice, from this point of view, is not only repeated social activity involving language, but is also, through its relocalization in space and time, the repetition of difference.

While Deleuze's repetition is not the same as Derrida's iterability (Bearn, 2000), the re-emphasis on time rather than place, on the centrality of repetition rather than originality, also underlies Derrida's argument. In his debate with John Searle concerning the type of speech acts that were excluded from

Austin's (1962) model of performativity (Austin excluded what he termed *etiolations*, language uses that were not serious or real, such as jokes and plays) Derrida (1982) argued that such exclusions raised an important point about language use: "Is not what Austin excludes as anomalous, exceptional, 'non-serious,' that is, citation (on the stage, in a poem, or in a soliloquy), the determined modification of a general citationality – or rather, a general iterability – without which there could not even be a 'successful' performative?" (1982, p. 325). For Derrida, then, the crucial issue was not so much one of trying to establish what made a performative felicitous – the right person saying it at the right time under the right conditions – but rather the way in which language use was made effective by repetition, by citation. "Could a performative statement succeed", Derrida asked, "if its formulation did not repeat a 'coded' or iterable statement, in other words if the expressions I use to open a meeting, launch a ship, or a marriage were not identifiable as conforming to an iterable model, and therefore if they were not identifiable in a way as 'citation'?" (p. 326). For Searle and Austin, a signature was a performative because, by signing one's name, one does the act of signing; Derrida asks whether such acts as signing do not gain their power from the general citationality and iterability of language rather than from these contextual acts of original authorship.

While Deleuze's repetition and Derrida's iterability are underlying and largely unintended patterns of language use, there are also acts of repetition that are more clearly intentional: the deliberate repetition of sameness in the form of mimicry and mimesis.[2] For B Fuchs (2001, p. 5), it is important to see mimesis "as a deliberate performance of sameness that necessarily threatens, or at least modifies, the original". As both Michael Taussig and Homi Bhabha have argued, mimicry of the dominant powers, arts and discourses unsettles those powers and creates a new relationship between colonized and colonizer. Michael Taussig's work on the ways in which modern Western images are incorporated into traditional arts (such as the RCA 'listening dog's' incorporation into traditional weaving, or the Cuna's figurines of white people) suggests that such mimesis becomes a weapon for the non-Western or colonized subject, a tool that undermines the status and distinction of the West.

As Taussig (1993, p. 8) observed, the Cuna's figurines depicting white people unsettled his position as anthropologist, since the "very mimicry corrodes the alterity by which my science is nourished. For now I too am part of the object of study. The Indians have made me alter to myself." In a similar vein, Bhabha (1985) suggests that the civilizing mission of colonialism is put under threat by colonial mimicry, by the ambivalence of being almost but not quite the same, of being both resemblance and menace. For Bhabha (1985, p. 131), mimicry "is like camouflage, not a harmonization or repression of difference, but a form of resemblance that differs/defends presence by displaying it in part, metonymically." Yinka Shonibare MBE's mimicry of paintings by Fragonard, Gainsborough or Raeburn, or his recreation of the 'Scramble for Africa' as fourteen brightly dressed, headless figures seated around a table, arguing over the colonial division of Africa, can similarly be seen as a process of destabilizing relations of colonial and postcolonial power.

Walcott (1997) makes a related observation in his discussion of Black diasporic language and culture: the extraordinary oppressions of slavery "produced spaces for particular forms of identity, identifications and disidentifications. Being forced to perform for the master in a number of different ways meant that a relationship to identity for diasporic black people manifested itself as something that could be invented, revised and discarded when no longer useful" (Walcott, 1997, p. 98). This understanding of identity performances as a form of resistance ties in with James Scott's (1985; 1990) discussions of the 'weapons of the weak', the 'hidden transcripts' that underlie the many local acts of resistance to domination. From poaching, squatting and desertion to gossip, rumour, carnival, social myth and dissident subcultures, the arts of resistance are often hidden and subversive. These "weapons of the weak … these simple acts of false compliance, parody, pretence, and mimicking are the strategies by which the marginalized detach themselves from the ideologies of the powerful, retain a measure of critical thinking, and gain some measure of control over their life in an oppressive situation" (Canagarajah, 2000, p. 122). Yet, in addition to being identities that can be discarded, in addition to allowing a measure of control through mimicry, such parodic strategies are also acts of sameness that create difference: they differ from the original and simultaneously change the original through relocalization.

Returning to Heraclitus' point that one can never step into the same river twice (that when we step again into a river we are both stepping into the same and not the same river, or we are and are not the same stepper), it is important to note that this view of the world takes change and flow as the norm; and it can therefore contain seeming contradictions that the river is and is not the same, that we are and are not. This ties in with a central contention of Thrift's (2007) non-representational theory that human life is best understood not in terms of the frozen states implied by grammars and languages as objects, but rather in terms of movement. Fritjof Capra's attempt to connect Eastern metaphysical philosophy – where the possibility of the unity of opposites had long been entertained – with the discoveries of new physics revealed that "the principal theories and models of modern physics lead to a view of the world which is internally consistent and in perfect harmony with the views of Eastern mysticism" (1985, p. 303). Capra overtly compares the "Greek 'Taoist'" Heraclitus with the Taoist philosopher Lao Tzu, since they shared "not only the emphasis on continuing change, which he [Heraclitus] expressed in his famous saying 'Everything flows,' but also the notion that all changes are cyclic" (1985, p. 116). Just as physics needed to accept the Daoist unity of opposites in order to accept the co-occurrence of waves and particles, so an understanding of language as a local practice needs to accept that in the relocalization of language, language acts do not enter the same flow twice: to say the same thing again, whether as an everyday language act or as an intentional act of mimesis, is to invoke difference through sameness.

Language as sedimented discourse

From one point of view, stability, structure, universality and commonality are the background against which language use occurs: languages are systems that can be used in different contexts: the underlying system remains the same but the recontextualization of use can bring about new meanings. Once we can establish the rules that exist irrespective of time and place, we can then show how context and human action creatively transcend these norms through the production of difference. An alternative position, by contrast, views such permanence, organization and unity as illusionary, a product of sedimented action. As both Hopper (1998) and Butler (1990) show, in their very different ways, accounts of underlying sameness (whether grammatical structure or gendered identities) mistakenly attribute structure/sameness to underlying rules instead of the effects of repetition. For Butler, the "subject is not *determined* by the rules through which it is generated because signification is *not a founding act, but rather a regulated process of repetition*" (Butler, 1990, p. 145; emphasis in original). For Hopper, the apparent structure or regularity of grammar is an emergent property that "is shaped by discourse in an ongoing process. Grammar is, in this view, simply the name for certain categories of observed repetitions in discourse" (1998, p. 156).

This is not merely an observation that languages are always changing and that grammar is always therefore, in the longer term, temporary, but rather that the notion of systematicity embedded in the concept of grammar is itself a product of repeated social action. According to Croft's (2001) *Radical Construction Grammar*, "grammatical knowledge is acquired through the use of language in utterances" and "social interaction determines the macro-processes of language change: variation, propagation, language contact, language divergence, language shift. At the microlevel, constructions arise and evolve in the course of language use … Syntax cannot be separated from its context" (p. 368). For Bybee and Hopper (2001), linguistic structure is seen not as an independent set of pre-given laws but rather "as a response to discourse needs" (p. 2). From this point of view, "grammar comes about through the repeated adaptation of forms to live discourse" (ibid.). The implications of this view for an account of language as a practice are clear: it is not that we use language as a pre-given entity in context, but rather that we produce language in our repeated local activities. Furthermore, these activities are parts of bundled practices, and as such they are always social, always historical and always local.

According to Bybee and Hopper, 2001 (p. 3), this understanding of grammar as *emergent* is akin to Giddens' (1979) understanding of *structuration*, a term he used to capture the relationship and the mutual interdependence of structure and agency. In this view, there is a constant reciprocal structuring, with social structures both the medium and the product of social action, or from the point of view of language practices, there is a constant reciprocal restructuring both of language and of the social domain. "The notion of language as a monolithic system has had to give way to that of a language as a massive collection of heterogeneous *constructions*, each with affinities to different contexts and in constant structural adaptation to usage" (Bybee and Hopper, 2001, p. 3). Thus, just as Butler (1999, p. 120) argues that identities are a product of ritualized social performatives calling the subject into being and "sedimented through time", so for Hopper "there is no natural fixed structure to language. Rather, speakers borrow heavily from their previous experiences of communication in similar circumstances, on similar topics, and with similar interlocutors. Systematicity, in this view, is an illusion produced by the partial settling or *sedimentation* of frequently used forms into temporary subsystems" (1998, pp. 157–58).

This view of repetition and sedimentation sits uncomfortably with a consensus that stresses prior interior being on two scores: on the one hand, by denying the existence of core rules and identities, it unsettles widely held beliefs about grammar and individuality; on the other hand, by rendering grammar and identity the products of repeated action, it can appear to remove all semblance of will and agency in favour of socially regulated behaviour. As I have been arguing, however, if we view sedimentation as a product of fertile mimesis, of repetition that is never the same, we can see the construction of apparent regularity of language and grammar in terms of relocalized difference. From this point of view, change, difference and flow are the norms, repetition is always different, and any apparent sameness needs to account for itself. Or to put things another way, the conundrum discussed earlier (where rule-breaking was the apparent norm and repetition ubiquitous) can be reinterpreted by seeing repetition as a form of renewal that creates the illusion of systematicity.

Taking difference as the norm, rejecting a model of commonality and divergent creativity, viewing structure as the apparent effect of sedimented repetition and bringing a sense of flow and time into the picture open up important new directions for thinking about language as a local practice. Such a position forces us to question assumptions about context, diversity, ownership and originality. It suggests a rethinking of the relation between competence and performance, since we can start to see the latter not so much as a secondary by-product of an underlying competence but rather as the primary context of repeated difference where the regularities of sedimented sameness are produced. As Bauman (2004, p. 10) puts it, "Approaching performance in terms of the dynamics of recontextualization opens up ways to a recognition of alternative and shifting frames available for the reconceptualization of texts. Successive reiterations, even of texts for which performance is the expected, preferred, or publicly foregrounded mode of presentation, may be variously rekeyed. A performed text may be subsequently – or, to be sure, antecedently – reported, rehearsed, translated, relayed, quoted, summarised, or parodied, to suggest but a few of the intertextual possibilities." Echoing Derrida's interest in the iterability of language, Bauman's emphasis on recontextualization and intertextuality – or as I am arguing here, relocalization – shows how apparent sameness becomes difference through its various repetitions.

As discussed in the previous chapter, a key text in the development of a theory of practice is Bourdieu's (1977) *Outline of a theory of practice*. And yet, as with the need discussed above to find a way of thinking about repeated social action that does not lock us into always doing the same thing over and over, so we need to be cautious with Bourdieu's thinking on language as social activity. In her discussion of speech acts and performativity, Butler (1997) critiques Bourdieu's "conservative account of the speech act" on the basis that it "presumes that the conventions that will authorize the performative are already in place, thus failing to account for the Derridean 'break' with context that utterances perform" (p. 142). The problem with Bourdieu is that his view of context is too confining. Yet Derrida's more generalized view that "the force of the performative is derived from its decontextualization, from its break with a prior context and its capacity to assume new contexts" (p. 147) is also problematic, since it takes us out of context. As Butler goes on to argue, "whereas Bourdieu fails to take account of the way in which a performative can break with and assume new contexts, ... Derrida appears to install the break as a structurally necessary feature of every utterance and every codifiable written mark, thus paralysing the social analysis of forceful utterance". (p. 150).

What we need instead is a way of thinking about language as a local practice that does two important things: it moves away from an account of language as pre-given structure and instead accounts for language as the product of practice, of repeated social activity; and at the same time, it develops a notion of locality rather than context, which itself is imbued with a sense of time and movement. Language practices cannot happen out of locality, but neither are they defined by it. This idea builds on Butler's understanding of performativity and the particular ways in which this can be taken up in relation to language (Pennycook, 2004; 2007a). Performative language use constitutes language; it creates what it purports to be in the doing. The account of language as a local practice that I am developing can help us get beyond the dilemma that Butler finds herself in here, caught between Bourdieu's over-determined social context and Derrida's decontextualized utterance. Understanding the performativity of language in relation to relocalization allows for an understanding of utterances as never outside a locality, nor determined by it.

Conclusion: language practices and relocalization

The ways in which repetition and change occur may be likened to the processes of evolution. Simply put, over long periods of time, the processes of natural selection operate in relation to minor and generally random changes in genetic transmission.[3] The reproduction of genetic material is not always reproduction. Every so often small differences occur and if these favour certain features or behaviours at a particular time, they may over time be reproduced more regularly. Likewise language and social practice. As I have argued, the notion of practice carries with it a strong sense of repeated action. How does difference happen? In two ways: humans are, of course, capable of changing things, though often much less than we like to think. By and large, we go on doing more or less the same thing over and over. But we can make intentional changes to what we do, and these changes may become sedimented over time. There are also small, unintentional slippages, changes to the ways we do and say things, and these too may start to be repeated and become sedimented practices. And, as I have argued in this chapter, what appears to be the same may in fact also be already different.

"Rap songs simultaneously celebrate their originality and their borrowing" (Shusterman, 2000, p. 65). As I shall argue in Chapter 5, this simultaneity of originality and borrowing, this "recycling of the old", this picture in which "there are no ultimate, untouchable originals, only appropriations of appropriations", this liberation of creative energy "to play with familiar creations without fear that it thereby denies itself the opportunity to be truly creative" (Shusterman, 2000, p. 64–65), starts to unsettle ways of thinking about origins. Once we see the possibility that to be original or authentic, as Yinka Shonibare MBE (he insists on the repeated and ironic use of his MBE) shows us, is not about what is supposedly tied to an apparent identity, but is rather a question of relocalization, then we can see that questions of origins become highly suspect. In Chapter 5 I will question the idea of 'language spread' that lies at the heart of much discussion of global English and instead suggest that it has multiple, simultaneous origins.

The problem that this chapter has tried to highlight is that the various strands of thought around originality, universality and individuality that underpin much common and current thought about language have tended to discard repetition, mimicry and similarity as non-creative. These assumptions have been built in to concepts such as competence and performance, with the former providing the conditions of possibility for the latter. The alternative discussed here, however, allows for a reversal of this view: the appearance of competence is a result of the sedimented practices of repeated performance. It is not so much a question of repetition occurring in creative language use, but rather that the ubiquity of creative language use and repetition (Carter, 2004) calls for a rethinking of common assumptions about language. Despite many disputes within applied linguistics as to what constitutes diversity, it is by and large a given that one is *for* diversity. Diversity, however, wears the face of discernible difference, and rarely includes sameness. Current debates about whether English presents a threat to the diversity of other languages, or whether in either its World Englishes centrifugal multiplicity or its lingua franca centripetal range, it presents an alternative diversity (for example, Rubdy and Saraceni, 2006), all operate with similar underlying beliefs in language cores with peripheral variation. In the centre is a language with common lexical, syntactic, morphological, semantic and phonological features. On the outskirts are forms that differ; difference remains a condition of human freedom that needs protection. Yet the focus of this chapter is that we need to look more closely at mimesis and repetition if we are to understand how language, and indeed human freedom, work.

A greater understanding of relocalization enables us to think in terms of the same item being different, while an understanding of difference as the norm and sameness as in need of explanation turns the tables on assumptions about diversity. Rather than a view of diversity that simultaneously supports the view of core similarity on which it is based, this position renders that difference the norm and requires similarity to account for itself. Instead of therefore assuming that English, for example, exists as an *a priori* object of analysis, with the diversity on its edges presenting a problem once it gets to be too different (as is the case often enough with Creole languages), the stability, indeed the ontology, of that core is perforce open to question as an illusion brought about by the misrecognition of sedimented performance in terms of underlying rules (Pennycook, 2007b). To understand difference not as intentional or unintentional divergence from a core, but rather as the repeated acts of quotidian language use, shifts the focus from stability to flow. The notion of repetition within a concept of difference does not make sameness primary: this is not a view of creativity as similarity. Rather, it is a view that questions the stasis and centrality of sameness in the dominant model of creativity, while opening up different ways of thinking about time and place and difference.

If we accept the possibility that the mimetic enactment of language may radically relocalize what superficially may appear to be the same, then a use of English, such as the imitation of an African American term in global hip-hop (Pennycook, 2007a; 2007c), may be full of multiple meanings of identification, localization, imitation and reinterpretation. This takes us back to issues of performativity and the point that language identities are performed in the doing, rather than reflecting a prior set of fixed options. The art of Yinka Shonibare MBE (he insists on the repeated and ironic use of his MBE) gains its force by the relocalization of images in a different time and space, by the reuse of Dutch wax fabric to recreate clothes that are both African and European, cheap cotton and expensive fabric. Any use of English, therefore, may not necessarily be tied to a past history of English use, but may rather be to perform English anew, to be involved in a "major radical act of semiotic reconstruction and reconstitution" (Kandiah, 1998, p. 100). If we assume difference, flow and becoming as the norm, then repetition, the use of apparently metropolitan English in non-metropolitan contexts, can be understood as acts of creative difference.

This chapter has sought to undercut these dichotomous assumptions about sameness and difference, creativity and conformity, repetition and originality. The message to be gleaned from dipping our toes in the clear and muddy waters of Heraclitus' river is that we need to understand that things both are and are not. At the very least, in order to understand language as a local practice we have to engage with the textual worlds of others rather than remain only in our own. And to do so may take an intellectual leap from the applied linguistic trajectory of thought that emphasizes difference as observable non-isomorphism to an alternative world in which we can never write the same thing, say the same words, use the same language, step into the same river twice. Language creativity is about sameness that is also difference, or to put it differently/similarly, language creativity is about sameness that is also difference.

4 Talking in the city
The linguistic landscaping of locality

Melbourne's graffiti have become a tourist attraction, so much so that groups of tourists head straight for some of the best-known alleys, such as Hosier Lane, just off Federation Square in central Melbourne. Two young Korean women, having seen Melbourne street art on Korean television, examine and photograph "a dense, lurid collage that ranges from rudimentary signatures drawn in marker pen to giant dayglo paintings and intricate paper prints pasted on the wall. 'Very good,' says one, indicating a playful image of a moon-faced Asian child hugging a docile killer whale. 'I like it very much'" (Jinman 2007, p. 11). "Head down Hosier lane on a weekend," suggests Coslovich (2005, np), "and you will see how the swirling, wild creations of the city's stencil and street artists engage the mainstream." This is not just a site for "wannabe rock stars seeking street cred for their new CD cover", but a much broader section of society who head for the backstreets to be "photographed against the gritty, glorious backdrop of street and stencil art". Tourists, passers-by, artists, brides and bridesmaids pause in front of Melbourne's graffiti to "secure a touch of urban chic" for their photographs.

Such graffiti tourism can be seen as part of the broader domain of hip-hop tourism (Xie et al., 2007), which in turn is related to music tourism more generally (Gibson and Connell, 2005). As Xie et al. (2007) explain, "The ghetto or the hood, which were once a source of sublime terror and fear, have been transformed by Hip-Hop into an enticing landscape for tourism: an image, a sound, graffiti mural waiting at a distance for visual and sensory consumption by those who come from farther afield" (p. 457). In addition to Hosier Lane in Melbourne, there are other well-known sites such as The Graffiti Hall of Fame at 106th Street and Park Avenue in New York, or Yokohama's graffiti wall in Japan. Although it is hard in many ways to mourn the disappearance of the Berlin Wall, we have nevertheless lost one of the world's great collections of artistic and political graffiti. *Berliner Mauerkunst* is still celebrated in museums, on postcards, in books, but it has gone as a living linguistic landscape.

The rise of British street artist Banksy, meanwhile, has greatly increased the value of some city walls, and has led to the inclusion of graffiti in some art exhibitions, either within galleries or as part of a tour round the city. In July

2009 there were long queues outside Bristol City Museum and Art Gallery to see some of Banksy's work on display, work that had moved from accessible city walls to the interior of a gallery. The 2008 Tate Modern 'Street Art' exhibition in London invited well-known street artists (Blu from Bologna, the Faile collective from New York, JR from Paris, Nunca and Os Gêmeos from São Paulo and Sixeart from Barcelona[1]) to create new works for part of the building's façade, while a collective of Madrid-based artists created a series of works around the city which people could visit on a walking tour. While such graffiti areas have become sanctioned (the tourist gaze, especially when supported by tourist dollars, plays a part in constructing the city), for many city officials, dwellers and visitors graffiti remain precisely that which should not be seen. Graffiti beckon from our peripheral vision as we traverse urban landscapes in cars, trains, buses, rickshaws or on foot, yet for many they are little more than passing flashes of indecipherable colour, reminders of anti-social tendencies and the ubiquity of global subcultures.

In this chapter, through a focus on graffiti and the struggles over urban space, I will look at the practices of locality, at the ways in which we create the spaces in which we live. Now that we have considered practices (Chapter 2) and language (Chapter 3) in greater depth, it is time to focus on the local. As already suggested in Chapter 1, a careful reconsideration of what is meant by the local can take us beyond accounts of context as inert backdrops against which we use language. A problem with the notion of the local is that it all too often operates only as a counterpoint to the macro, the global, the universal, the big. While this focus on the local as micro may be very welcome, useful, grounded and practical, the use of the term local in this context reduces the potential meaning of the term to the contextual or small-scale. Discussing 'language planning in local contexts' for example, Liddicoat and Baldauf (2008) make a good case for the need to view language planning not just in terms of top-down governmental decision making, but also in terms of local, individual, educational and community action on language: "Considering language planning only as the property of those who hold the institutional power to effect their decisions, ignores the interplay between the macro and the micro which is fundamental to all language planning work" (p. 11).

The common strategy in such approaches to the local is to define the macro category against which the local will be juxtaposed and then proceed with contextual studies of language policy, education or language use. Once the work has been done to define the context of locality – in opposition to global, macro, national top-down approaches – work then proceeds at this level of analysis without further consideration of the meaning of locality. The local is here, this place, this minority language, this activity (Guernsey French, the Maltaljan variety of Maltese in Australia, the role of the Kadazandusan Language Foundation in Malaysia). This focus on the context of language policy, on the often-overlooked, on rarely discussed languages, is of course generally a great advance over the work that remains only at the level of the common and the macro. What I want to argue, however, is that if we confine the notion of the local always to the small and the overlooked, the micro and the contextual, we run the risk of constraining the potential of the local at the same time that we explore it.

We need to understand how language planning often builds on small local actions, on decisions made in communities, on local publications. Such a focus on local action is a useful corrective to the bland work on language planning that has held sway for too long, doing little more than describing national policies. At the same time, however, we need to be cautious lest a focus on the local remain only on the 'bottom-up', the micro, the contextual, and is thereby bereft of more powerful interpretations. Amongst other things, we need to bring in an understanding of space here, and, as Thrift (2007) warns, in doing so, we need to avoid the reduction of space and locality to notions of scale or closeness. Indeed we need to banish "nearness as the measure of all things" (p. 17). When we think in terms of locality, we should not be concerned with either smallness or proximity. Focusing on the local, as Canagarajah (2005a) observes, is far more than merely looking at particular contexts, since it entails "radically reexamining our disciplines to orientate to language, identity, knowledge, and social relations from a totally different perspective. A local grounding should become the primary and critical force in the con-struction of contextually relevant knowledge if we are to develop more plural discourses" (p. xiv). From this point of view, taking locality into considera-tion is also about taking seriously local understandings of locality.

I intend to push these insights further by looking in much greater depth at locality as spatial practice. In addition to the practices turn discussed in Chapter 2, a 'spatial turn' has also influenced thought across the social sci-ences, including education (Edwards and Usher, 2008; Gulson and Symes, 2007a; 2007b). These turns, along with the linguistic, somatic and ecological (see Chapter 6), share a great deal in common. All come in the wake of post-structuralist/postmodern emphases on the *constructedness* of social life: all emphasize that we cannot take language, the body, the environment, space as given entities with evident meanings. Humans endow their surroundings and themselves with layers of meaning that are not in the end separable from the thing itself. While this might suggest a reluctance to engage with 'reality' through these turns, there is also at the same time an emphasis on bodies, actions, locations, spaces, environments, contexts. If reality has been set at a slightly greater distance (reality is a less knowable thing because of the ways we construct our worlds), the focus of attention has also moved more locally, to what we do, say, perceive.

The spatial turn draws on insights from writers such as Lefebvre (1991/1974), Soja (1989; 1996) and Massey (1992; 1994). More broadly, as suggested by the contributors to Crang and Thrift (2000), many key thinkers, from Bakh-tin, Bourdieu and Deleuze to Fanon, Foucault and Said, can be considered as spatial thinkers. For Lefebvre, space is socially produced, and social relations can only be understood in relation to the space in which they are constituted. He gives the example of the Mediterranean, which in addition to its basic geographical features is also a socially produced space with a particular focus for Northern Europeans as a leisure space. For French Hip-Hop artists of North African origin, by contrast, this becomes a 'black Mediterranean' (Swedenburg, 2001, p. 69), a metaphorical space where musical influences flow back and forth. The notion of the black Mediterranean is a reference to Gilroy's (1993) earlier notion of the Black Atlantic, referring to the many cultural and linguistic influences between West Africa, the Caribbean, North America and the UK. The French Atlantic (Miller, 2008) is also a focus of study in terms of similar relations between France, West Africa (Mali, Gabon, Senegal, Côte d'Ivoire) and the Caribbean and North America (Martinique, Guadeloupe, Haiti, Quebec). Where French slave routes formerly operated, complex mixes of music and culture now flow (Pennycook, 2007a). Indeed, 'oceanic cultural studies' (Ghosh and Muecke, 2007) is an emerging field of study, looking at oceans as cultural spaces of trade, exchange, movement, social relations and imagination. The spatial turn is thus both a reaction to changing conditions of movement – diasporic movements, labour migration, media connectivity – and a rethinking of the ways in which space has been understood.

At the core of the spatial turn is the observation that rather than being a neutral setting, a backdrop, a blank canvas against which social relations are acted out, space is a central interactive part of the social. For Soja (1996), drawing on Lefebvre (1991/1974), space is the "third existential dimension" (p. 3) that needs to be considered alongside, as well as deeply interwoven with, the social and the historical. This spatiality/historicality/sociality nexus, argues Soja, affects not only the ways in which we consider space but also the ways in which we understand history and society. Several basic concerns emerge from thinking through space. Claims to universality, to aspatial abstraction, become highly suspect. All thought, theory, ideas and writing need to be located geographically. Nothing happens non-locally. As I have already suggested, and will be exploring further in following chapters, this idea of the relocalization (rather than recontextualization) of language practices draws on these ways of thinking about space and locality.

A problem here, as with all turns, is that space (like language, the body, practice, ecology) may become little more than a generalized metaphor within social theory, "the everywhere of modern thought. It is the flesh that flatters the bones of theory. It is an all-purpose nostrum to be applied whenever things look sticky" (Crang and Thrift, 2000, p. 1). The same might be said of the so-called linguistic or discursive turn (Eagleton, 2004), with its constant call that everything is constructed in language. An overemphasis on space, as May and Thrift (2001) point out, has come about in part from the continued use of the time/space dichotomy. Even those who sought to challenge the conception of time as dynamic and space as static by reversing this polarity (e.g. Soja, 1989), have maintained the distinction. Indeed, the elevation of space over time in radical geography and social theory, while moving away from a "debilitating historicism" (p. 2) has led, according to May and Thrift

(2001), to a potentially equally debilitating spatialization. What we need, following Massey (1994), is a dissolution of this divide, an appreciation that space and time are indissolubly interlinked.

Recent thought on space, therefore, has sought to move beyond the remnants of a Kantian version of space as fixed and immutable, towards space that also encompasses a notion of time and change, space as process. From this point of view, we can look at "practice as an activity creating time-space not time-space as some matrix within which activity occurs" (Crang, 2001, p. 187). This insight is crucial for the arguments I am developing in this book: space (place, location, context) is not a backcloth on which events and language are projected through time. Rather, language practices are activities that produce time and space. The invocation of the *everyday* – practices are very much part of the focus on everyday activities – suggests not only the temporality or frequency of things that occur over and over in a mundane way, but also an everyday locality: our everyday activities are always in places that become part of the process. A local language practice – writing graffiti, talking about it, writing a policy to remove it – does not simply occur in time and space; time and space are part of the doing, and indeed are produced in the practice.

This is not therefore only about the local as opposed to the global, about the here and now, about the contextual, about micro rather than macro. Nor is it only about local understandings, language ideologies and the pluralization of discourse. Rather, it is about how we construct the local through what we do and say. This is not only about de Certeau's 'walking in the city' but also about 'talking in the city'. To explore what I mean by this, I shall turn to a discussion of space and movement. Graffiti as a spatial practice and tourism as mobile practice will help shed light on these issues. Graffiti are one of the ways in which cities are brought to life and space is narrated. Graffiti, as both products of artists moving through an urban landscape and as art viewed in motion, are part of the articulation of the cityscape. That graffiti are deemed a threat to property, propriety and pristine walls has to be seen in terms of struggles over the preferred semiotics of a city. Insistently and colourfully reminded that graffiti will farewell and welcome them from city to city, the possible discomfort for global travellers needs to be understood in terms of the flattened class images of the global that tourism produces.

Graffiti as counter-literacies

My interest here is not centrally with the textual scribblings on toilet walls often associated with the term graffiti, but rather the large hip-hop-style picture-texts, or the more recent development of stencil art, and in particular how these operate as local language and spatial practices. There is a great deal that can be said about graffiti as text, not only in terms of the political and social messages they may convey, but also in terms of the playful and transgressive language use. Jørgensen's (2008b) analysis of a graffito on the foot of the

Marx–Engels sculpture memorial in Berlin, for example, which reads 'LE KAPITAL C'EST FUN, LE COMMUNISME C'EST NUF', points to the use of the K within the French to refer to Marx's key work *Das Kapital*, and the *verlan* use of 'nuf' – a reversal of the English/French[2] 'fun' – as part of the complex polylingual language play here. The focus of this chapter, however, will be on graffiti 'writing' as one of the four core elements of the broader hip-hop culture (rapping or MCing, scratching or DJing, and break-dancing being the others), and as part of a move towards transmodality rather than the narrower confines of what is normally deemed to be 'language' (Penny-cook, 2007a). A classic hip-hop crew might be made up of one representative of each of the four elements, though graffiti has also developed into a distinctive subculture of its own, with attendant terminology such as *tag* (the most basic form of graffiti, a writer's logo or stylized signature with marker or spray paint), *buff* (the removal or covering up of graffiti), *blockbuster* (big, square letters, often tilted back and forth, usually in two colours), *throwup* (variously used to mean a quickly painted piece with one layer of spray paint and an outline, or also bubble letters of any sort, not necessarily filled), *bomb* (to cover an area with tags, throwups etc).

Doing graffiti, the practice of graffiti writing, then, can be understood as part of a subcultural activity that is about participation in a hip-hop/graffiti crew: it may be the process of writing/drawing illicitly, as much as the subsequent traces of that writing that matters. As Hansen (2005) shows, for a number of graffiti tourists to Melbourne (from Sweden, Germany and the US), the point is not to come and observe but to participate. Christen (2003) goes as far as to claim that graffiti crews "resemble medieval guilds or trade unions, with apprentices assisting on works designed by masters, often painting backgrounds and filling in outlines in preparation for the finer detailed work" (p. 63). Rahn (2002) likewise suggests that graffiti writing "provides a structure of traditional skills, mentors, and codes" (p. 191). While a case can therefore be made that participation in graffiti production may have important social, cultural and educational values, it is its unsanctioned deployment in public space that is of central importance to the arguments here. Although graffiti artists may do commissioned or legal work (rather than attempt to enforce 'zero tolerance' strategies (see below), some councils commission well-known artists to produce works on commonly painted walls in order to discourage others, bringing both respect and suspicion from other street artists), graffiti largely depends on its confrontation with the lines of authority around public space.

A common argument among graffiti artists is that the legally sanctioned billboards and advertisements that adorn urban environments are a greater eyesore than graffiti, and it is only the fact that capitalist-influenced laws make one legal and the other not that turns their art into an underground activity. As Melbourne street artist Vexta puts it, "I don't want to live in a city that's really bland and covered in grey and brown and advertising. I never said it was OK to put a billboard on the top of Brunswick Street,[3] so who's to say that I can't put up a small A4 size image in a back laneway" (cited in Coslovich, 2005; and see Hansen, 2005). Scollon and Scollon (2003) argue that the occurrence of graffiti "in places in which visual semiosis is forbidden" (p. 149) render them as *transgressive*, since "they are not authorized, and they may even be prohibited by some social or legal sanction" (p. 151). Rather than accepting this predefinition of the authorized and the transgressive, however, with its unproblematized distinction between the permitted and the proscribed, it may be more useful to take up Conquergood's (1997) under-standing of graffiti writing as "a counterliteracy that challenges, mimics, and carnivalizes" the relations between text, private ownership and the control of public space: "This outlawed literacy grotesquely mirrors and mocks the literate bureaucracy that administers licenses, receipts, badges, diplomas, ordinances, arrest warrants, green cards, and other deeds of power and possession. What distinguishes graffiti writing from other subaltern literacies is its criminaliza-tion: more than an illegitimate literacy, it is illegal" (pp. 354–55). Graffiti writing challenges assumptions about who has access to public literacy, who controls the space, who can sanction public images and lettering, who gets to decide on what a city looks like.

City souls and buffed landscapes

Cities are always being cleaned, scrubbed – *buffed* as the graffiti world calls it – to present an acceptable face to the world. This battle has a long history, as Castleman (2004) shows, since to be seen to be easy on graffiti may be seen as being light on crime. Indeed, it is not uncommon for cities to have specific 'graffiti management' plans. As the City of Melbourne explains (City of Melbourne, 2007), its "whole-of-Council approach to graffiti management ... is committed to providing a clean, vibrant, safe and welcoming atmosphere for all city residents, workers and visitors". When Melbourne hosted the Common-wealth Games[4] in 2006, the anti-graffiti campaign was intensified so that any graffiti in the inner city (suburbs, where visitors were less likely to wander, were of far less concern) would be removed within 24 hours. As a media release (Minister for Police and Emergency Services, 2005) explained, "a spe-cialist anti-graffiti police taskforce" was to be set up "to crack down on graffiti". It would "initially target inner Melbourne and Commonwealth Games venues and precincts". As the Minister explained, "Graffiti is an act of vandalism. Graffiti is not only ugly and unsightly, it is a serious criminal offence ... This blitz on graffiti will make sure Melbourne is looking its very best in the lead up to the Commonwealth Games." As this 'blitz' was repor-ted in the press, the "rapid-response clean-up crew ... as part of a round-the-clock attack on graffiti during the Commonwealth Games" aimed both to keep clean those parts of the city likely to be seen by visitors, as well as "to catch vandals in the act and to remove graffiti" (Kelly, 2006, np).

The classification of graffiti as vandalism is an important discursive move. The City of Melbourne plan in fact acknowledges that "vandalism in the form of graffiti" may only be responsible for "diminishing *perceptions* of the city's cleanliness and safety" (City of Melbourne, 2007, my emphasis), thus suggesting that the problem may be that graffiti produce negative images of the city rather than being detrimental themselves. This is akin to what is known as the 'broken window' view: like an unrepaired broken window in a building, graffiti will invite more vandalism. This also invites us to reflect on whether it is the graffiti themselves that are the problem or the practice of graffiti writing. This emphasis on vandalism, on graffiti as destruction, has to be seen in relation to a long history of discrimination along lines of class, race, gender and ethnicity that constructs the sullied other. As Metcalf (1995) makes clear, colonial discourse was insistent in its construction of native populations as dirty and disease ridden. In her study of conflicting images ('turf wars') of a contemporary urban community, Modan (2007, p. 141) points out that "Much discrimination and persecution is partially accomplished by language of cleanliness and filth." And for those who do not know how to read the signs of the graffiti world, as Milon (2002, p. 87) suggests, tags are often seen as "incomprehensible hieroglyphic signatures that aggressively pollute the visual space of the inhabitant, a type of filth that damages the City's attractiveness. These marks are felt as dirty, exterior marks on the City." This struggle over urban space is as much about class as it is about crime: It is about whose semiotic practices can participate in the making of the city.

From a graffiti artist's worldview, by contrast, this is not vandalism but public art; it is an issue of adorning rather than destroying public space. For the perpetrators, makers or writers of graffiti, their work is about style, space, identity and reimagining the city. Melbourne, some suggested, was overlooking the tourist potential of its recently acclaimed status as 'the stencil capital of the world' (Smallman and Nyman, 2005). As reported in *The Age*, while "more than four kilometres of graffiti has already been erased from venues and transport routes", for the artists, "Melbourne's graffiti is itself a colourful tourist attraction and painting over it on rail corridors makes a boring view for commuters and Games visitors" (Edwards, 2006a, np). As Jake Smallman suggests, Melbourne "was known as one of the top 10 street art cities in the world and the clean-up was a shame" (ibid.).

There is more at stake here, then, than competing views of what constitutes art, or whose vision of the preferable look of a city should prevail. What *is* being buffed when the authorities wipe the city clean, and what might we be able to learn about urban semiotics if graffiti were more readily incorporated into a possible vision of a city for both internal and external consumption? As I shall argue in the next section, an understanding of *global graffscapes* in relationship to urban landscapes, space and movement, presents us with alternative ways of thinking about how we interact with cities, and a focus on graffiti writing as a local practice (not in contrast to global graffscapes but as part of them) draws our attention to the fact that buffing a city is not only about controlling urban semiotics, but also about regulating language practices. As Coslovich (2005, np) asks, referring to the graffiti and stencil art in Hosier Lane, Melbourne, "Who needs the Harbour Bridge" (a reference to Sydney's famous tourist icon, and the long-term Sydney–Melbourne rivalry) "when your city has soul?" It is to an understanding of graffscapes as city souls that I shall now turn.

Graffscapes, place, style and movement

While the texts on toilet walls may vary from the graphic ('For good cock, call 8653002') to the cryptic ('Back soon – Godot'), hip-hop graffiti are not generally aimed at easy public consumption. Not intended to be interpretable by people outside the subculture of hip-hop/graff writers, graffiti are about style and identity: as van Treeck (2003) argues, the different graffiti styles – from tags to throwups, and from local city styles to where they are positioned (under bridges, on the sides of bridges, on trains, inside tunnels, on derelict buildings, high up, low down) – are an important part of identity formation. From risk taking, to opposition to bourgeois sensibilities, from mapping parts of the city, to developing a recognizable style, from placing pieces in juxtaposition to officially sanctioned signage (commercial advertising, street signs), to locating oneself within a particular spatial, class and ethnic subculture of the city, graffiti are about establishing particular types of identity.

While much is often made of graffiti and turf wars, about the role graffiti play in urban territorial claims, it is important to understand that graffiti writing is equally about style, identity and reinterpreting the public space. In the same way that *parkour*[5] – the art of fluid, physical movement through urban landscapes developed in the suburbs of Paris and other French cities – reclaims the drab concrete environments designed for working-class and pre-dominantly immigrant communities by reinterpreting the cityscape through physical movement, so graffiti are not, as a bourgeois reading would have it, only about bespoiling the public space, but rather are about the semiotic reinterpretation of urban environments. *Parkour* is not just another extreme sport, or a form of gymnastics, but is also a way of marking out the city through physical movement: that its practitioners are known as *traceurs* and *traceuses* (from the verb to trace) ties it to Derrida's (1976) notion of the trace, as something left behind by a sign, something that is absent in the presence of the sign. Graffiti and *parkour* transform cities into different kinds of places that carry not only the designs of urban planners but also the redesigns of urban dwellers.

Graffiti are therefore concerned with the redesigning of urban landscapes. In his work on how people, especially tourists, 'consume place', Urry (1995) starts with a distinction between land and landscape "as distinct forms of belongingness to place" (Urry, 2005, p. 19). Unlike the physical, tangible land on which we dwell, landscape is based around appearance and "emphasizes leisure, relaxation and visual consumption by visitors" (p. 20). Thus the land to which Indigenous Australians, for example, are tied in complex ways (and these connections are far more than physical dwelling but are also deeply bound up with narratives of the Dreamtime) becomes the landscape to be viewed and photographed by outback tourists. Cannadine (2000) makes a related distinction in his book on class in Britain: by the same token that we can see landscape as "what culture does to nature", so it is possible to view class "as being what culture does to inequality and social structure: investing the many anonymous individuals and unfathomable collectivities in society with shape and significance, by moulding our perceptions of the unequal world we live in" (p. 188). Cannadine's view of landscape, which draws on Schama's (1995) work on landscape and memory, makes salient the ways in which landscape is not only produced in terms of planting, cutting, diverting, and shaping (landscaping) but is also "the process whereby those trees, rivers and flowers become invested with meanings and morals and myths, and that process is as much a matter of perception and politics, of language and rhetoric, of feeling and sentiment, as it is the result of the conscious acts of landscaping themselves" (Cannadine, p. 188).

This helps us to move beyond the sociolinguistic trap whereby places and contexts are understood in terms of the scenery in which language occurs, and instead to engage in "progressively more acute analyses of the ways in which places in time and space come to have subjective meanings for the humans who live and act within them" (Scollon and Scollon, 2003, p. 12). Socio-linguistics, Coulmas (2009) reminds us, "is the study of language in urbanized settings, its proper object being the multidimensional distribution of languages and varieties in the city, as opposed to the regional distribution of varieties of language investigated in traditional dialectology" (p. 14). Yet the sociolinguistic study of the multidimensional distribution of languages and varieties in urbanized settings is only useful if it takes on board a dynamic account of that relationship, an account of how urban spaces are given meaning through local language practices, rather than assuming the city to be a space of inert geography. Drawing a distinction between a view of graffiti on the one hand as scars on the landscape [*paysage*] that "pollute the visual space of the inhabitant," and on the other, as part of the urban face [*visage*], "expressions that fully participate in the life of the City", Milon (2002) argues that graffiti can be seen as "integral parts of the City; they contribute to the definition of its exterior aspect, its size, as well as to the definition of its interior design, its soul" (p. 87). From this perspective, these "expressions that shape the City's landscape" (p. 88) can be seen not as scribblings that cover up a landscape whose interpretation is complete, but as part of the mobile expression of the changing face of the urban, part of a city's soul.

Landscapes are not static spaces: "The language of landscape is ... a lan-guage of mobility, of abstract characteristics", since "landscape talk is itself an expression of the life-world of mobile groups" (Urry, 2005, p. 25). Space, as spatial theorists from Soja (1989), via Massey (1994) to Thrift (2007) have noted, is far more than a physical world in which we act. Space is a "social construct that anchors and fosters solidarity, oppression, liberation or disintegration" (Ma, 2002, p. 131). Space is "a practical set of configurations that mix in a variety of assemblages thereby producing new senses of space" (Thrift, 2007, p. 16) (thus space is both material and productive of new understandings, cultural, social, political, historical); space therefore also forms "a poetics of the unthought, … a well-structured pre-reflective world" (ibid.) (thus is part of our internal and unarticulated mapping of the world); and space also "has more active qualities designed into its becoming" (ibid.) (and thus is always part of a complex and dynamic interaction and transformation). When we talk, then, of language as a local practice, the local is not just here, now, small, non-global, fixed, traditional, in a particular place, but rather is part of spatial practices that have both a physicality and a sense of movement, assemblage and transformation.

Talking in the city

The location of graffiti around transport (bridges, trains, railways) suggests not only the availability of writable walls and the cult of daring that makes a virtue of tagging inaccessible public space, but also the importance of movement and visibility: just as Tibetan Buddhist prayer flags are strung across windy areas so that they can flutter in the breeze, and prayer wheels may be either turned by hand or made to rotate by water in small mountain streams in Bhutan, so graffiti are not only about placement but also about movement. This is not merely a case of urban mobility, but rather the construction of meaning from movement. While graffiti may be oppositional, "it is not formless or disorganized. Like other guerrilla formations, it has its own internal structure and highly efficient strategies for mobilizing meaning" (Conquergood, 1997, p. 358). Indeed meaning is mobilized in several senses.

The idea of movement is central to Thrift's (2007) non-representational theory "as a means of going beyond constructivism" (p. 5). Human life, he argues, "is based on and in movement" (p. 5). A focus on movement takes us away from space being only about location, and instead draws attention to a relationship between time and space, to emergence, to a subject in process – performed rather than preformed – to becoming (see Chapter 3). As I have tried to emphasize, and as will be discussed at greater length in the next chapter, this notion of the local as dynamic, about movement and fluidity, helps us to get beyond a vision of the local as static, traditional, immobile. This is of particular importance when we juxtapose the local with the global. The latter term tends to accrue, whether positively or negatively, ideas of change, movement, dynamism, while the former is all too often reduced to the unchanging, the immobile, the static. To make the notion of the local useful, however, we need to give it the dynamism of notions of space and movement. Thrift's (2007) non-representational theory is thus concerned with "the anti-substantialist ambition of philosophies of becoming and philosophies of vitalist intuition equally – and their constant war on frozen states" (p. 5).

De Certeau's (1984/1990) well-known discussion of walking in the city "as a space of enunciation" (p. 98) captures this dynamic well, since in this view it is the act of walking that gives meaning to the urban system.[6] Pushing this insight further, however, we might want to suggest that rather than walking in the city giving meaning to the prior system of urban structures (the enunciation of *la langue*), it is rather movement through the city that performatively produces meaning. Moving through the urban landscape does not so much bring meanings to life as it makes meanings possible: it is a spatial realization of place. Graffiti, as São Paulo graffiti artist Ninguém explains, "is about conquering space. What I like is that I can draw or illustrate the places I move in and out of all the time – the trains, buses, etc. Better said, I can use these places to imagine. Imagination is key to graffiti and it is what attracted me" (cited in Pardue, 2004, p. 426). Graffiti is thus far more than a string of individual identity marks or tags but rather involves a process of narration and *imaginação* (imagination).

In his discussion of 'driving in the city' Thrift (2007) argues that de Certeau's work on walking in the city "needs to be reworked to take into account the rise of automobility and the consequent changes in how space is ordered, changes which cannot easily be subsumed into his account of the city" (p. 75). Similarly, as I have been suggesting, graffiti gains its strength from mobility, and this is often precisely because of its placement in relation to cars and trains. For de Certeau (1984/1990) spatialization is a practice, the making of meaning and the inscription of time onto urban space. If we think about (re) localization as a spatial practice, then language as a local practice is also about particular ways in which things we do with and through language give meaning to the spaces in which we do them. Delivering a sermon in a church, calling the faithful to prayer from the minaret of a mosque, or giving a lecture in a classroom are not only language practices that reflect the space in which they happen, but also give meaning to that space. Likewise, singing 'happy birthday' round a birthday cake, talking about food distribution in a refugee camp or writing in a ship's log in the Southern Ocean are both linguistic and spatial practices.

If, as Thrift (2007) suggests, we need to look at driving in the city as well as walking in the city, we might also consider the practice of *talking in the city*. It is perhaps the very fact that de Certeau ties walking in the city to the enunciation of language that the practice of talking in the city has been overlooked as a practice of urban semiotics. One of the many pleasures of living in a large, multilingual city such as Sydney, with over 30 per cent of the population speaking a language other than English at home, is to enjoy the plurilingual, polylingual or metrolingual (see next chapter) flow of languages in urban spaces. It has not always been the case that 'home languages' have been used with comfort outside the home: the use of languages other than English in public spaces has not always been so readily accepted and assumed. In different suburbs today, however, English may be dominant or virtually non-existent. Commonly it operates as a lingua franca when speakers of one community language, say Vietnamese, have to negotiate with speakers of another language, say Arabic (though English is not the only language that serves this function between different communities). In spaces in between, on beaches, at parks, concerts, festivals, the languages of Sydney and its many visitors swirl around as people talk and walk and eat and drink in the city.

Talking in the city is related to public space. It is very noticeable in cities with long, hard winters, cities such as Montreal, that talking goes inside for those winter months, but comes out again with a vengeance in the summer, when people sit on their porches, barbecue in their back yards, eat out in street cafés, wander the pedestrian zones with the street musicians and performers. These cities are full of talk in the summer. In milder climates, people talk in the city all year round, sitting in piazzas, coffee shops, along the walls of the harbour. The mobile phone has added a very particular dynamic because of the introduction of certain types of talk – whether personal or business – into the public space. It is also useful, especially for those for whom such talking in the city is the norm, to consider how new and particular this is. Until mobile phones arrived, talking on a phone in the city was boxed up: the archetypal British telephone box, with its distinctive red colouring, door and windows, was a separate space one entered to make a call, isolated from the surrounding city. Elsewhere, if there were no boxes, telephones were nevertheless attached to buildings, parts of phone booths, one type of street furniture. We had to make our way to them, and by and large no one could call us; we could only call out. The mobile phone makes us immediately locatable within a city. All of this, at a very simple level, has significance for how we understand ourselves in relation to the cityscape. To talk on a mobile phone while walking down the street, sitting in a restaurant, attending class, is to engage in a linguistic and spatial practice.

Graffscapes, contested zones and stained-glass windows

To talk of graffscapes is to invoke several significant ways of thinking: by locating graffiti within an understanding of landscapes as constructed, interactive, expressive, semiotic resources, we can start to see such street art not as immobile text on static city walls, but rather as part of the integrative life of the city that gives it meaning. The term graffscapes also draws on Appadurai's (1996) vision of global ethnoscapes, mediascapes, technoscapes, financescapes and ideoscapes, which, in accord with the discussion of landscapes above, "are not objectively given relations that look the same from every angle of vision but, rather, deeply perspectival constructs, inflected by the historical, linguistic, and political situatedness of different sorts of actors" (p. 33). Appadurai's understanding, furthermore, that we are living in "a world of flows", that "we are functioning in a world fundamentally characterized by objects in motion" which include "ideas and ideologies, people and goods, images and messages, technologies and techniques" (2001, p. 5) allows us to see that it is not only the city dwellers that are in motion but also the graffiti.

Graffiti artists weave new imaginary relations across the urban landscape as they create intertextual city links; and graffiti are perceived by people in motion, as tourists, commuters, drivers, cyclists, walkers pass through these global graffscapes.

Graffiti move across a globalizing world, adorning walls from Reykjavik to Rio,[7] greeting new arrivals in a city with a sense of urban familiarity. In the same way that the *global semioscape* (Thurlow and Aiello, 2007) offers both commonality and difference across space, global graffscapes are intertextually linked across urban landscapes, moving the traveller across and within cities. Graffscapes are a reminder of both the locality of global style and the globality of local style. Graffiti are also, however, as Milon reminds us, "the translation of social unrest" (2002, p. 87), an image of the city that reflects not only the desired objects of the bourgeois gaze – history, tradition, architecture, investment – but also those more threatening urban stories of subcultural struggle, class and social disquiet. Graffscapes also remind us that in this battle over what texts are permissible in public space, there is a struggle over possible ways of making sense, not the urbanity of international multilingualism but the intertextual world of urban semiotic resources (Makoni and Pennycook, 2007).

When the 'zero-tolerance' campaign got under way in Melbourne before the Commonwealth Games, artists responded in a number of ways. As reported in *The Age* (Edwards, 2006b, np), "In the graffiti war, it seems you can fight city hall – as long as you keep moving." As Melbourne City Council and police continued their widely publicized crackdown on graffiti in order to keep the city 'clean' during the Commonwealth Games, a group of artists developed a roaming graffiti wall, made up of five large panels of stencil art, carried through the central business district of the city, passing along laneways that had formerly carried extensive graffiti art (see Pennycook, in press a). According to local artist Patrick Jones, "We received a lot of support, especially from international visitors, with lots of people taking photographs and talking to us" (cited in Edwards, 2006b). Melbourne's graffiti art scene was widely respected, he explained, and visitors were often more interested in the immediacy of a moving graffiti wall than in the bourgeois estrangements of art galleries.

A more challenging reaction came from the internet, however. Police found that not only did they have to follow a walking wall of graffiti around the city, but the battle had also moved into a different space, or rather into the interactive space between the internet and city walls: "Police are investigating one website running the 'Melbourne Graffiti Games' and offering gold, silver and bronze medals. Categories include most daring placement, best caricature of the mayor or councillor, most seditious piece and largest graffiti piece" (Kelly, 2006, np). Soon the use of a modified version of the Games' logo – the two running and jumping figures in the original were now seen holding spray cans – was banned as the police put pressure on the site owners to stop their promotion and display of "dozens of photos of illegal graffiti – some with

vandals pictured in the act" (ibid.). While the Commonwealth Games continued, and while Indigenous Australians made their own protest under the
banner of the 'Stolenwealth Games', graffiti artists waged a new battle for
public space and imagery. Even if graffiti in the city would be buffed within
hours, a digital image could be placed online and people could vote according
to the various categories.

A rather different response from the zero tolerance campaign being fought
out in Melbourne comes from Father Gwilym Henry-Edwards of St Luke's
Anglican Church, Enmore, Sydney, which he describes as a "traditional
church, in that we acknowledge that God works in many different ways". As
he goes on, "The stained glass windows that we have – some of them are very
historic over a hundred years old – and that medium of stained glass spoke
very clearly to the people of the past, and this", he continues, gesturing to the
wall of graffiti behind him, "speaks to people of the present and the future."
He goes on to explain that this wall of graffiti, painted by Sydney graff artist
Mistery, has received "a lot of very positive comments. There's a lady in one
of the houses just down the lane who sits up in her window and has been
watching Mistery working on it, and saying how wonderful it is to see such
artistry on the wall. Because this expresses something which is important to
people, and important to Mistery. It expresses his faith, his beliefs and people
can see that and they appreciate it" (Compass, 2006). Like a number of more
enlightened urban dwellers, Father Henry-Edwards can see the benefits of
engaging with the stained-glass windows of the twenty-first century, a contemporary semiotic resource that tells an alternative story of the world.

We might be tempted to consider stained-glass windows as the opposite of
graffiti: they are inside rather than outside, permanent rather than temporary,
admired in wonder rather than despised in passing, religious rather than vulgar,
aimed at uplifting the spirit rather than lowering the tone of the neighbour-
hood. These points of difference, however, depend very much on their locus of
enunciation. As Cresswell explains, "Our actions in places are evidence of our
preferred reading. Kneeling in church is an interpretation of what the church
means; it also reinforces the meaning of the church" (1996, p. 16). Similarly,
looking at stained-glass windows in a church is an interpretation of what the
church and the windows mean (see Cowen, 2005; Lee, Seddon and Stephens,
1976), and looking in a particular way reinforces particular meanings of the
church. So too graffiti, and if the vicar of St Luke's Anglican Church, Enmore,
can see graffiti as a semiotic practice of the twenty-first century, so might
more people be able to see the ways in which particular spatial and semiotic
practices construct the city. This dissolution of the division between the
sacred (stained-glass) and the profane (graffiti) invites us to reflect on what
texts are sanctioned, what urban literacies allowed, what voices heard, which
windows broken, which souls saved (and which buffed).

Graffiti writing, as Conquergood (1997) points out, "performatively constitutes middle-class and public spaces into contested zones of contact, site-
specific theaters of defiance where excluded others re-present themselves"

(p. 358). To treat graffiti only in terms of dirt or vandalism, to present a 'buffed' cityscape, is to project middle-class sensibilities onto the urban landscape, to create the *bourgeoiscape*. To present only the buffed *paysage* rather than the living *visage* of the city is to reduce the possibilities of urban meaning-making. To travel though cities with an eye only for sanctioned texts is to operate within a very particular position on class, culture and the city. To overlook global subcultural commonality is to turn one's back on global flows of meaning in favour of a sanitized, class-based image of the local. To ignore the local upswelling of urban unrest depicted through graffiti is also to ignore the local in favour of a flattened class image of the global. Fortunately, graffiti, like language, are hard to control: just as Singlish in Singapore reclaims the buffed linguascapes imposed by the state's 'speak good English' campaigns (Wee, 2005), so graffiti artists reclaim the buffed cityscapes that cannot last. Graffiti highlight several ways in which the buffed cityscape and the overlooked graffscape unsettle global relations of space.

The understanding of graffiti that I have been trying to open up here suggests a need to include a dynamic account of space, text and interaction: readers and writers are part of the fluid, urban semiotic space and produce meaning as they move, write, read and travel. The styles and locations of graffiti are about identity; they are statements of place, belonging, group membership and style. Landscapes are more than the environment in which texts and images are drawn; they are spaces that are imagined and invented. Urban graffscapes are animated by the movement and interactions of city dwellers. If we view language in terms of practices, as an activity, in terms of 'languaging' (e.g. Shohamy, 2006), so too is it useful to see graffscapes in terms of 'graffscaping', implying not only intertextual urban spaces but also the discursive creation of the landscape. We need to view the landscape not as canvas or as context but as integrative and invented environment. The importance of movement, of interactive spaces, takes us beyond studies of audience and reception, towards a focus on space as dynamic, on city landscapes as having been graffscaped. Graffiti, as the stained-glass windows of the twenty-first century, give cities soul.

Linguistic landscaping as local practice

The notion of linguistic landscapes has clearly resonated with researchers interested in social and political roles of languages (Shohamy and Gorter, 2009): it emphasizes that language is not something that exists only in people's heads, in texts written for institutional consumption or in spoken interactions, but rather is part of the physical environment. At least in urban contexts – as Coulmas (2009) points out, a better term might indeed be linguistic cityscape – language surrounds us, directs us, hails us, calls for our attention, flashes its messages to us. Linguistic landscapes take us into the spatiality of language; we are invited to explore what Scollon and Scollon (2003) call from a related perspective *geosemiotics*: "an integrative view of these multiple semiotic systems which together form the meanings which we call place" (p. 12). As Shohamy and Gorter (2009) explain, linguistic landscape (LL) "contextualizes the public space within issues of identity and language policy of nations, political and social conflicts ... LL is a broader concept than documentation of signs; it incorporates multimodal theories to include sounds, images, and graffiti" (p .4).

At the same time, the ways in which the study of linguistic landscapes has often proceeded have constrained the possibilities of seeing linguistic landscapes in more dynamic terms (Pennycook, 2009b). Both the concept of language embedded in the 'linguistic' and the concept of context embedded in the 'landscape' have been commonly viewed from perspectives that limit the possibilities of thinking about language and place in different ways. Put simply, the most common construction of language has been as an indicator of a particular language, with the focus then being on the representation of different languages in public space; this has been linked most often to questions of language policy and multilingualism in an attempt to address questions about which languages are used for particular public duties, how official language policies are reflected in public signs, how local sign making may present other forms of diversity, and so on. At the very least, we might want to ask about the easy rendition of a sign–language relationship. In public, globalized spaces, is it so clear that signs are 'in' one language or another?

Take this sign on the front of a building in Kuala Lumpur, Malaysia, for example: **Pub dan karaoke**. Is this a trilingual sign (with 'pub' in English, 'dan' (and) in Bahasa Malaysia (BM), and 'karaoke' in Japanese)? But the fact that I don't need to offer a translation here of karaoke suggests it is already an English word, so perhaps this sign is just in English and BM. But how integrated are the two terms – pub and karaoke – into BM anyway? Maybe this is a monolingual sign in Bahasa Malaysia. Similar questions may be asked about the 'trilingual' graffito analysed by Jørgensen (2008b) (above): 'LE KAPITAL C'EST FUN, LE COMMUNISME C'EST NUF', which, he suggests, combines German (because of the 'K' in Kapital), French and English (Fun). To ask what language these are in is perhaps to ask the wrong question. If asked if this is (a) monolingual, (b) bilingual, (c) trilingual, or (d) none of the above, I think I'd prefer (d). To render diversity contingent on the numerical representation of languages is to focus on languages as entities rather than on linguistic resources, on the quantitative strategy of language enumeration rather than the qualitative understanding of the traffic of meaning (Jørgensen, 2008a; Kramsch, 2006; Makoni and Pennycook, 2007; Pennycook, 2008).

If we are prepared to accept graffiti as the stained-glass windows of the twenty-first century, and that both graffiti and stained-glass windows are part of the linguistic landscape, the notion of what counts as 'linguistic' clearly is also opened up to a broader semiotic domain. Much of the focus of linguistic landscapes has been on sanctioned text in public space, but as many recent studies of multimodality (e.g. Kress and van Leeuwen, 2001) have suggested, it may make little sense to try to separate text from image. Graffiti and stained-glass windows generally transcend notions of language as text and language as separable entity, and present instead a broader domain of social semiotics. As Father Henry-Edwards suggests, furthermore, such images 'speak to people', or, put another way, they address passers-by in different ways.

And this also takes us back to talking in the city, and the ways in which the use of language in cityscapes is part of the production of meaning in place. If the notion of landscape is taken to mean little more than the public backdrop of the city, the spaces on which official and unofficial signage are embedded, we lose the chance here of looking at landscaping in more active terms. Malinowski's (2009) question 'Who authors the landscape?' becomes not only a question as to who has written what sign, but also how our landscapes are made through language. In order to understand signs in landscapes, we need signographies rather than sign cartographies. A dynamic account of *linguistic landscaping* as the active production of space through language, therefore, allows us to see how different linguistic resources are used, different worlds evoked, different possibilities engaged in as people use the linguistic where-withal around them. Language as a local practice, therefore, understood in terms of linguistic landscaping, helps us see how we make our surrounds linguistically.

5   Kerala tuskers

Language as already local

It's an ancient culture, with a new name

Vulk Makedonski and Raceless of Melbourne-based hip-hop artists Curse ov
Dialect suggest that the origins of hip-hop can be found in multiple cultural
resources: according to Vulk Makedonski, "hip-hop is the culture of people
that were oppressed at one stage, and a lot of cultures have songs about
oppression in their folk tales. To me, that's hip-hop. They're expressing
themselves through song, through dance – which hip-hop is – through graffiti,
you know the old way when people used to write on rocks or whatever. That's
hip-hop." Hip-hop, he suggests, has to be seen in relation to both diverse
cultures and spaces and as having a long history: hip-hop "is too powerful to
be modern, that's why I believe it's more ancient. It's an ancient culture, with
a new name. And the new name is hip-hop, that's the modern name, but the
elements that come out of hip-hop go back – way, way, back." The elements
of hip-hop, he suggests, should not be seen in terms of breaking, rapping and
so forth, but rather as part of forms of music and dance that have been part
of different cultures for centuries. Hip-hop, asserts Raceless, is about "bringing back old things, and reappropriating it" (CoD Interview 23/09/06[1]).

Drawing analogies with issues of localization in hip-hop (see also Alim and
Pennycook, 2007; Pennycook, 2007a), this chapter argues that processes of
localization are more complex than a notion of languages or cultures
spreading and taking on local forms; rather, we have to understand ways in
which they are already local. Debates over the implications of the global
spread of English all too often assume this metaphor of spread, suggesting
that English spread from the centre (England/UK/USA etc.) until it was
eventually adapted locally, leading to distinct local varieties of English. Imagine a stone dropped into a pond. The ripples move out as concentric circles,
affecting ever new areas of water. The focus of World Englishes has been on
the ways in which these ripples take on local characteristics, how the movement from the centre is also about change. But let us consider another aspect
of this. It is not the water that moves outwards, but the energy created by the
falling stone that passes through the water. By and large, the water in different
parts of the pond simply moves up and down as the ripples move through.

Our focus, therefore, might be equally on the water or language that is already there: it is not that English spreads like ripples from the centre but rather that a certain force passes through, and languages move up and down to accommodate this. Ripples, like language, are not localized; they pass through, leaving the water or language that has always been there rocking slightly. "A language never spreads like a liquid, nor even like a disease or a rumour" (Fabian, 1986, p. 8).

In this chapter on the locality of language, I shall ask what happens to ideas about the global spread of English if we look at it as a local language. As we have already seen in Chapters 3 and 4, rethinking space and time in relation to language opens up different possibilities for how we think about locality. This does not mean, then, that English as a local language should be understood in terms of local adaptations made to English – new lexical items, locally influenced pronunciation, grammatical structures that differ from the centre norms – but rather as a practice embedded in the local. As Vulk Makedonski and Raceless remind us, English is too powerful to be modern; the elements that make up English go way, way, back. The issue is not one of English spreading and being locally appropriated but of English bringing back old things, and reappropriating them. To grasp this argument is to address particular ways of thinking about the locality of language.

Current debates about the inapplicability of a World Englishes framework to current conditions of globalization, or concerns that a focus on English as a lingua franca presents a new form of homogenization (see Rubdy and Saraceni, 2006), miss the point that we need to react not only to new conditions of postmodernity but also to the postmodern imperative to rethink language. This suggests the need to articulate a new sense of history and location, avoiding narratives of spread, transition, development and origins, and thinking instead in terms of multiple, heterogeneous and simultaneous histories that the dominant historical narrative has overlooked. If we question the linearity at the heart of modernist narratives about language origins and spread, we can start to see that global Englishes do not have one point but rather multiple, co-present, global origins. Just as hip-hop has always been Aboriginal, as MC Wire claims (see below), so has English. Such an understanding of global Englishes reshapes the ways in which we can understand global and local cultural and linguistic formations, and takes us beyond the current debates between monocentric and pluricentric models of English.

To take these arguments further, I shall approach this from several directions. First, I shall return to the discussion of hip-hop and locality in order to open up discussion of the coevalness of origins. This will be followed by a discussion of the locality of English in Kerala, with particular reference to temple elephants. Once we start to view global Englishes in terms of local language practices, our attention is drawn away from a language entity called English with peripheral variants. We are directed instead to the doing of language in particular localities. This doing of language, as argued in Chapter 3, is part of the production of language, and as argued in Chapter 4, it is both a spatial and linguistic practice. Local language practices do not reflect the local reality but are part of its production.

English and hip-hop have always been local

Curse ov Dialect – from the name of their band to the clothes they wear and the identities they perform – like to challenge received notions of language and ethnicity. They take issues of language, culture, ethnicity and multiculturalism and twist, flaunt and change them. Their view that hip-hop is very old and links to other cultural trajectories presents us with a different sense of origins. Such a view is only possible within a reconceptualization of time, space and localization. The processes of localization are more complex than global hip-hop or global English taking on local flavours. While an analogy with World Englishes may bring us pluralization, so that we can view either hip-hop or English as pluralized entities – hip-hops and Englishes – there are many limitations to such a strategy. It is not so much the case that hip-hop merely takes on local characteristics, but rather that *it has always been local*. As Indigenous Australian Wire MC says, "Hip-hop is a part of Aboriginal culture, I think it always has been" (Interview 31/03/06). Not only have indigenous styles of clothing, dance, vocal styles, stances and movements combined with hip-hop styles to form indigenized hybrids where US hip-hop is no longer the host culture, but hip-hop is seen as having a direct link back to traditional ways of singing, dancing and telling stories (Pennycook and Mitchell, 2009).

One way to view this, as Somali-Canadian hip-hop artist K'Naan explains, is that it is easy to see the connections between traditional African practices and hip-hop in the West African tradition of *griots* and the East African traditions of oral poetry:

> I'm certain that any country, any given country in Africa, you will find an ancient form of hip hop. It's just natural for someone from Africa to recite something over a drum and to recite it in a talking blues fashion, and then it becomes this thing called hip-hop.
>
> (K'Naan interview 25/04/06)

This sits well with those Afrocentric arguments that draw strong connections between contemporary African American cultures and their African origins. But rather than viewing hip-hop as an American cultural form with African origins, K'Naan suggests that it is first and foremost an African form that has been Americanized. Senegalese hip-hop group Daara J likewise claim hip-hop as their own, not merely as an act of appropriation but rather as a claim to origins. According to their track 'Boomerang', "Born in Africa, brought up in America, hip-hop has come full circle," (Daara J, 2004). As their MC Faada Freddy explains, the traditional Senegalese form of rhythmic poetry, *tasso*, is the original form of rap. From Daara J's West African perspective, African Americans "brought out all that culture that was slumbering at the bottom of their soul". But now, rap music "is coming back home because it is about time that we join the traditional music, we join yesterday to today" (Daara J, Interview 05/03/05).

Here, then, we have a different possibility from the image of hip-hop emerging from US urban ghettoes and spreading around the world. Daara J take up the Afrocentric argument that traces all such movements back to African contexts. From this point of view, the arguments over the multiple influences of the Black Atlantic (Gilroy, 1993; and see Chapter 4) or the Jamaican role in the development of hip-hop become subsumed under a wider argument that all are part of the wider influence of the African diaspora. The development of hip-hop in Africa, from this point of view, is merely a return to its roots. Thus, while Perry (2004) rightly critiques "romantic Afro-Atlanticism" (p. 17) for overlooking the point that "Black Americans as a community do not consume imported music from other cultures in large numbers" and thus ultimately the "postcolonial Afro-Atlantic hip hop community is ... a fantastic aspiration rather than a reality" (p. 19), this in turn may overlook the point that African American hip-hop is only a part of a much wider circuit of musical and cultural influences.

Yet Daara J's image of the boomerang points to a problem with this story too. It brings us spinning in a circle back to Indigenous Australia and Wire MC:

> The reason I was attracted to it was the song and dance aspect to it, because the culture I come from, The Dreamtime, we always expressed our stories, our beliefs, our fears, our superstitions through song and dance. So being an Abo-digital in the 21st century, it was a natural evolution for me to move into hip hop and continue the corroboree, but with the modern day aspect.
>
> (Wire MC, interview, 31/03/06)

Consequently, this is not a question only of whether hip-hop started in Africa and then returned, but that hip-hop has always been Aboriginal Australian, just as it has always been African. Hip-hop from this point of view is a continuation of indigenous traditions; it draws people into a new relationship with cultural practices that have a history far longer than those of current popular music. Yet in doing so, it also changes those cultures and traditions, rendering them anew. From rappers in Berlin of Turkish background who draw on the traditions of medieval Turkish minstrels (*halk ozani*), acting as "contemporary minstrels, or storytellers, ... the spokespersons of the Turkish diaspora" (Kaya, 2001, p. 203), to Fijian Australian MC Trey's invocation of the connections between hip-hop and Pacific Islander cultures (Pennycook, 2007a), hip-hop becomes not merely a cultural formation that has spread and been locally taken up, nor even one that has its origins in Africa and has returned, but rather one that has always been local. Put another way, rather than trying "to sort out the autochthonous from the borrowed, we need to consider the uses musicians make of hip-hop, how they understand its relationship to their own condition, and what new meanings are generated by its use" (Urla, 2001, p. 185). Similarly with English, rather than trying to sort out the local from the derived – the constant comparison between peripheral and metropolitan forms of English – we need to consider what language users do with English, how they understand its relationship to their own condition, and what new meanings are generated by its use.

Such a view is of great significance for how we see varieties of English. The analogy I am trying to draw here between global Englishes and hip-hop suggests that common images of English or hip-hop as having spread around the world, with varying degrees of adaptation to local contexts, inadequately portray their local use. It is a far more dynamic and diverse process than this suggests, involving a constant struggle between identification, rejection and engagement with local cultural forms, as well as uses of language that not only localize but also transform what it means to be local. Ultimately, therefore, whether we are dealing with the global spread of English or the global spread of hip-hop, we need to move beyond an image only of spread and adaptation, to include not only pluralization (global Englishes and global hip-hops) but also an understanding of the already local. If we take Wire's view seriously that hip-hop has always been Aboriginal, we are confronted by the need to articulate a new sense of history and location.

The global locatedness of hip-hops demands that we rethink time and space, and adopt what Mignolo (2000) refers to as a historiography that "spatializes time and avoids narratives of transition, progress, development, and point of arrivals" (p. 205). If we can allow for "multiple, heterogeneous, and uneven temporalities and histories that the dominant historical narrative, often presenting itself as singular and linear, suppresses" (Inoue, 2004, p. 2), it becomes possible conceptually to question the linearity at the heart of modernist narratives about origins. As argued in Chapter 3, if we take seriously the idea that we can never step twice into the same river, then the reorganization of time and space that this implies allows for what is apparently the same also to be different. Global Englishes do not have one point of origin but rather multiple, co-present, global origins. Following the arguments in Chapter 4, furthermore, which draw attention to processes of linguistic landscaping and the fact that languages do not adapt to their surrounds so much as create them (see also Chapter 6), then Global Englishes are not what they are because English has spread and been adapted, but because local practices have been relocalized in English. Just as hip-hop has always been Aboriginal, so has English.

The most ideal tusker from Kerala forests

Recent debates in World Englishes have focused on the one hand on the applicability to the twenty-first century of the World Englishes (WE) framework with its nation-based concentric circles (Bruthiaux, 2003), and on the other hand on the question of whether either the World Englishes or the English as a lingua franca approach has the best handle on diversity. Yamuna Kachru and Nelson (2006), for example, arguing that it is indeed the strategy of pluralization that best succeeds here, juxtapose World Englishes with terms such as 'world English' (Brutt-Griffler, 2002), 'English as an International Language' (Jenkins, 2000), and 'English as a Lingua Franca' (ELF) (Seidlhofer, 2001) on the grounds that they "idealize a monolithic entity called 'English' and neglect the inclusive and plural character of the world-wide phenomenon" (p. 2). Yet, in order to address such questions we need to get beyond simple questions of pluralization (English versus Englishes), since they leave unexamined both the question of relative scale and broader issues of epistemology. While at one level there may be an important distinction here between a WE approach, with its centrifugal focus on local variation, and an ELF approach with its centripetal focus on the development of regional varieties (European and Asian English), at another level, this may only be a matter of relative scale (see Pennycook, 2009a; in press b).

Here I want to focus on two very particular concerns in relation to language as a local practice that have particular importance for how we think about the notion of locality. The first issue is one that questions the way we conceive of language spread. As I have argued above, the way in which language spread is commonly considered rests on a number of questionable assumptions to do with time and place, assuming that languages move across space and through time, and in doing so adapt to new environments (for further discussion of this last point, see Chapter 6). The second has to do with the locatedness of language. World Englishes has attempted to account for local language use by dint of a model based on a concept of regional, and particularly national, variation. Hence it is common to talk in terms of Indian, Malaysian, Nigerian or Philippine Englishes but less common to talk in terms of Tamil Nadu, Kerala, Rajasthan, Kelantan, Negeri Sembilan, Perak, Ebonyi, Abia, Edo, Siquijor, Cebu or Bohol Englishes. The World Englishes framework, as Bruthiaux (2003) notes, is something of a mixture of history, politics, linguistics and geography, and in fact rarely engages in any sustained way with questions of locality. Let us look, however, at a typical local newspaper (*The New Indian Express*) article from Kerala, in India's South: 'Jumbos driving Tripunithuraites crazy' (22 December 2006). "With festive season round-the-corner, Tripunithuraites are gearing up to welcome some of the prestigious tuskers who will line up to carry the idols of gods and goddesses" (Varma, 2006, p. 3). As the article goes on to explain,

On January 3, Thiruvambadi Shivasundar will carry the thidambu of Lord Siva of Kannankulangara Mahadeva temple as part of thiruvathira celebrations. The festival committee of Pottayil Bhagavathy temple is busy designing attractive flex boards of three tuskers, Thechikkottu Kavu Ramachandran, Pambadi Rajan and Naanu Ezhuthassan Sreenivasan, as part of the annual festival of the temple on February 28. Thechikottu Kavu Ramachandran, the famous tusker from Bihar, will leave the town

only after attending the thalappoli of Muradu Kottaram Bhagavati temple
in the first week of March.

(Varma, 2006, p. 3).

Although Kachru and Nelson (2006) argue that there is considerable variation across writing conventions and genres in different varieties of English
around the world, we might nevertheless observe that there is little here in
terms of grammar or text type that is particularly noteworthy: it is a fairly
unremarkable announcement of an upcoming event, common to many local
newspapers. It is clearly in the domain of vocabulary that this becomes more
interesting. From the point of view of describing Indian English, we might
point to the use of 'tuskers' and 'flex boards' as regional variants (though the
term *tuskers* is also used in parts of Africa). Yet its distinctiveness lies surely in
the local references to festivals ('thiruvathira celebrations') and temples and
elephants. The locality of this article derives therefore not so much from the
use of 'flex boards' but from the fact that the local temple is busy designing
such boards with pictures of famous elephants.

What we have here, then, is a range of local religious practices involving
elephants (which are named and well known in the region). As a subsection of
the article explains, "From time immemorial the most famous tamed tuskers
in Kerala were the senior-most members of the Aana Tharavadu (Punnathoor
Kotta) of Guruvayoor Devaswom. The tusker that topped the list in yester-
year was the celebrated Guruvayoor Keshavan. Now Guruvayoor Padma-
nabhan tops the list" (Varma, 2006, p. 3). Height of elephants is important,
but only in the context of overall body proportion, shape of the tusks and
number of nails in the fore limbs: "Thechikottu Kavu Ramachandran with a
height of 10.3 ft is second in demand. Though he stabbed the celebrated tusker
Thiruvambadi Chandrasekharan, Ramachandran is still the hot favourite."
But there is also strong support for local elephants. Thus, "Among the nadan
(born and brought up in Kerala/Mysore forests) tuskers, Pambadi Rajan tops
the list. With more than 10 ft height, fleshy trunk that touches the ground,
beautiful tusks and wide ears, the tusker enjoys the status of the most ideal
tusker from Kerala forests" (Ibid., p. 3).

Despite its occasional gloss (the explanation of 'nadan' for example), the
article largely assumes local knowledge, and an appreciation of local practices
and elephant aesthetics. It is more useful, therefore, to look at this article in
terms of the relocalization of local practices rather than in terms of Indian
English. This relocalization does include English as part of this language
practice, and doubtless this use of English would not have occurred but for
the role of English under colonialism, the subsequent role of English in
India (including the North/South divide) and the more recent dominance of
English as a global language. And yet, this is surely also more than a localization of English. These are local practices relocalized in English. The very
notion of Tripunithuraites makes this local before it is anything else, but not
as a form of Kerala English, or Indian English, but as a relocalized set of

practices involving English. It is local not because it is in Kerala (as opposed to Mumbai, Tokyo or New York) but in terms of the relationship between particular practices and their linguistic relocalization. Looking at this in terms of the relocalization of local practices inverts the relationship between language and practice: instead of assuming the ontology of English and its local variants, we start with local practices and look at their linguistic instantiation.

The local practices surrounding temple elephants in Kerala are here relocalized as a set of language practices in a newspaper. As I have suggested in Chapter 3, and will argue at greater length in Chapter 6, this notion of relocalization of language practices is central to an understanding of relations between language and locality, and, as we shall see, can help us move beyond common, yet suspect, claims about relations between language, culture and place. Here I want to pursue this observation further in relation to the localization of language. It is often argued that English has become localized in such contexts, that English, as a language that has spread around the world, here takes on local characteristics. From the point of view of language as a local practice, however, we need to look at this from a different direction. Instead of starting with prior assumptions about languages as arrangements with variations, we can start by looking at local practices as they are relocalized in language. In the same way that thinking in terms of practices may reverse assumed relations between language and its realization in discourse (discourse produces language rather than the other way round), so this perspective may reverse assumptions about the notion of spread and localization (the local produces the spread rather than the spread becoming local).

The local and the worldly

Taking a step back from the arguments about who has the most pluralistic version of English (World Englishes or English as a lingua franca), we may now wish to question the ways in which a thing called English is considered to exist in the first place. It is assumed *a priori* that there is such a thing as English, a view reinforced by excluding those types of English and, as Mufwene (2001) notes, those types of speakers, that don't fit what is deemed to be English, and by then employing the circular argument that if it doesn't fit, then it isn't English. For a World English to be such, it must adhere to the underlying grammar of central English, demonstrate enough variety to make it interestingly different, but not diverge to the extent that it undermines the myth of English (Pennycook, 2007b). If we acknowledge Creole languages, however, if we refuse to draw a line down the middle of a Creole continuum (exclaiming that one end is English while the other is not), if we decide that those 'Other Englishes' may be part of English, then we are not dealing with a language held in place by a core structure with variation on the edges, but rather with a notion of language that cannot hold together. Paraphrasing Harris (1990, p. 45), the question is whether the concept of English or Englishes, as defined by the camps currently slugging it out round the global spread of English – linguistic imperialism, World Englishes or English as a lingua franca – corresponds to any object of analysis at all, whether social or individual, whether institutional or psychological. This also means, on the other hand, that, as with the discussion of signs in the previous chapter, we should no longer be trapped by the necessity to account for something being 'in English'.

These approaches to global English – whether linguistic imperialism and language rights, or World Englishes and English as a lingua franca – remain stuck within twentieth-century frameworks of languages and nations (Bruthiaux, 2003). The central concern that the debates between these rival conceptualizations leave uncontested is how we can understand diversity outside those very frameworks that are part of the problem. Neither a defence of national languages and cultures, nor a description of a core of English as a lingua franca, nor even a focus on plural Englishes, adequately addresses questions of diversity under new conditions of globalization. As Canagarajah (2005b) argues, to deal seriously with the local is both to engage with particular forms of time and space and to question received epistemologies: "The local will always have a questioning effect on established paradigms, deriving from the non-systematized, unorthodox, and simply messy features of its existential practice" (pp. 19–20).

To speak of language as a local practice is to address not only the embeddedness of language in place and time, but also the relation between language locality and a wider world. One way I have been trying to address this over the years is through the notion of the worldliness of language, drawing on various postcolonial thinkers to do so. One of Edward Said's (1983) goals was to find a way of dealing with the 'worldliness' of texts: "Is there no way", he asked, "of dealing with a text and its worldly circumstances fairly?" (p. 35). The issue here is of finding a means to understand textual contextuality, and thus avoiding on the one hand the removal of texts from the world as if they existed independently of the world, while on the other hand avoiding the opposite pitfall of seeing texts only as reflections of material existence. Indeed, Ashcroft and Ahluwalia (1999) see the notion of worldliness as central to Said's overall intellectual project, since "we cannot separate this political concern for the state of Palestine, this concern with his own identity and the identity of Palestinians in general, from the theoretical and literary analysis of texts and the way they are located in the world" (p. 3). Taking up Said's view of worldliness, I argued (Pennycook, 1994) against an idea that English, or any other language, could somehow be considered 'neutral', could be discussed without consideration of its worldly circumstances.

I suggested at the time – and this still holds to a large extent today – that the main ways in which English as an international language was discussed lacked an understanding of a broad range of social, historical, cultural and political relationships. This was what I called the worldliness of English: its relationship to class, education and culture, the materiality of its imposition on students, the implications of their eventual success in and through English.

I argued that English should be thought of as worldly by dint of its vast global expansion, in the sense that a person may be called worldly: it has been and is constantly in the process of being changed by its position in the world. English, I argued, was in the world, part of the world; to use English is to engage in social action which produces and reproduces social and cultural relations. The worldliness of English, in this formulation, referred both to its local and to its global position, to the ways in which it both reflects social relations and constitutes social relations. The worldliness of English, I argued, was always a question of cultural politics (Pennycook, 1994, pp. 33–34). Yet, there was a danger here that, as Said (2004) later put it, the notion of worldliness was "a rather crude and bludgeon-like term to enforce the location of cultural practices back in the mundane, the quotidian, and the secular" (p. 336).

In more recent work (Pennycook, 2007a), therefore, I tried to develop the term worldliness as a counterpoint to globalization, to account for the local resistances to the forces of globalization. Drawing on Mignolo's (2000) distinction (which in turn draws on the work of Renato Ortiz, and Edouard Glissant) between globalización/globalization and mundialización/mondialization (which on one level may be read as synonymous), I suggested that on the one hand globalization may be used to refer to the homogenizing forces of global designs, while the latter, which I translated as worldliness, could be seen in terms of "local histories in which global histories are enacted or where they have to be adapted, adopted, transformed, and rearticulated" (Mignolo, 2000, p. 278). Worldliness in this view is the site of resistance, change, adaptation and reformulation, akin to what Canagarajah (1999) describes as a 'resistance perspective', highlighting the ways in which postcolonial subjects "may find ways to negotiate, alter and oppose political structures, and reconstruct their languages, cultures and identities to their advantage. The intention is not to reject English, but to reconstitute it in more inclusive, ethical, and democratic terms" (p. 2). Whereas in my earlier formulation of worldliness I used it to encompass both the globality and the locality of English, here I reduced the scope of the term to refer to local appropriations.

There are problems with such a formulation, however, since the juxtaposition of worldliness with globalization renders globalization as non-local: the local is worldly, the global is not. As I have been arguing in this book, we need to understand that everything is local. Accordingly, I want to shift the perspective a little once again, since to emphasize worldliness only as resistance and appropriation is to narrow its scope too far. Taking up Radhakrishnan's (2007) use of the term worldliness as "part of a sensitive and hermeneutically generous vocabulary, anchored in a phenomenology that acknowledges that the very one-ness of the world can only be understood on the basis of an irreducible perspectival heterogeneity" (p. 313), we can move beyond both the all-encompassing version I started with and the resistance-oriented version I moved to. This version of worldliness also takes into account that what is global, part of the very one-ness of the world, can only be understood through the locality of perspective, in a way that includes the standpoints, the worldviews, the local articulations through which the global occurs.

A focus on the worldliness of English therefore demands that the very one-ness of English can only be understood on the basis of local perspectives of difference. This is not a question of pluralizing Englishes but of understanding the way different language ideologies construct English locally. Questioning the ways in which we have come to think about languages within colonialism and modernity, and regarding the grand narratives of imperialism, language rights, linguae francae or World Englishes with suspicion, this perspective looks towards local, situated, contextual and contingent ways of understanding languages and language policies. Like Radhakrishnan, therefore, I want this term to do several things, in particular to suggest both localization and epistemological alternatives. It is unfortunate that in much discussion of globalization, localization has been confined to various narrow options: nothing more than globalization on a small scale, traditional cultural practices, or one pole of the dialectic pull between macro and micro forces. From the perspective I am raising here, however, localization is part of worldliness and is thus also a cultural, linguistic and epistemological challenge to globalization.

Connell and Gibson (2003) argue that we need more active terms than 'global' and 'local', or their insipid elision in the term 'glocalization', since these "reify the status of geometric space over the dynamic conditions under which space is actively constructed and consumed by companies, institutions of governance and by individuals" (p. 17). Certainly, as already suggested, the notions of global and local as commonly used present us at the very least with some difficulties: if the global is always manifested locally, and the local is always part of the global, then the global may mean little more than the sum total of all localizations, and the local little more than particular moments of the global. Connell and Gibson (2003) propose instead 'fixity' and 'fluidity', which "reflect more dynamic ways of describing and understanding processes that move across, while becoming embedded in, the materiality of localities and social relations" (p. 17).

From this point of view, fixity is about place, tradition, sources, heritage, authenticity, 'roots' and so on, while fluidity has to do with migration, tourism, cultural flows, hybridity and so forth. While this does give us a more dynamic set of tools, it runs the danger of place and locality always being tied to fixity, tradition and heritage while space is dynamic, fluid, constructed and open. To the extent that I am trying to maintain a sense of the local and locality here, and that at some level this will need to be related to place, I also want to divest the local of notions of fixity and tradition. Following Massey (1994), I see space and place as intertwined rather than juxtaposed, place being a specific articulation of space, and both, as discussed in Chapter 4, being far more dynamic categories than mere context. Worldliness and locality, therefore, are intended to address both the text and its worldly circumstances, both fluidity and fixity, both the global and the local.

Rethinking and relocating language

The local and perspectival emphasis of worldliness suggests that we also need to revisit the ontology of language, raising many questions about the grand narratives or sweeping epistemologies that underpin many discussions of World Englishes, linguistic imperialism or English as a lingua franca. This points instead towards local, situated, contextual and contingent ways of understanding languages and language policies. While the notion of worldliness insists on the one hand that we cannot ignore the material relations between English and globalization, it also suggests we cannot explore the contemporary worldliness of English through twentieth-century tools. In order both to unravel the ways in which languages and metalanguages have been constructed as part of modernity and statist narratives, and also to account for current modes of linguistic landscaping, we are obliged to reconsider our ways of thinking about language.

As a first step, a historical understanding of the interwoven projects of colonialism and language study sheds light on ways in which languages have been constructed. Linguists, as Errington (2008) explains, "can be regarded as a small, rather special group of colonial agents who adapted European letters to alien ways of talking and, by that means, devised necessary conduits for communication across lines of colonial power" (p. 4). As a result, the description of languages was intimately linked to the wider colonial emphasis on human hierarchies, so that "the intellectual work of writing speech was never entirely distinct from the 'ideological' work of devising images of people in zones of colonial contact. It means also that language difference figured in the creation of human hierarchies, such that colonial subjects could be recognized as human, yet deficiently so" (Errington, 2008, p. 5). Language descriptions cannot be abstracted from the colonial imperatives to control, subdue and order. The description of languages, therefore, has to be seen not so much as a scientific division of a language spectrum along natural lines but rather as a colonial project in the defining and dividing of colonized people. As Irvine and Gal (2000) describe the process of 'linguistic description' of Senegalese languages by 19th-century European linguists, "The ways these languages were identified, delimited, and mapped, the ways their relationships were interpreted, and even the ways they were described in grammars and dictionaries were all heavily influenced by an ideology of racial and national essences" (p. 47).

In his discussion of the imposition of Bahasa Indonesia, Heryanto (2007) suggests that "It took European colonialism to introduce the idea of 'language' before the old word *bahasa* came to articulate this newly-acquired concept." Thus, although this was a regional language being used for regional communication, and although the term *bahasa* was a local term, lurking behind this language policy was an ideology both of language and of the nation that had its origins elsewhere. "Language was – as it is today – believed to be a universal property of human species, in all its variations, existing in a separate sphere from, but universally referring to, more or less one and the same objective world" (p. 43). This introduced concept, Heryanto suggests, did not accord with local understandings of language, since "at least in the two most widely spoken and influential languages in Indonesia, Malay and Javanese, there was no word for 'language'. More importantly, there was neither a way nor a need to express its idea until the latter part of the 19th century" (p. 43). This newly introduced concept of language entered "a world with no language", in the process replacing vernacular views of language and how it worked. In speaking of 'language-free communities', the point, to be sure, is not that these contexts involved any less language use, but rather that these language users did not speak 'languages'.

As Sinfree Makoni and I (Makoni and Pennycook, 2005; 2007) have argued at length elsewhere, current approaches to diversity, multilingualism and so forth all too often start with the enumerative strategy of counting languages and romanticizing a plurality based on these putative language counts. While opening up questions of diversity with one hand, at the same time such strategies also reproduce the tropes of colonial invention, overlooking the contested history of language inventions, and ignoring the collateral damage that their embedded notions of language may be perpetrating. By rendering diversity a quantitative question of language enumeration, such approaches continue to employ the census strategies of colonialism while missing the qualitative question of where diversity lies. They continue to use the underlying ideology of countability and singularity, where language-objects are physically located in concepts of space founded on a notion of territorialization. As Heller and Duchêne (2007, p. 11) remark, we need to "rethink the reasons why we hold onto the ideas about language and identity which emerged from modernity. Rather than assuming we must save languages, perhaps we should be asking instead who benefits and who loses from understanding languages the way we do, what is at stake for whom, and how and why language serves as a terrain for competition."

This construction of language, either as an autonomous object or as a linguistic system, has been challenged from several directions that suggest that linguistics has profoundly misconstrued language through its myths about autonomy, systematicity and the rule-bound nature of language, privileging supposedly expert, scientific linguistic knowledge over everyday understandings of language. Following Harris's (1990) argument that the concept of languages as separate entities within orthodox modern linguistics does not correspond to any clear object of analysis, we are forced to conclude that colonial and postcolonial language projects alike (Errington, 2008) produced not only languages that did not fit local language use but also a body of knowledge about language that could not adapt to the locality of language. Returning to the question of English, the focus of much of the analysis, as Canagarajah (2007) points out, "derives from the dominant assumptions of linguistics, informed by the modernist philosophical movement and intellectual culture in which they developed. To begin with, the field treats language as a thing in itself, an objective, identifiable product." By focusing on form, on language as a "tightly knit structure", descriptions of English neglect "other processes and practices that always accompany communication" (p. 98). Indeed, it is not only practices that accompany communication that we need to focus on but the fact that language is a set of practices in itself.

English as metrolingual practice

The question that has started to emerge, then, is whether these old categorizations of language – varieties, code-switching, bilingualism, mother tongue, multilingualism, borrowing – as well as the identities that are assumed along lines of language, location, ethnicity and culture really work any more. Developed in contexts very different to those in which English now finds itself, many of these concepts simply do not seem to address the forms of hybrid urban multilingualism in which English now partakes. Indeed, there are strong reasons to question the very notion of English, or any language, as a discrete entity that is describable in terms of core and variation. There are two sides to this: on the one hand, the changing realities of urban life, with enhanced mobility, shifting populations, social upheaval, health and climate crises, increased access to diverse media and engagement with new forms of popular culture, are leading to fresh language mixes and possibilities. On the other hand, a serious consideration of the ways in which ideas about language have been constructed and invented forces us to consider anew not only emergent language mixes but the terms in which we think about them.

Bosire (2006, p. 192) argues that the "hybrid languages of Africa are contact outcomes that have evolved at a time when African communities are coming to terms with the colonial and postcolonial situation that included rapid urbanization and a bringing together of different ethnic communities and cultures with a concomitant exposure to different ways of being." At the same time, "young people are caught up in this transition; they are children of two worlds and want a way to express this duality, this new 'ethnicity'" Out of this mix, emerge new language varieties, such as "Sheng", a Swahili/English hybrid, which provides urban youth with "a way to break away from the old fraternities that put particular ethnic communities in particular neighborhoods/estates and give them a global urban ethnicity, the urbanite: sophisticated, street smart, new generation, tough" (Bosire, 2006, p. 192). Also looking at English in different domains in East Africa, Higgins (2009) argues for the need to look not so much at local forms of English, but rather at ways of thinking about how "languages work together in multilingual societies by placing multilingual practices at the theoretical center" (p. 2). Focusing on English as a local language, Higgins thus draws attention to the ways in which English participates in local multilingual practices, how "East Africans exploit the heteroglossia of language to perform modern identities through localizing global linguistic and cultural resources while generally maintaining the multiple layers of meaning from both the global and the local" (p. 148).

Rather than thinking in terms of English and its peripheral varieties, therefore, this work moves towards an understanding of local language practices that draw on a range of language resources, whether these be from different varieties, registers or languages. This is, consequently, an attempt to move away from nation-based models of English and to take on board current understandings of translingual practices across communities other than those defined along national criteria. The interest here is in "the communicative practices of transnational groups that interact using different languages and communicative codes simultaneously present in a range of communicative channels, both local and distant" (Jacquemet, 2005, p. 265). These transidiomatic practices, Jacquemet explains, "are the results of the co-presence of multilingual talk (exercised by de/reterritorialized speakers) and electronic media, in contexts heavily structured by social indexicalities and semiotic codes." For Jacquemet, such practices are dependent on "transnational environments," the mediation of "deterritorialized technologies", and interaction "with both present and distant people" (p. 265).

Jørgensen's (2008a) analysis of 'polylingual languaging' among children and adolescents in Denmark comes to a similar conclusion: it makes more sense to look at the use of diverse language resources, or *features*, than to consider whether a phrase is in one, or two or three languages. Jørgensen (2008a) and Møller (2008) propose the notion of *polylingualism* in place of *multilingualism* in light of the idea that "speakers use features and not languages" (Jørgensen, 2008a, p. 166). As Møller (2008, p. 218) asks, "What if the participants do not orient to the juxtaposition of languages in terms of switching? What if they instead orient to a linguistic norm where all available linguistic resources can be used to reach the goals of the speaker?" If indeed the local understanding of language use does not fit an externally imposed notion of code-switching, then "it is not adequate to categorise this conversation as bilingual or multilingual, or even as language mixing, because all these terms depend on the separability of linguistic categories. I therefore suggest the term *polylingual* instead." While this notion of polylingualism shares much with the ways of looking at language that I am developing here, it might still be argued that, like plurilingualism and multilingualism, it tends towards a pluralization of singular entities (languages).

The changing cultural and linguistic worlds in which many English users live pose challenges for how we conceive of culture, ethnicity and language. As Maher (2005) describes it in the context of Japan, students are rejecting fixed ascriptions of cultural identity and instead playing with notions of *metroethnicity*: "Cultural essentialism and ethnic orthodoxy are out. In Japan, metroethnicity is in. Cool rules" (p. 83). Metroethnicity, he explains, is "a reconstruction of ethnicity: a hybridised 'street' ethnicity deployed by a cross-section of people with ethnic or mainstream backgrounds who are oriented towards cultural hybridity, cultural/ethnic tolerance and a multicultural lifestyle in friendships, music, the arts, eating and dress" (p. 83). People of different backgrounds now "play with ethnicity (not necessarily their own) for aesthetic effect. Metroethnicity is skeptical of heroic ethnicity and bored with sentimentalism about ethnic language" (p. 83). As language learners move around the world in search of English or other desirable languages, or stay at home but tune in to new digital worlds through screens, mobiles and headphones, the possibilities of being something not yet culturally imagined mobilizes new identity options. And in these popular transcultural flows, languages, cultures and identities are frequently mixed. Code-mixing, sampling of sounds, genres, languages and cultures becomes the norm (Alim, Ibrahim and Pennycook, 2009).

In order to capture how language is used in such contexts, we can talk in terms of *metrolingualism* (Otsuji and Pennycook, 2010). Drawing on Maher's (2005) metroethnicity, metrolingualism is a product of modern, urban interaction, which, as Coulmas (2009) reminds us (and see Chapter 4), is the central focus of sociolinguistics. Metrolingualism describes the ways in which people of different and mixed backgrounds use, play with and negotiate identities through language; it does not assume connections between language, culture, ethnicity, nationality and geography, but rather seeks to explore the contingencies of these categories; its focus is not on language systems but on languages as emergent from contexts of interaction. As a result, while part of the focus here is on hybridity and play, metrolingualism carries a very serious intent. As with many studies of language play – from Rampton's (1995; 2006) studies of *crossing* and the language of late modernity in school classrooms, or Lin's (2000) and Luk's (2005) studies of language play in Hong Kong, to studies of multilingual creativity in hip-hop (Lin, 2009; Omoniyi, 2009) – the focus here is not on elite game playing but on the ludic possibilities in the everyday. While the focus of metrolingualism, therefore, may include forms of chic, privileged playfulness in elite bilingualism – acquired bilingual capacity for the upwardly mobile in a global world (De Meija, 2002) – it includes a much broader view of contexts of translingual activity.

Canagarajah's (2007) discussion of Lingua Franca English (LFE) makes a similar point. This distinction between English as a lingua franca and Lingua Franca English is an important one, since the former tends towards an understanding of a pre-given language that is then used by different speakers, while the latter suggests that LFE emerges from its contexts of use. According to Canagarajah, "LFE does not exist as a system out there. It is constantly brought into being in each context of communication" (2007, p. 91). From this point of view, "there is no meaning for form, grammar or language ability *outside the realm of practice*" (2007, p. 94; my emphasis). That is to say, LFE, or any other language, has to be located in forms of local practice to have any meaning. "LFE is not a product located in the mind of the speaker; it is a social process constantly reconstructed in sensitivity to environmental factors" (2007, p. 94). This is consistent with the argument I have been making for the need to escape the predefinition of a language user by geographical location or variety and instead to deal with language as a local practice. Put another way, if we adopt a translingual model of language (Pennycook 2007a; 2008; 2009a) to look at English use, the relationship to be understood is among interlingual resources (what language resources people draw on), colingual relations (who says what to whom where) and ideolingual implications (what gets taken from what language use with what investments, ideologies, discourses and beliefs).

English has always been local

Once we start to think in terms of language as a local practice, the ideas of language use in context or of languages spreading to take on local character-istics become suspect. The very notion of English as a describable entity is destabilized; the notion of local Englishes determined along national lines is likewise contestable. Instead, we can start to consider the relocalization of different practices in language and the translingual practices of language users drawing on different resources. Ganesh, "an engineering student and an ardent adorer of tuskers" who has "taken a tusker on lease" explains that although "the tuskers brought from Bihar like Thechikkottu Kavu Rama-chandran are taller than the tuskers from Kerala, they do not have the beauty of Kerala tuskers" (Varma, 2006, p. 3). This, as I argued before, is less about Indian English as a variety, as a localization of some other English, than about local practices – leasing and enjoying elephant aesthetics, with parti-cular local orientations (Kerala tuskers are more beautiful than their Bihar rivals) – relocalized in interviews (was this in English or Malayalam or something else again?) and relocalized again in a newspaper article.

If it is clear that the ways we think about language are inevitably products of particular historical contexts, then an age of globalization suggests that we need both to reflect on how and why we look at languages as separate, countable, describable entities in the way we do, and to consider that lan-guages may be undergoing such forms of transition as to require new ways of conceptualization in terms of local activities, resources, or practices. Like other arguments in this book, this signals a switch in direction. Just as I argued in Chapter 3 that language may be a result of discourse rather than discourse a result of language, or in Chapter 4 that talking in the city may produce locality as much as context determining the talk, so here I am sug-gesting that if we look from the bottom up, if we take both practices and locality sufficiently seriously, then instances such as the above are not so much local varieties of English as relocalizations of practice. This suggests not only that language is here embedded in local practices, but also that the origins of English use are not to be found in the idea of a language that spread from the centre to the periphery, but in the multiple, simultaneous origins of locality. Rather than seeing English in different parts of the world as all part of this thing called English that has been spread and locally adapted, we can start to see that this notion of English is only a confusing patina that obscures the local origins of language use. From this point of view we can transcend the arguments over pluralization – is WE more concerned with diversity than versions of ELF? – and engage instead with the possibility of multiple, co-present, local origins of English. This view of global Englishes as local language practices reshapes the ways in which we can understand global and local cultural and linguistic formations, and suggests that English has always been local.

6 *Alibangbang* and ecologies of local language practices

Talking about fish and ropes

Two different language practices in which I engage fairly regularly are fish-
and rope-naming. When underwater, scuba diving is not in itself a very
talkative domain, and the local, nonverbal language practices we engage in
are limited. Once back on the surface, however, the unvoiced experiences of a
long dive may need quick relocalization in discourse. Talk of fish is common:
Did you see the Yellow Masked Angel Fish under the rock? What was that
fish with the blue and yellow stripes? The one I saw had a high dorsal fin, and
so on. In the more formal contexts of fish identification that I do as part of
reef conservation projects in the Philippines[1] (we're supposed to know the
name of that fish with the blue and yellow stripes), there are more specific
language practices involved particularly with species identification. One of the
problems here, however, is that fish tend to get called many different things in
different languages, and even within the same language. A difficulty with
gaining knowledge about shark attacks (which in itself is not a good term,
since although attacks remain a concern for those of us that swim in certain
waters, they are more often instances of shark taste tests), for example, is that
they are known by different names in different waters. The Bull shark
(*Carcharhinus leucas*) in Australian waters is also known as the Whaler shark,
the Zambezi shark (or Zambi) in South Africa, the Ganges shark in India,
and the Nicaragua shark in Central America.

Take the family of *Chaetodontidae* (from the Greek for brush and teeth),
of which there are about 120 species globally. Popularly known as Butterflyfish in English, these particularly colourful tropical fish are significant
indicators of the state of a coral reef: since they feed on coral polyps, their
abundance and diversity can be a measure of coral health. Their names
vary from language to language and also from region to region. The
Threadfin Butterflyfish – *Chaetodon Auriga* (auriga: charioteer, groom) –
named in English after its long filament running from the dorsal fin, is known
in French as Chaetodon Cocher (cocher: a coachman), in German as
Fähnchen-Falterfisch (Falter: butterfly (an alternative to Schmetterling) and
Fähnchen – the diminutive form of Fahne, a flag, meaning banner or pennant),

and in Japanese as トゲチョウチョウウオ (togechouchouuo) (トゲ spike; チョウチョウ butterfly; ウオ fish). While these names all draw attention in different languages to the salient feature of the dorsal fin – as a thread, whip, pennant or spike – in other instances, as we shall see later, different aspects of different fish contribute to the mutiplicity of naming practices.

Rope-naming is something I do when sailing (if I am not below the water, I like at least to be on it). And sailing, as many know, has a vast range of particular terms and language practices. This is not so much a question of rope identification in the same way that we need to identify fish species, but rather of the relocalization in language of the complex practices of managing a sailing boat. It may surprise non-sailors, for example, that there are in fact no ropes on a boat (except possibly a bell rope – the hanging rope used to ring a traditional ship's bell): there are halyards, sheets, shrouds, stays, reefing lines, painters, topping lifts, boom vangs, downhauls and many more. Woebetide a novice sailor who asks What's this rope for? Only to be met with a vitupera-tive response from a bearded, weather-beaten sailing master on the names of things on a boat (There are no bloody ropes on a boat (except maybe a bell rope)). Now, also of interest is that in French, for example, there is no *cordage* (rope) on a boat either, only *un étai* (stay), *un hale-bas* (vang or downhaul), *un hauban* (shroud), *une drisse* (halyard), *une écoute* (sheet), *une amarre* (painter) and so on. I shall return to the significance of this observation later.

Locating languages in ecologies

These examples link not only to questions of language and locality – and in particular to ways in which languages cut up the world – but also to language and ecology, or questions about how language relates to the natural environ-ment. A central interest of this chapter will be the notion of language ecology, since this raises important concerns for how we think about the locality of language. Theorists in a number of fields have suggested that language ecology, or an 'ecology of languages paradigm', enables us to better relate languages in complex ways to their contexts, and to close the gap between micro- and macro-sociologies of language. Ricento (2000, p. 20), for example, suggests that a new generation of language policy studies has emerged, based on a "synthesis of elements of critical theory with an ecology of languages approach." Leather and Van Dam explain that "an ecological approach to the study of language acquisition sees the individual's cognitive processes as inextricably interwoven with their experiences in the physical and social world. ... " and "aims to avoid unjustifiable appeals to normativity – in both research designs and the interpretation of data" (2003, p. 13). According to Fettes (2003, p. 45), "ecological explanations offer a more promising foundation for critical rea-soning than any of the alternatives (Marxism, poststructuralism, gender theory and the rest) ... ".

The notion of language ecology has become both popular and productive as a way of understanding language and environment, drawing our attention to the ways in which languages are embedded in social, cultural, economic and physical ecologies, and also in relationship to each other. For Leo van Lier (2004), echoing some of the arguments I make in this chapter about an ecology of language practices, an ecological approach to language learning "offers a theory of language integrated into a theory of semiotics, and a theory of learning as activity-in-the-world" (p. 20). It has reopened discussion about the ways in which languages cut up the world differently, and thus what may be lost when a language dies (Evans, 2010). And by drawing an analogy between environmental concerns about endangered species and cultural concerns about endangered languages, it has been able to appeal politically to those who have been more concerned about the death of various animals than the death of various languages. Indeed, as Mühlhäusler puts it, "The ecological metaphor ... is action oriented. It shifts the attention from linguists being players of academic language games to becoming shop stewards for linguistic diversity, and to addressing moral, economic and other 'non-linguistic' issues" (1996, p. 2).

The different ways in which we approach a relationship between language and the environment put different conceptions of language, reality and agency into play. I have discussed (Pennycook, 2004) the distinctions and terminology in different approaches to language and ecology elsewhere (Fill, 2001; Fill and Mühlhäusler, 2001), and it will serve no purpose here to reiterate these in detail.[2] Briefly, however, we can distinguish among various related positions. One approach to language ecology emphasizes the point that languages must always be considered in relationship to their context: as Nettle and Romaine (2000, p. 79) put it, a "language is enmeshed in a social and geographical matrix just as a rare species is enmeshed in an ecosystem". A variation on this, sometimes called linguistic ecology, is interested particularly in the capacity of languages to describe their environment. As Mühlhäusler (2001, p. 163) puts it, "Western languages have many gaps in their ability to express aspects of the environment. The number of edible plants the average Westerner can name contrasts very unfavourably with the many hundreds of names known to the average speaker of a South American Indian language."

A different perspective again, which may be termed an ecology of languages, is more concerned about relationships between languages. For Mufwene (2001, p. 166) "answers to diverse questions about language evolution, such as why a particular language was restructured and in what specific ways, or why a particular language was/is endangered, are to be found in its ecology, both internal and external, and both structural and nonstructural". Finally, there is ecolinguistics, a form of critical discourse analysis with an interest in the environment. Halliday (2001, p. 198), for example, suggests that 'growthism' (an ideology that bigger is better), along with class prejudice, is grammatically encoded in English: "Growthism and classism are our two major ideological menaces; and ideologies are constructed in language." Schleppergrell (2001, p. 228), in a debate over what constitutes "a truly green grammar", argues that it "is a grammar that reveals the real forces and institutions that result in environmental destruction". As Alexander (2009) puts it, since "a major function of language is that of distortion, obfuscation, deception, if not straight mendacity", it is incumbent on linguists to engage in critical analysis of the "'misrepresentations' of ecologically relevant issues which take place via language" (p. 12).

Clearly, across a broad range of different approaches to language and ecology, there is a great deal to be gained from this engagement between language and an understanding of the environment. And yet, although language ecology is both powerful and useful as a way of understanding language diversity, it is also hazardous. At the very least, a critical exploration of the notion of language ecology points to the need to be wary about the metaphors or analogies we use. As Crawford (1998, p. 155) points out, the language ecology metaphor can be misleading: "Unlike natural species, languages have no genes and thus carry no mechanism for natural selection. Their prospects for survival are determined not by any intrinsic traits, or capacity for adaptation, but by social forces alone." It is perhaps impossible, he suggests, to avoid "biomorphic metaphors like *ecology, survival, death,* and *genocide*", but we should be cautious since "such metaphors can lead us into semantic traps, and these traps have political consequences".

Several questions emerge, therefore, when we start to relate language to the environment: What versions of language are put into play in different forms of language ecology? What kinds of relation are envisaged here between languages and other social practices? What are the political consequences of biomorphic metaphors or the mapping of direct relations between language and the environment? Stephen May (2001, p. 3) has noted several concerns with these ecological ways of thinking about language: by suggesting that the demise of languages may be "an inevitable part of the cycle of social and linguistic *evolution*," they may ironically promote a political quietude towards language politics at the same time that they are hoping to raise awareness of language concerns. The emphasis on a relation between language and the environment, furthermore, tends to "obscure the wider social and political factors at work in language loss" (May, 2001, p. 3) and to "understate, or simply ignore, the historical, social and political *constructedness* of languages" (2001, p. 4).

This point about the constructedness of languages takes us back to the discussion in the previous chapter. As I have suggested at several junctures in this book, to understand languages as separate, countable entities is to operate with a very particular language ideology. While some ecological approaches to language take ecology largely as a metaphor, and thereby allow for a view of languages as complexly interrelated within a linguistic ecosystem, others take ecology fairly literally, and tend towards an apparent equation between threatened languages and species, suggesting that both need to be similarly saved from extinction. As Mufwene (2004) has observed, such discourses of language preservation often overlook humans in favour of language: if people start to change their patterns of language use because of social and economic change, and this change looks as if it will lead to a language no longer being used, they are urged to put linguistic richness before personal wealth, to pre-serve their language for the sake of linguistic diversity. Batibo (2009) observes that "poverty is a crucial factor in language maintenance, as speakers of any language tend to identify themselves with the most socioeconomically presti-gious language" (p. 23). While the dual measures of language codification and economic development may assist, missing in much of this discussion is the mediating realm of an understanding of local language practices.

When loggers move into forests in the Amazon or Indonesia, forcing forest dwellers, or those who gain their livelihood from the forest, to change their ways of living; when crops fail and people move to urban environments in East Africa; when new industries are introduced in Pacific islands, from mining to new ways of fishing, from new cash crops to carpentry for the tourist industry; when people start to take up a new religion – Islam in sub-Saharan Africa, or Christianity in Papua New Guinea; when Gabonese rap artists in Libreville mix French, verlan, Fang, Téké and English in their lyrics; when Indigenous Australian kids blend Kriol and other languages, we need to understand the local language practices they are engaged in and how these are changing in relation to other social practices. We cannot map language onto the environment as if there were some representational symmetry here; we need to think in term of language practices. And we need to be wary of mapping language ideologies onto these contexts without understanding how language is understood locally.

In the rest of this chapter I shall look at ways in which a notion of language ecology puts into play various relationships between languages and the physical environment. Of particular interest will be questions as to how we understand language, culture and the world, and whether languages adapt to the world or create the world. As I have argued in previous chapters, it is important to understand language in relation to space, movement and locality, since local language practices are far more than the use of language in particular con-texts. Different people's language practices work in relation to the local organization of space, since language as a local practice is not so much a question of locally embedded language use as of the production of locality. This observation will have particular implications for the discussion in this chapter, since it suggests a move away from any idea that languages as entities reflect their surroundings, and instead draws attention to an understanding of how language practices are involved in the creation of our surroundings.

Language organicism

Mapping relations between language and the world of biology is nothing new. While the notion of language ecology is generally attributed to Haugen (1972), as Edwards (2004, p. 468) argues, it can be traced back "at least to Aristotelian concepts of 'design in nature'". Explicit comparisons between the evolution of languages and species emerged in Europe in the nineteenth century, with Darwin and many others drawing analogies with the constructed family trees of language origins in order to introduce their radical theories of the origins of species and humans. Thus, evolutionary theory and biology (as well as geology and other sciences) drew on linguistic (comparative philology) models to develop their explanation of evolutionary theory (Alter, 1999). The successes of comparative-historical philology in the genealogical reconstruction of the "obscure linguistic past" gave evolutionary thinkers the opportunity to open the door to speculations on parallel biological changes (p. 147).

Yet such analogies came bundled up with a range of related correspondences. The "central philological trope" of comparative philology and missionary linguistics, Errington (2001, p. 32) points out, was the conception of "language as organism" which "informed images of language change in natural, entelechial processes of articulation, predetermined by languages' originary conditions and communities". This led to constructions of language families, organic differences between language types, language trees, and a host of language–biology analogies, a move closely tied to the scientific racism of the nineteenth and twentieth centuries. A set of biological/linguistic metaphors arose towards the end of the nineteenth century, with Darwinian evolutionary theories being mapped against ethnic, racial and linguistic categories. In this circular movement, the linguistic, ethnic and racial maps of the European empires were remapped onto evolutionary theory. These analogies that placed human evolution alongside plant and animal evolution emerged by no means coincidentally at the acme of European empire, as attempts were made to relate racial, linguistic and biological order.

Language sciences, from early in their development, were already playing a major role in the development of ways of thinking not only about language but also about biology, culture, race and human hierarchies. The study of languages (philology) had already equated language evolution and family trees before this was taken up in other areas of scientific inquiry. Errington (2008) suggests two ways in which philological images of language were influential beyond the academy. On the one hand, they contributed to the "broadly organic view of history which helped to explain Europe's superiority in a colonial present, naturalize its ongoing civilizational advancement, and frame linguistic difference as human inequality in a colonial world" (p. 71). On the other hand, as a peculiarly German science, philology turned the past into a "resource for nationalist ideologies in an industrializing Europe" (p. 71).

As Cameron (2007) makes clear, assumptions about a close organic link between language and culture have a long and problematic history. The moral force of preservationist arguments "lies in the perception of a natural bond between a community and the mother tongue that uniquely expresses its culture and worldview" (p. 280). This view constantly recalls the history of the *Volk*, one people, one language, one culture. Hutton (1999) explores this point in depth, pointing out that "race science took its lead from the study of language" (p. 3). As he argues in his study of linguistics and the Third Reich, many of the concepts we use today in linguistics – from native speaker to speech community – have their origins in the 'nationalist organicism' that developed as part of European nationalism and found its apotheosis in Nazi Germany.

These "seemingly natural metaphors – half-conscious bonds of logic among distinct fields of knowledge – draw upon the aesthetic sensibility of a given time and place: they ground the communicative strategies and plausibility structures of science in juxtapositions that are as much imaginative as they are cognitive" (Alter, 1999, p. 1). Although on the one hand, then, the metaphors linguists use – language trees, language spread (see Chapter 5), language ecology – may open up useful ways for reflecting on language, such analogies are also bound up with the cultures and ideologies of the times and places in which they emerge. As Alter suggests, comparative philology "had the inherent benefit of combining a scientific method and a romanticist, antiquarian spirit, an association that could have emerged so prominently perhaps only in the nineteenth century" (p. 148). The parallel concern, then, is what it is about a notion of ecology, a biological metaphor, that appeals so much to people working with language at this historical juncture. The scientific and romanticist spirit of comparative philology that was adopted into evolutionary theory appears to have been preserved in aspic, to be reborrowed in recent times for a language politics that seeks both the hard aura of science and the soft feel of environmentalism, both the appeal of environmental politics and the romanticism of language revivalism.

The implications of drawing on biological models to understand language relationships, and treating languages as analogous with species, can be seen in recent research in the biological and applied mathematical sciences. The metaphor has now passed back in the opposite direction once again, so mathematical modelling usually employed for evolutionary prediction and explanation may now be applied to languages as biological entities. Two articles in the scientific journal *Nature* epitomize this approach. Using complex statistical models to compare biological and linguistic diversity and extinction risks, Sutherland (2003, p. 277) concludes that "languages are more threatened than birds or mammals. Rare languages are more likely to show evidence of decline than commoner ones. Areas with high language diversity also have high bird and mammal diversity and all three show similar relationships to area, latitude, area of forest and, for languages and birds, maximum altitude". Sutherland also concludes, however, that while these correlations may explain language, mammal and bird diversity, similar factors (altitude, density and insularity) do not explain the numbers of endangered languages.

Now while this finding is quite interesting as a counterpoint to arguments for a direct, causative relationship between biological and linguistic diversity, this way of understanding languages as similar to bird or mammal species is perilously reductive. This becomes even more apparent in Abrams and Strogatz's (2003, p. 900) models of language death: "the model we describe here idealizes languages as fixed, and as competing with each other for speakers" and "we also assume a highly connected population, with no spatial or social structure, in which all speakers are monolingual". In the conclusion, the authors admit that "contrary to the model's stark prediction, bilingual societies do, in fact, exist", before going on to erroneously suggest that "the histories of countries where two languages coexist today generally involve split populations that lived without significant interaction, effectively in separate, monolingual societies. Only recently have these communities begun to mix, allowing language competition to begin." Such views of monolingual societies in competition with each other, and of bi- or multilingualism not as a sustainable practice but as a result of the convergence of monolingual populations, are precisely the result of drawing analogies between ecologies, species and languages.

Kibbee (2003, p. 51) strongly refutes the possibility of drawing this analogy, arguing that this "'language equals species' equivalency" that emerged in the nineteenth century is as problematic now as it was then: "A language is a behaviour, not a physical characteristic. If two languages are in contact, then they influence each other. If a dog lives in the same house as a bird it does not grow wings, nor does the bird sprout paws. If two languages are in contact, they create a new language." If species are the cornerstone of biological ecologies, how do we deal with the vast differences between species and languages? Species, for example, cannot, by definition, interbreed, whereas languages, perhaps by definition, do. Scientists have recently developed transgenic methods of transferring genetic material from one organism to another; languages have always had this capacity.

The re-emergence of these analogies at this particular conjunction of time and politics needs careful consideration. At the same time that a particular social, economic, cultural and political world order is emerging, so too are attempts to biologize the world to match that order, to find biological explanations (either in hard science through DNA modelling or in the softer sciences such as evolutionary psychology) for gender relations, sexual orientation, states of mind, ways of being. Language ecology, whether seen as a metaphor or as a relationship between languages and the natural environment, is inevitably tied to this cultural climate to negate the social, cultural and political. The use of the notion of language ecology, then, needs to be understood in relationship to this broader reactionary stance to naturalize the world as it is, to make the cultural natural, to render language biological, to normalize social and sexual relations as hard wired, to make genetics the science of everything, to counter an emphasis on difference. There are deep ironies here, since many language ecologists consider diversity to be inherently good, but such are the risks that emerge from the use of biomorphic metaphors.

Language, the world and adaptation

If a focus on language ecology may thus suggest troubling relations with a history of language-culture-nation homologies, it also opens up for examination significant concerns to do with a relationship between language and the world around it. As suggested above, many of the language endangerment, preservation or ecology arguments hinge on a twofold set of relations between language and culture and language and the world. If we lose a language, it is argued, we lose the culture that goes with it, and we also lose its capacity to describe the world. Thus we lose both a way of representing the world and a particular cultural orientation towards doing so. It is not hard to see a contradiction in this proposition: either the issue is a relation between language and reality (the capacity of language to describe the world), or it is a question of language and culture (the ways in which language is used as part of a particular worldview, cutting the world up differently). Unless we argue that language, culture and the world are easily mappable onto each other, we have to concede a need for a more complex relationship here among language and culture, language and reality, and culture and reality.

A core argument of language ecology is that language diversity is part of human diversity and, like biological diversity, this is inherently good. On the face of it, this looks a useful and sensible argument, yet it has a number of flaws. The biological argument is one that hinges on, first, the position that biological diversity is crucial for biological sustainability. The reasons for this can at times be oddly anthropocentric (we don't know what value species may have for human medicine and so forth, so we should protect them for unknown future benefits for humans), but are also grounded in the general proposition that the greater the genetic diversity, the greater the possibilities for biological survival. Second, it is an argument that humans should not intercede in ecologies but let them run their natural course. Thus, whatever we may object to in the natural domain (animals killing each other and so forth), this is natural and we should not intervene. While there are a number of debates to be had here (such as the benefits of eradicating certain organisms that create immense human suffering and death), the general argument appears sustainable. The question, then, is should we not also work to sustain the cultural diversity that is crucial for the maintenance of human existence?

The human diversity argument, however, is a different one. It is not one about human biology, but one about human behaviour. Humans do many things, some of them estimable, many not: murder, torture of many and gruesome proportions, mass killing and the development of diverse means to do so, rape, violence against women, abuse of children, homophobic brutality, malice, spite, cruelty, avarice, mendacity, vindictiveness, an extraordinary diversity of bigotries and much more are, alas, all too human. While the balance of human activity may, perhaps, verge towards a positive account, it is clear that vicious and abusive behaviour is deeply human, sitting at the heart of familial and social life. And surely a continuing hope is not that this part of the rich tapestry of human diversity should be preserved, but rather that this is a vast domain of human life that we desperately need to try to change. The point, then, is that human cultural diversity is not something of inherent value; it is something to be struggled over. Let me be very clear about this argument here: I am not as a consequence suggesting that there are good and bad languages, that we should be choosing which languages to maintain and which to eradicate, but rather that the analogy is wrong. Human diversity is not inherently good in the same way that biological diversity may be. And while it would be foolish in the extreme to judge languages, the same cannot be said of language practices: the 'rich tapestry' of diverse human language practices is something we need to struggle over, since they include anything from magical moments of language creativity to hateful moments of deepest bigotry.

As Halliday (2002) asks, we need to consider why we would assume that what is good for species and languages is good for humans in general (see, for example, Skutnabb-Kangas, 2000), and why, ultimately, the assumption is made that the diversity of languages is assumed to be the central way of understanding linguistic diversity: "How do we reason from diversity of species – biodiversity – to diversity of languages – glossodiversity, let us say?" (Halliday, 2002, p. 13). Halliday's distinction between glossodiversity – the diversity of languages – and semiodiversity – the diversity of meanings – points to a key issue here. What kind of diversity are we after and "exactly what is the value that attaches to such diversity, for the human race as a whole?" (p. 13) This distinction questions both the supposition that the enumeration of languages is the best measure of diversity, and the supposition that such diversity is inherently beneficial. What we need to start to explore, then, is this relation between diversity of meaning and local language practices.

This leads us to questions of adaptability: "Languages, like species, are highly adapted to their environments," suggest Nettle and Romaine (2000, p. 43). In an interesting critique of the notion that English is a language that adapts easily to its environment, Mühlhäusler suggests that "English in many places has been an exotic language, in the sense of ill-adapted to the new environments to which it was transported ... those who argue that English can be nativized and adapt to new conditions tend to underestimate the time it takes – and that in the meantime considerable collateral damage can be caused" (Mühlhäusler, 2003, p. 77). Mühlhäusler goes on to discuss the ecological damage caused by the lack of adaptability of English to a sudden new environment in Pitcairn (following the mutiny on the *Bounty*). While Mühlhäusler's point about the damage caused by the slow adaptability of English (and this damage has been in far more domains than just the environmental) is an interesting counterpoint to the suggestions all too easily made within World Englishes discourse that English adapts well to all new environments (see Chapter 5), we need to be cautious about this notion of adaptability.

Languages are always adaptable, while species are not. Certain species are tied very much to a specific locality, food source, climate – a niche – and if that changes, they may be instantly threatened. Other species are more adaptable, rats and cockroaches being among the most successful. It is tempting, perhaps, to push the analogy: English, Spanish, Chinese, and other widespread languages are like cockroaches, rats, goats, seagulls, pigeons: adaptable omnivores. But there is a danger here, since although some languages seem akin to the niche species, it cannot be the case that a language is not itself adaptable: species are relatively fixed biological types (apart from some fast-mutating viruses and bacteria), whereas languages are not. Language death arises not from the non-adaptability of a language to a changed environment, but because (amongst other things) the speakers use another language increasingly adaptable to their changing needs. This shift may be enforced through education, language policy, economics and so on, but it is not so much that the language cannot adapt to a new environment as that speakers of that language start to use another language in its place. Once again, we can see here the problem of making the notion of 'a language' and its adaptability central to any understanding of language and locality. It is not the language that adapts or does not adapt, but rather that people adapt their language practices to new social and economic conditions.

The death of Indigenous Australian languages came about, and continues drastically today, not because they became less adapted to a changed physical environment, nor because English is better adapted to that environment, but as a result of colonization, genocide, racism, educational practices and shifting social, cultural and economic practices. It was not the adaptability of the languages but the enforced changes on the Indigenous people. So here we touch on the crucial role of human agency, an element all too often missing in these accounts of languages as entities struggling with each other for survival.[3] We need to consider the development of language as a human artefact rather than an entity in the world that exists independently of human action. Languages do not adapt to their environment; humans produce linguistic diversity that cuts the world up differently. Of course environments exist: there are trees, leaves, rocks, plants, animals and so forth, but the naming of these is a human activity. Biological, geographical and environmental sciences may present us with a certain set of classifications along certain lines, but humans classify the world in their own terms. Although this is an adaptation to the environment in the sense that particular divisions of plants, fish, sails, ropes and so forth are being made, it is an agentive categorization of the world, not an objective reflection of a material world.

There appears, then, to be a contradiction between competing ways of understanding language and the world. At one level, the issue is simply that certain terms for natural items and their use may be lost when a language is no longer used (Evans, 2010). At another level, however, we have a tension here between a language ecological view that stresses the different ways in which languages cut up the world (the argument being that if we lose a language, we lose a unique way of understanding the world) and an ecology of languages position that emphasizes a direct relation between languages and their environment. If we stress the former, then we are placing language-specific categorizations over non-language-specific biological definitions: the world is crucially divided into non-biological, language-specific understandings of diversity. If we stress the latter, it is the facts of non-language-specific biological diversity that form the parallel with languages.

If we also wish to make an analogy between languages and species, then we need to decide which version of the world we want. Given that languages cut up not only the world but also the world of languages differently, there is something of a gap between the quasi-biological species-type accounting of the world's 6800 languages and the language-specific division of some 40,000 names for languages arrived at by asking speakers what they speak (see Ethnologue, 2009). The truth of language diversity does not lie with either figure, or even somewhere in between, but rather in the disparity itself. The different ways in which languages are constructed suggest problems for the quasi-scientific status of the analogy between languages and biological species, and raise complications for both preservationist accounts of diversity and mappings between language and environment. What matter are local language practices.

The strong arguments for a causative link between linguistic and ecological diversity are also thus exposed to critical scrutiny. It has been observed that there is a correlation between forms of diversity in certain regions of the world, leading to an argument that "it might not only be a correlational relationship. It may also be causal: the two types of diversities seem to mutually enforce and support each other" (Skutnabb-Kangas, 2003, p. 36). Maffi (2000, p. 17) makes the point that "the concurrent ongoing loss of linguistic and cultural diversity on the planet is largely due to the same global economic, political, and social factors that are affecting biodiversity". This is, up to a point, a reasonable assumption, though we might still want to ask whether standardized education, for example, which is a serious factor in language decline, also has a similar negative effect on biodiversity. Maffi goes on to argue, however, that "these two 'extinction crises' are convergent … , one reinforcing and being reinforced by the other", and that "the persistence of vigorous, thriving linguistic diversity around the world may afford us our best chance of countering biodiversity loss and keeping the planet alive and healthy" (p. 17). The argument, then, is this: biological diversity is essential for the planet; different languages cut the world up differently; linguistic diversity therefore helps maintain biological diversity because we can talk about it differently in different languages; and biological diversity helps produce linguistic diversity by presenting more diverse realities for languages to describe.

> Different languages have developed distinct vocabularies to express those differences that are important to their speakers. One would not expect to find dozens of words for different types of snow or reindeer in the languages spoken in the Sahara desert, or scores of words for different types of sand and camels in the languages of the far North. In this sense, languages have been called « the DNA of cultures » – they have encoded the cultural knowledge that people have inherited from their ancestors, and each generation continues to add to this heritage.
>
> (UNESCO – Terralingua, 2003, p. 20)

The reinvocation of the old Eskimo Snow Myth muddies the waters here. As Martin (1986), Pullum (1989) and others have shown, not only has this become something of an urban language myth – with the number of words for snow varying from a handful to a hundred – but it is also based on a real mis-understanding of these languages: "Among the many depressing things about this credulous transmission and elaboration of a false claim is that even if there *were* a large number of roots for different snow types in some Arctic language, this would *not*, objectively, be intellectually interesting; it would be a most mundane and unremarkable fact" (Pullum, 1989, p. 278). While it may be interesting to show that there are different vocabulary items in differ-ent languages, this once again conflates diversity within languages and a diversity of languages (semiodiversity as opposed to glossodiversity).

If it is the case that biological diversity and linguistic diversity are connected, this connection would be one of diversity within languages rather than a diversity of languages. If languages are different ways of cutting up the world, then a diversity of languages gives us different ways of looking at the same thing. To be sure, to lose a language is to some extent to lose forms of knowledge about the world, and much local knowledge is "at great risk, as long as it is only available in little-known languages spoken by just a few hundred people, since a shift to another language can cut off its transmission" (Evans, 2010, p. 22). It is also worth noting, however, that the vast majority of plant and animal life is simply not described in natural languages anyway. There are millions of microscopic forms of life that languages have never even bothered about. Indeed, an irony here is that it is the scientific description of these – usually done in Greek or Latin (supposedly a dead language) – that gives us the closest relation between language and species diversity. It is the semiodiversity of Latin that is increasing.[4]

So let us return to the butterfly fish. Across different languages we find a general commonality in terms of naming – reference to the butterfly family and various descriptions of salient features. This is also, of course, a result of mutual influence. While not direct translations of each other, they exist alongside each other, in relations of mutual borrowing: they all agree these are butterfly fish (French uses both the scientific name, *Chaetodon*, and the French *Papillon* (butterfly)), yet with a variety of descriptors – this line, that fin and so on. There is also, however, considerable variation within languages. The *Chaetodon speculum*, for example (*Chaetodon à miroir* in French) may be either a Mirror or an Ovalspot Butterflyfish in English. *Chaetodon lunulatus* may be either a Pinstriped or an Oval Butterflyfish. The *Chaetodon bennetti*, which has two distinctive blue lines (hence in French, *Chaetodon à deux lignes bleues*), but also a dark mark surrounded by a lighter circle, is variously Bennett's Butterflyfish, Eclypse Butterflyfish, or Bluelashed Butterflyfish. In Japanese it is ウミ ヅキチョウチョウウオ – チョウチョウ butterfly, ウオ fish, ウミ sea, and ヅキ moon:[5] thus, sea moon butterfly fish.

Now, on a very basic level, this does not help us classify and count butterfly fish as part of a marine survey. In the end we try to use the 'scientific name' so that either within or across languages we know what we are talking about. Another option, of course, would be to use the local terminology, since this might capture more about local divisions and significances. Many people spread across the islands that make up the Philippines have lived from the sea; indeed a number of people's names are derived from fish names. What is immediately obvious, however, is that the world is cut up rather differently in Philippine languages, and along different lines of need. *Lapu-Lapu* for example, is a widely used Visayan[6] term for grouper (*Serranidae* family, *Cephalopholis* and *Epinephelus* genera), covering a large number of species, called anything in English from Peacock Hind (*Cephalopholis argus*) to Speckled grouper (*Epinephelus magniscuttis*). Likewise, the many butterfly fish, which some languages so carefully separate, are generally referred to as *Alibangbang*.[7] The Mirror, Ovalspot or Eclypse Butterflyfish are all *Alibangbang* (White, 2001). On the one hand, we do indeed lose something when the Kunwinjiku (in North Arnhem Land, Australia) term *bokorn* is dropped in favour of 'spangled grunter' and 'white apple' (the term refers to both the fish and the tree) since the "ecological link" between the two – the fish eats the fruit when it drops into billabongs – is lost (Evans, 2010, p. 22). On the other hand, access to an understanding of aspects of diversity may also be locally obscured.

In the context of words for ropes, or many other nautical practices, it is a fairly mundane observation that languages in which such practices do not occur – the languages of landlocked nations such as Nepal, for example – do not have words for such things. Languages in which sailing is done do have such terms. This has to do with the relocalization of sailing practices in local language practices and the question of register. Just as divers and marine biologists may use particular registers and terminology to talk about fish, so sailors have similar language practices to do what they need to do. This has more to do with particular language practices than with separate languages. Kramsch (2006) draws attention to a similar concern when she points out that if one American speaks of "options and opportunities" and the other of *optiones y opportunidades*, they may in a sense be speaking the same language. "Many Europeans", she suggests, "talk the same globalspeak even as they speak German, Italian or Dutch about minority rights, women's rights, race and ethnicity concerns. Many Chinese or Koreans now speak an American neo-liberal discourse of consumerism, entrepreneurship and economic competitiveness even as they speak Chinese or Korean" (p. 102). I shall return to related issues in the discussion of mission statements in the next chapter.

Language, difference and creativity: speaking the world otherwise

The strong argument for a causative relation between language and biological diversity depends on the questionable claims that diversity is language specific (glossodiversity rather than semiodiversity), that the diversity recognized linguistically is closely linked to species diversity, and that linguistic diversity is a result of environmental diversity (if this is indeed a two-way argument that it is not only linguistic variety that supports biological diversity but biological diversity that supports linguistic diversity). It may be the case that the threats to linguistic and biological diversity are the same, though Sutherland's study showed that while "patterns of language, bird and mammal diversity are similar, the reasons for extinction risk differ between cultural and biological diversity" (Sutherland, 2003, p. 279). One question missing from all this is how we account for linguistic diversity in the first place. Is linguistic diversity, as an environment–language homology argument would suggest, a result of different languages adapting to different environments, or is there something else at stake here? As George Steiner pointed out in his classic book *After Babel*, the diversity of human languages has all too often been explained by a "facile" argument in "casually evolutionary terms: there are many different tongues because, over long stretches of time, societies and cultures split apart and, through accretion of particular experience, evolved their own local speech habits" (Steiner, 1975, p. 56).

   A model of Darwinian adaptation simply does not work here: species survive because of their adaptation to the environment; they die out when they can no longer adapt to change. Languages have not adapted to their environment, apart from a very superficial level of lexical recognition. The diversity of Indigenous Australian languages is not so much a result of their adaptation to physical environments but of their creation of a cultural world; it is the human construction of complexity in an arid environment that is at stake here, not a mapping between language and the world. As Steiner asked:

> What can possibly explain this crazy quilt? How are we to rationalize the fact that human beings of identical ethnic provenance, living on the same terrain, under equal climatic and ecological conditions, often organized in the same types of communal structure, sharing kinship systems and beliefs, speak entirely different languages? What sense can be read into a situation in which villages a few miles apart or valleys divided by low, long-eroded hills use tongues incomprehensible to each other and morphologically unrelated?
>
> (1975, p. 54)

The question already points to problems in any view that the environment itself produces diversity. If we look at Papua New Guinea (PNG), for example, which has remarkable linguistic diversity, it is not clear that a causative link can be made between environment and diversity. It is not, as might be assumed, a result of physical isolation, since there has long been a great deal of mixing, trading, intermarriage and multilingualism. Thus, Nettle and Romaine complicate the picture of languages adapting to the environment when they suggest that it was human action in maintaining difference, not physical environment that brought about this diversity. It was the will to belong and to be different that produced diversity. Thus linguistic diversity in PNG is a result of both "the ecological background, which favoured small, self-sufficient, scattered local groups, and the cultural environment, in which a preference for local social capital kept a large number of local languages very much alive" (Nettle and Romaine, 2000, p. 89).

For Steiner, the answer lies rather in understanding language as the main instrument of human "refusal to accept the world as it is ... Ours is the ability, the need, to gainsay or 'un-say' the world, to image and speak it otherwise" (1975, p. 217–18). An understanding of the origins of human speech and the multiplicity of tongues, he argues, needs to be sought not so much through 'a theory of information' as through a 'theory of misinformation'. It is in the human capacity to make the world anew through language that we need to pursue a notion of diversity, which brings us back to language ideologies and language practices. We need to understand how language works as a local practice, which includes the language ideologies that generate particular understandings of language and particular ways of orienting towards language (an emphasis, for example, on creating difference from other linguistic communities), as well as the ways in which language operates as part of complexes of other social practices.

Staying in Papua New Guinea, let us look for a moment at the Maiwala, Kaluli and Urapmin communities, and changes that have been going on in relation to their language practices in the context of Christianity (Pennycook and Makoni, 2005). A project aimed at "reconstructing the Maiwala culture" and "reversing the language-mixing situation" (Nagai and Lister, 2003, p. 89), for example, starts with the concern that although "most of the community members come to the cricket ground on Saturday, only 10% of them attend the Sunday morning church service" (p. 90). Thus, they quite rightly see that cricket, if not quite the work of the devil, is at the very least part of a range of changing social practices that are interconnected with the increase in borrowings and mixed code use between Maiwala, Tok Pisin and English.

And yet, when they point out that to counter this, "we came up with the idea of translating the Lord's Prayer into Maiwala" with the help of a colleague, who has just begun the "Maiwala Bible Translation Project because of his concern about the situation of the heavy borrowing of English words" (p. 95), they are surely constructing a strange and, it must be said, disingenuous version of cultural and linguistic purity combined with church-going. This is not to discount church-going (or cricket) as a local practice: the notion of local practice needs to be carefully disentangled from discourses of preservation, tradition and maintenance. Cricket and church-going may be local practices in PNG, and like many cultural practices they have implications for language practices. Yet we cannot claim that church-going is unproblematically connected to language maintenance as if it were not also part of a series of changing cultural and linguistic practices which bring about social transformation. Likewise, we cannot condemn cricket and code-mixing as if these cultural and linguistic practices were inevitably changes for the worse.

Looking at the introduction of literacy into the Kaluli community in PNG by Australian missionaries, for example, Schieffelin (2000) notes how this "challenged and changed Kaluli notions of truth, knowledge, and authority, thereby affecting Kaluli linguistic as well as social structures" (p. 294). The introduction of various practices – clothing, eating, hygiene, reading – was bound up with changing language practices. These also have to be seen in relation to local understandings of language – language ideologies – which make particular sense of language use. As Schieffelin (2000) makes clear, "everyday language practices, local metalinguistics, and language ideologies that are embedded in complex cultural and historical moments intersect in ongoing processes of social reproduction and rapid cultural change" (Schieffelin, 2000, p. 296). It therefore does not make much sense to decry language change, code-mixing and cricket while at the same time insisting on language purity and church-going. This is where a notion of language ecology in terms of an *ecology of language practices* can take us forward, since it gives us a way of thinking about language practices within changing social and cultural practices.

A similar observation can be made in relation to Robbins' (2001) discussion of language ideologies, religion and the Urapmin of PNG. As he points out, we need to understand the language ideologies that are tied to different religious practices, and the ways in which these relate to local language practices and ideologies. Protestantism, for example, with its rejection of formal ritual, "is prone to appear as a religion that is fundamentally, one might say, almost exclusively, constituted through language" (p. 904). Protestant linguistic ideology is linked to broader modernist ideologies in which intention and meaning are closely coupled "in the postulation of a speaker who has both an ability and an inclination to tell the truth" (p. 905). As Robbins goes on to show, for the Urapmin of Papua New Guinea, this presents an ideological dilemma, for "while they recognize that as modern, Christian subjects they are supposed to speak truthfully at all times by accurately and openly representing their inner states in speech, their traditional linguistic ideology does not constitute them as subjects capable of performing in this way" (p. 906). Urapmin linguistic ideology, Robbins argues, maintains "a very general skepticism toward the reliability of the spoken word" (p. 904). As a result, this interaction between Urapmin and Protestant ideologies changes both the ways in which Christian prayer is used and the semiotic resources of the Urapmin community.

The introduction of new language and literacy practices, particularly in the context of wider changes to social and cultural practices, or the introduction of religions, schooling and new forms of economic activity, affect local language ecologies by changing the language practices in which people engage. The point is not only that literacy is used as a means to convert people to Christianity, but that in the process of these literacy and language projects, language and literacy practices are changed. The so-called preservation, maintenance or reconstruction of vernacular languages has to take into account the ecology of local language practices – what people are doing with languages in relation to other social and cultural practices (playing cricket, praying, selling yams at a local market) – if it is to make any sense. Languages are not, as I have repeatedly argued in this book, entities that exist outside human relations and interactions, but are embedded in ecologies of local practice.

Preservation, change and local language ecologies

One of the problems that a language ecology perspective presents us with is its analogical goal of preservation. Just as we need to protect delicate ecologies, to fence them off, to create national parks, to collect DNA, so the solution to unbalanced language ecologies is to protect endangered languages in order to preserve them. This notion does not embrace change easily. Languages are not organisms that interact with the environment, or fixed, static systems, but rather shifting, changing cultural artefacts. Some aspects of them can be preserved in books, dictionaries and grammars, but to preserve a language is, like collecting butterflies, an activity potentially inimical to language. As Muehlmann (2007) makes plain, discourses of language preservation put very particular ways of understanding indigeneity into play: "The endangered language movement builds its discourse on the assumption that safeguarding indigenous languages helps protect nature because indigenous people have a natural interest in sustaining ecological relations" (p. 30). A romantic dream of ecological sustainability as the bedrock of Indigenous life becomes a key part of an argument for language preservation.

As well as this "vernacularist nationalist organicist strain" in language preservation discourse, there is also, according to Cameron (2007), "an exoticizing or 'orientalist' strain" leading to "the implicit exoticism of images like 'our rich human landscape', and more generally, the discursive depoliticization of preservation and revitalization movements" (p. 281). Preservationist rhetoric, with its exoticizing and romanticizing view of local people locked in time, runs the danger of overlooking the language practices and language ideologies of local populations. As de Souza and Andreotti (2009) argue in the context of Brazil, 'preservation' may be seen by Indigenous communities not so much as the maintenance of the same but rather as the constant need to acquire difference and newness in order to remain the 'same'. This resonates with the discussion in Chapter 3 of the ways in which staying the same may be a process of renewal, and repetition may be a practice of difference. While outsider views focus on the preservation of language and culture, particularly through education, from a local perspective, survival may be guaranteed by constant change, through the acquisition of newness, through difference.

Hence Block's (2008) concern that the metaphor of language loss may often be quite inappropriate, and his call to "listen to the voices of those who have actually lived through language maintenance and loss, so as to avoid romantic depictions of such experiences" (p. 201). Part of the problem, as Duchêne (2008) makes clear, is that minority languages that need to be preserved are constructed as the flip-side of majority national languages, a view that tends to "reify language in its fixed and delineated dimension" and is thus incapable of "integrating the complexity of the social, economic and political factors that are involved in any process of linguistic, cultural or other minorization" (p. 9). For Torres Straits Islander Martin Nakata (1999, p. 14), "the most damaging aspect of the principle of culture preservation and promotion ... is that it has not only become a panacea for all our ills but has also become so regulatory that it precludes Islanders such as myself and Indigenous people all over this country from pursuing the issues that we want to pursue".

As long as languages are seen as species-equivalent entities in ecologies, we can retain the fiction that it is possible to count and preserve languages, but once we acknowledge that languages are very different, open systems, such a notion is harder to maintain. Kibbee (2003, p. 52) argues that "in an ecological conception of languages, all lexical, phonological, morphological or syntactic borrowings are attacks against a language, an artificial deformation that can be contrasted with a 'natural' development (historical evolution without external influence)". Here the language ecologist orientation towards a liberal concept of diversity encounters its contradictory nemesis through a notion of language purity, since the preservationist and language-realist orientations of language ecology may all too easily exclude the possibility of change, borrowing, hybridity and difference. Yet, if we are to do more than preserve the rare examples of standardized codes, we have to work with the very non-species-like fuzziness, changes, hybridities and peculiarities of languages.

Looking at fish in the Philippines once again, several points emerge: things are named according to human interest. Fishermen and -women are interested in grouper generally (*lapu-lapu*) as good eating fish, and not very interested in distinguishing between butterfly fish (*alibangbang*). Local naming practices do not seem to have done much good for the fish, since there are major problems with fish shortages, caused by over-fishing as well as destructive fishing practices (dynamite, destruction of substrata). There is certainly no easy connection to be made here between indigenous people (always a contentious notion in places such as the Philippines and many other parts of the region), fish names and preservation of the environment. While languages in the Philippines do have numerous words for fish, there are fewer terms than in languages spoken by those with a particular interest in fish categorization. The terms for fish cut across different languages (though deciding what counts as a language is always an impossible task) so there are regional terms for fish across the Visayas, for example. There may also be more local terms for some fish, though there is no obvious case to be made that these are in different languages.

Most users of English, or French or Japanese or languages in which there are many names for such fish (from *Chaetodon à deux lignes bleues* to Eclypse Butterflyfish to Umitsukichouchouuo) do not generally know these terms, just as they do not know the difference between a shroud, halyard, backstay or boom vang (*un étai, un hale-bas, un hauban, une drisse*), which takes us back to the question of what it means to claim that something is 'in' a language or that a language has a number of terms for certain things. Local naming does not necessarily lead to preservation, and diversity of local species does not necessarily lead to naming. There is no obvious link between diversity of species and diversity of languages. There is not even an evident link between species diversity and diversity within languages, since fish names can be common across languages, and diversity within languages may be local descriptions of the same thing. We do need to understand local naming practices because these can shed light on significance, diversity and social and cultural networks, but we should give up once and for all trying to map all this against languages as inventories of the world, and especially trying to map numbers of languages against numbers of species.

Ecologies of local language practices can help shed light on interrelationships among reef ecologies, fishing practices, naming practices, the establishment and monitoring of marine protection areas, the local economy, community organizations, the supplement of income in the face of declining fish stocks, local education and so forth. One of the things that involvement in environmental projects such as Philippine reef conservation has helped me understand is the complexity of ecologies. Coral reefs in the Philippines and elsewhere are under threat from several directions: over-fishing, in part because of population growth, which in turn is related to gender relations, access to contraception and the role of the Catholic church; particular fishing practices as a result of new technologies, faster boats, finer nets, and the use of dynamite; and warming seas, pollution, tourism and different levels of economic development across the region all have various effects on the condition of the reefs. We can gain certain understandings of the health of a reef by the number and diversity of butterfly fish (as long as we agree on what they're called), but in order to do something about it, we have to look at water supplies in local villages, land use and ownership, the use of fertilizers, gender relations and religious practices, community leadership and local language practices. Such local language practices have little to do with mapping languages against physical environments; rather they are to do with the array of ways in which the environment is constructed through language.

Diversity and ecologies of local language practices

My concerns about certain versions of language ecology have been concerns about how we understand diversity. Viewing linguistic diversity in terms of numbers of languages, and relating these languages to a representational relationship to the environment, overlooks the complex ways in which language practices are part of the way we create locality, as discussed in the two previous chapters. Language practices are activities we do with the semiotic resources of language, and are always interrelated with other cultural and social practices. One of the concerns above has been the place we want to give to culture. As we saw in some versions of language ecology, one approach to questions of language, diversity and locality is to draw a close connection between language and culture – they become two sides of the same coin – and to relate both of these closely to the local environment. One of the advantages of thinking in terms of language as a local practice is that it starts to give us a more useful way of thinking about culture.

The notion of practice can help us see that what we do with language is always part of the everyday, of repeated activity, of social organization. As such, it is deeply tied to a notion of cultural practice, but not in terms of those monoliths of language and culture that have been mapped against each other along the lines of nationhood, but rather as much more localized ways of doing difference. Breton and Welsh fishermen have been able to talk to each other in their boats in the stormy Atlantic ocean, not only because of the shared backgrounds to their Celtic languages and cultures, but because they are fishermen. People who live near or on the sea use a lot of terms for water, fishing, boats and so forth, and people such as the Neverver in Vanuatu, who have migrated from the coast to inland settlements, find little use for their fishing-oriented lexicon and lack useful terminology for local flora and fauna (Barbour, 2006). So local language practices need to be understood in relation both to local language ideologies – the ways in which the roles and functions and meanings of language are understood locally – and to other social and cultural practices. To suggest that languages are somehow indelibly tied to and representative of their environment is to overlook the ways in which humans creatively construct the world through language.

This perspective does not of course deny that there is a decline in the use of certain linguistic codes and that these may be linked in various ways to environmental degradation. As Muehlmann (2007, p. 31) explains

> There is no doubt that language obsolescence and environmental degra-
> dation are processes deeply implicated in the organization of social
> inequality. It is the disempowered whose languages 'die' and the margin-
> alized and poor who suffer the effects of environmental degradation most
> immediately. But from this fact alone we cannot conclude that saving
> languages or rainforests will reverse the social processes that marginalize
> some groups in the first place.

The point here, quite simply, is that language practices are much more com-
plex than simply using given languages in context. While local language practices will inevitably be linked to social and cultural practices, to poverty, change, disadvantage and marginalization, it does not help to construct these as indelibly linked to a certain linguistic code and then to hope that by pre-serving a semiotic system we can preserve an environment, or that by preser-ving an environment a language will be saved.

An ecology of local language practices can be useful if we use it to under-stand, on the one hand, the ways in which language practices are deeply embedded in local, social and cultural activities; and on the other, if it can help us to get away from viewing diversity in terms of segregated, enumerable language entities. An ecology of local language practices views language within the total complex of the environment. If communities are working to maintain certain language and cultural practices, this always has to be understood in the context of health, employment, education, and more (rather than the all-too-frequent attempts to urge preservation only through education) so that the social, cultural and economic reasons for change can be addressed. We need to know how the language practices of different people work in relation to the local organization of space, since as we saw in previous chapters, language as a local practice is not so much a question of contextual language use as the production of locality. And any model of language maintenance needs to incorporate an understanding of change, so that communities can stay 'the same' by embracing difference.

7 'Molding hearts … Leading minds … Touching lives'

Practice as the new discourse?

"Molding hearts … Leading minds … Touching Lives," reads the vision statement of the St Isidore The Farmer Catholic School in Lazi, a small town on the island of Siquijor in Negros Oriental in the central Philippines. Printed in white text against a blue background, the statement is fixed to the faded wall of the former convent, said to have been the largest in Asia. Sitting opposite the St Isidore Labradore Parish Church, and surrounded by giant acacia trees, the former convent was originally built using coral stone and local hardwood between 1857 and 1891. Below this vision, the mission statement explains that the school aims to "Provide a wholistic and holistic development of students through an effective basic education curriculum that would prepare them to pursue higher levels of learning and assume a vital role in building the family, the church, and the community." The mission statement is supported by a series of objectives, such as "Strengthen school-faculty-parent-community relationship" and "Deepen the students' spiritual life through effective religious instructions, retreats and liturgical celebrations" or "Heighten one's abilities in and appreciation for the arts, culture and sports."

This blue glossy mission statement is apparently a revised version of the older, hand-painted statement fixed further along the wall. Here the vision is less succinct: "To be dynamic Catholic institution of basic education in the municipality of Lazi, offering high quality academic education molding citizens on the tenets of Christian virtues so they become worthwhile and God-centred citizens of the country." In the older version, there are four mission statements instead of the one, starting with "To develop well-disciplined and well-rounded students guided by the Christian virtues of love, brotherhood and peace". Many of the Objectives have been sharpened considerably in the later version, and now the mission of the school is not only to ensure that pupils acquire the necessary skills, but also, for example to "Enhance leadership and management skills of administrators and faculty members through conferences, in service trainings and other related activities". Other objectives have changed less, so the vocation-oriented "Acquire productive and entrepreneurial skills, a work ethic, and occupational knowledge essential both for making an intelligent choice as regards one's career and for specialized training in one's occupation" has only received minor modification, to read "Provide for the development of livelihood and entrepreneurial skills and occupational knowledge essential both for making an intelligent choice of a career and for specialized training in one's occupation".

Now what is all this doing here? Two of the major imports in these texts are well known: Catholicism came during the Spanish colonial occupation of the Philippines from the mid sixteenth century to the end of the nineteenth century, and has long been deeply embedded in many aspects of Philippine life. English came with the American colonial period in the first part of the twentieth century and was consolidated under different regimes following independence, so much so that it is now, alongside Filipino, an official language, playing a major role in education (as part of a bilingual education policy), the media, business, the export of workers and many other parts of Philippine life (Rappa and Wee, 2006). Both English and Catholicism have been deeply appropriated; they have been relocalized in Philippine lives, localities and letters. These mission statements, however, are clearly more recent appropriations, apparently drawing on the corporatist world of mission statements. While both the form and language of these statements echo this world of corporatism (Graham, Luke and Luke, 2007) – 'Develop a cohesive and committed team of teachers' – they also incorporate elements of other discourses, especially a blend of the religious and the educational.

This is not uncommon in many domains: Amnesty International Australia, for example, broadcast its 2009–14 Vision on postcards that announce on one side its commitment to the broader Amnesty International Agenda: "By 2014, Amnesty International Australia will protect and defend the human rights of more people by: Inspiring 500,000 people every year to take action; positively influencing and informing key opinion formers and decision makers" and so on. On a more local level (the back of the postcard), Amnesty International Australia will "Demand Dignity for all; stand with Indigenous communities to end human rights abuses; campaign for an effective National Plan to Stop Violence Against Women" and so on. There are many things going on in both these Amnesty International and St Isidore Primary School vision statements: the changes from the old to the new, the interdiscursive and intertextual echoes of other texts and discourses, the use of generic textual form (vision, mission, objectives; to provide, initiate, deepen, enhance and so on), the placement on the exterior walls of the convent, the production of a particular way of thinking about a relationship between school and community.

At one level it matters that these texts are 'in English' since English plays a significant role in the Philippines, and particularly in education (Tupas, 2006). Yet at another level, as suggested in the previous chapter, drawing on Kramsch (2006), the use of different languages may be of less importance than the language practices we are engaged in. These are global, generic mission statements, and English is a language in which many of these occur. And yet, as Cameron (2003) observes, "A McDonald's restaurant in Budapest must serve its customers in Hungarian, but it will be Hungarian spoken according to the same norms of interaction which govern the company's service in Chicago" (p. 33). Or if we look at the Social Sciences and Humanities Research Council of Canada (SSHRC)/Conseil de recherches en sciences humaines du Canada (CRSH), we find, very obviously, parallel statements of purpose: "At SSHRC, we are continuously seeking to improve our processes and practices as part of our ambition to promote quality, strengthen connections and increase impact." "Afin d'atteindre ses objectifs – promouvoir la qualité, favoriser la connexion et accroître l'impact, le Conseil de recherches en sciences humaines (CRSH) s'efforce continuellement de bonifier ses processus et ses pratiques." (SSHRC, 2009). What such texts suggest is not so much a process of translation across different languages as the global spread and relocalization of certain language practices.

A major focus of this chapter will be to relate the discussion in previous chapters of language practices to other available terms such as discourse and genre. Clearly, we can shed light on these texts by looking at both genre and discourse, or put very simply, at their form and content. Mission statements have both evident textual patternings – they are textual practices that are repeated over time – and evident discursive content – they are repeated messages of corporate intention. What different perspective might a notion of language practices bring to this? If language practices are repeated acts of language use that achieve a certain stability over time, how do they differ from genres, which have been defined, for example by Blommaert (2008), as the "complex of communicative-formal features that makes a particular communicative event recognisable as an instance of a type" (p. 43)? This is what allows us to recognize that something is a 'joke' or a 'lecture' or a 'newspaper article' or a 'poem'. Genres, Blommaert explains, guide us through the social world of communication, helping us to know how to put together a particular type of textual performance, and how to interpret it. There are, then, formal features, as well as expectations and responses. What do the notions of practice and genre do differently that might lead us to use one or the other?

Schatzki (2001), on the other hand, as we saw in Chapter 2, suggests that practice may be 'the new discourse'. In this sense, he is clearly pointing to the broader social scientific use of the term, which, drawing on Foucault, refers to those frameworks of meaning that give sense to social life. The notion of practice, for Schatzki, potentially replaces this broad notion of discourse as a way of making sense of how it is we come to do the things we do. In Gee's (1999) distinction, this is 'Big D' Discourse. As a way of describing language activity, however, the notion of language practices also covers some of the ground of Gee's 'small d' discourse, since it is clearly about language in use. As I shall argue later, the notion of local language practices allows us to get away from these awkward distinctions. Before exploring this in greater detail, however, it may be useful to look at a couple of other language practices or genres that sit on either side of the mission statements discussed above, the one highly regulated, the other very open.

Two language practices – regular, repeated social activities involving language – are airline safety instructions and writing postcards. Both are fairly common and easily recognizable, though they differ in a number of ways. The airline safety instructions are highly regularized. The answer to why this is so is not hard: they are regulated to be so. From national and international air regulations and the particular interpretations of airlines, there is only a certain amount of leeway. Typically they include information about safety belts and their buckles (how to do them up, why you should keep them on at all times), lifejackets (where they are – different in business and economy – how to put them on, do them up and so on), escape routes (your nearest escape exit, the lights on the floor), the brace position (can you reach the seat in front of you?), oxygen masks (put your own on first). These instructions may differ across airlines (almost always the same within) – the Qantas safety check starts with the odd line 'Subtly, every airplane is different' (for discussion see Wajnryb, 2009) – but they generally convey the same information in similar ways. Indeed this is one of the well-known problems with them: most passengers have heard it before, or think they have. This is partly because this is such a closed domain, but it is also because they are not so much socially regulated as industry mandated.

One way in which postcard writing and safety instructions are superficially different is that one is oral and the other written, at least so it appears. As literacy studies have long told us, however, this distinction is problematic (Gee, 1990): while an airline safety check is spoken, it is always scripted. There is supposed to be as little variation as possible. At another level, it is also generally written to be a spoken text. Clearly, we need to think in terms of register here, rather than mode. It is the nature of the text rather than the fact that it is spoken or written that matters. Postcards present a rather different case. At one level they may look like the opposite of the airline safety check: a written text in oral register, rather than an oral text in written register: 'Hi. Having a fabulous time here … '. But postcards are much harder to pin down (we can pin them up but not pin them down). On the one hand, we might observe, for example, that the common missing pronoun is something of a generic convention (perhaps with its origins in spatial limits), not simply an oral convention. On the other hand, like email (which may also operate at times as an oral register in writing), we in fact have a much more messy and unmanageable category. If you look through collections of postcards (you can find them for sale in some flea markets and second-hand book stores), it is in fact remarkable how diverse the texts may be: some are formal (depending on the writer, the addressee, the topic, the period it was written and so on), some minimal ('See you next week'; 'bon anniversaire'; 'This is from Daddy who hopes you are a good little girl'). In fact, although we might be able to describe some form of generic characteristics to certain sorts of postcards, written by certain sorts of people, in a certain era, postcard writing is a widely variant activity. I shall return to the implications of this point later.

Understanding language from underneath

As Schatzki (2001, p. 1) notes, to speak in terms of language practice "is to depict language as discursive activity in opposition to structuralist, semiotic, and poststructuralist conceptions of it as structure, system, or abstract discourse". To talk of language practices, therefore, is to move away from the attempts to capture language as a system, and instead to investigate the doing of language as social activity, regulated as much by social contexts as by underlying systems. This takes us usefully beyond structure versus function divides, since both structuralist and functionalist accounts of language ultimately privilege language system over language practice: the one may take structure as a given and have little interest in how it got there (or try to account for it in evolutionary cognitivist terms), while the other may be more interested in trying to account for structure as a response to function, but both end up with descriptions of structure. As Bourdieu (1977) observed, the structuralist legacy was never able "to construct practice other than negatively" (p. 28), either ignoring the modes of production of communicative regularities or relying on abstract constructs of underlying structure. A view of communication that draws on a notion of practices derived from Heidegger, Wittgenstein and Donald Davidson, as Rouse (2001, p. 192) argues, avoids the reliance on a normative set of underlying linguistic principles: "Shared meanings or beliefs are not the preexisting facts that would explain the possibility of communication, but the norms presumptively invoked in the course of interpreting someone or something as communicative." This reversal of common (applied) linguistic assumptions, which has already been discussed in previous chapters, has very real implications for how we understand language, genre and discourse.

In some ways, conversation analysts have known all along that we need to focus on the everyday doing of language. Drawing on the ethnomethodological turn away from broad social theory, conversation analysis (CA) has sought to show how turn-taking, pauses and the micro-interactions of ordinary language are a central site of the management of everyday life. Conversation analysis, as Drew and Curl (2008) put it, is concerned with "the norms, practices and competences underlying the organization of social interaction" (p. 22). The "central sociological insight of CA", they go on to argue, "is that it is through conversation that we conduct the ordinary, and perhaps extraordinary, affairs of our lives" (ibid.). CA has its origins in the ethnomethodology of Harold Garfinkel (1967), which as a field of sociological inquiry rejected the macro-sociologies of the time by seeking to understand how everyday structures of social order were produced, maintained and understood. Rather than assume the orderliness of society, ethnomethodology sought to understand how it was achieved through the potentially disordered procedures of daily life. From these insights, and the work of Ervin Goffman (1969) and then Sacks, Schegloff and Jefferson (1974), CA developed as a means to understand the ways in which talk-in-interaction was ordered and thus larger social order was achieved, or as Schegloff (1992, p. 1296) explained, while on the one hand "talk-in-interaction is a primordial site of sociality", it is also, on the other hand, one of the "preconditions for, and achievements of, organized life".

"As conversational order is achieved order", argues Liddicoat (2007, p. 8), "and the achievement is done through the deployment of practices in particular contexts", conversation analysts focus on naturally occurring instances of talk in order to shed light on the ways in which conversational interaction is part of social interaction. This focus on *achieved* order is part of a key CA tenet that "order does not occur of its own accord nor does it pre-exist the interaction, but is rather the result of the coordinated practices of the participants who achieve orderliness and then interact" (Liddicoat, 2007, p. 5). In the highly regulated context of pilot interactions in the cockpit (not as scripted as the safety check discussed above, but nevertheless carefully regulated), for example, Nevile (2008) shows that "moments of overlapping talk can be evidence of *trouble in the routine and unremarkable temporal order of actions for work*" (p. 45, italics in original). This move to see social order not as a set of pre-given rules but rather as an achieved outcome of social practices is akin to the argument emerging here about language practices: language is an achieved outcome rather than the implementation of a set of rules.

While CA and the ethnomethodological turn share some similarities with the perspective on language as a local practice that I am developing here, including an emphasis on local activity, order as achieved and the importance of practical reason, there are a number of differences. By putting such emphasis on the analysts' objective ability to understand social ordering while ignoring the subjective experience of the participants, it denies that other crucial part of the local: not only is the local something that happens here and now in this place, but it is also deeply perspectival. Language as a local practice needs to be understood through the emic lenses of anthropology as much as the etic lenses of sociology. It matters that local participants understand things in certain ways, and to render the local only in terms of the small-scale is to overlook the ways in which all language is always local. While shedding light on conversations in process, the sometimes obsessive interest in detailed analysis of transcriptions all too often fails to inform us about anything but its own internal framing of conversation. The same, of course, might be said of a number of frameworks for genre or discourse analysis, which start out with the goal of looking at social processes, interaction, or the social construction of meaning through forms of language analysis, yet all too soon slide back into a micro-analysis of linguistic tokens seemingly for their own sake.[1]

Finally, by focusing on the doing of sociality, the tendency in CA has been to eschew broader social theory: ethnomethodological concerns bracket away prior assumptions about the social. Like a practices focus on language that asks how language emerges from the doing of communication, rather than assuming we use a pre-given language in context to achieve communication,

CA starts not with the idea of a pre-given social order but looks instead at the production of social order in conversation. To the extent that it thus works admirably from a bottom-up perspective, CA fits well with a practices orientation, but to the extent that we also need to be able to theorize the social at the same time, it traps us in its bottom-up locality. This is why Hacking (2004) suggests we need to combine Foucault and Goffman, on the one hand because Foucault leaves us short when we need to look closely at texts, but on the other because Goffman leaves us short when we need to fix our scope more broadly. This starts to look a bit like little d and Big D discourse again, however, so it may be the *meso-political* space of language practices that can give us a way forward here.

Repeating language regularly: genres and getting things done

Ramanathan (2002) points out that "any social theory of language has to account for how particular conventions give rise to texts of a more or less predictable nature" (p. 69). This is a central question we need to deal with here: how do we account for the regularities in the ways we speak, interact, put texts together and so on? What makes an airline safety announcement, a mission statement and a postcard what they are? As van Leeuwen (2005) explains, texts can be seen as typical – generic – when they share certain features with other texts. These characteristics of form, content or function, he suggests, come about because text producers follow certain 'rules' – prescriptions, traditions, ingrained habits, role models and so forth (p. 123). From a number of perspectives, a focus on genre is centrally on regular patterns of textual organization. In the field of literature, the focus may be on those conventional structures (rather than the content) that make a fairytale or a novel or a poem recognizable as such (openings and closings, textual structure and sequence and so on). In other areas of work – from the so-called Australian or Sydney genre school (e.g. Martin, 1993) to work on languages for specific purposes (e.g. Swales, 2000) – the focus has been on describing those regular patterns of textual organization that characterize reports, recounts, narratives and so forth, or which, by contrast, can account for differences between, say, abstracts for academic papers in different disciplines.

If we understand language practices as repeated and regular social activity involving language, there is clearly a certain affinity with this notion of genre. Genres, as Paltridge (2006) explains, "are ways in which people 'get things done' through their use of spoken and written discourse" (p. 84). Paltridge's view that genres are how we 'get things done', however, points to a tension in this field of study. When genre is viewed from this point of view of activity, as social process, as doing things with words, we inevitably end up with a view of text that is more open ended than when we look from the other direction, at text as product. As Kress (2003) notes, the focus on the generic construction of text has tended to construct too fixed an idea of genre that does not take into account a much greater mobility of textual organization. Genre, he argues "responds, flexibly, to social environment, because the makers of genre are immersed in the demands of social lives and are constantly responsive to those demands" (p. 100). Thus, although the Australian genre school takes care to locate genres as social activities, defining genre as a "staged, goal oriented social process" (Martin, 1993, p. 121), and insisting that "texts are patterned in reasonably predictable ways according to patterns of social interaction in a particular culture" (Cope and Kalantzis, 1993, p. 7), there is always the problem that once genres are described as textual artefacts, they become frozen in time.

In many ways, this is the old problem of linguistic description: if we want to get a snapshot of language use, we have to freeze the frame. While discourse, genre and conversation analysts may decry the static world of invented sentences that characterizes areas of linguistics, they nevertheless face the difficulty common to all analysts of language, that freezing the frame stops the flow. The problem comes when we start to mistake those fleeting moments of apparent regularity for 'rules', underlying structure or social and cultural regulations rather than the contingent practices they are. For Kress (2003), genre is one of three main factors in the constitution of text, the others being discourse and mode. Genre, from this point of view, is that aspect of textual organization which "realises and allows us to understand the social relations of the participants in the making, the reception and the reading/interpretation of the text" (p. 94). Texts are recognizable as genres – lists, rules, regulations, reports and so on – because of "the social organization from which these texts come" (p. 100). Genre is thus "a social category: it is made by people in their social encounters, and when it has become text it gives us insight into the make-up of the social world in which it was made" (p. 100). This takes us back to the notion of the relocalization of social activity in language discussed earlier.

Although it is suggested that "Social patterning and textual patterning meet as genres" (Cope and Kalantzis, 1993, p. 7), and thus, as with Fairclough's (2003) view of a close relation between social and discursive orders, genres are seen as part of a social world of interaction, their description tends always towards fixity. As Luke (1996) points out, this 'logocentric' view of text that insists that genres can be both described and prescribed (taught in order to provide access to powerful ways of forming texts) overlooks the problem that "it is impossible to theorise or study empirically the social or intellectual 'function' of texts independent of the complex ideological forces, powers and struggles implicated in the social formation and organization of technology and knowledge" (Luke 1996, p. 310). As Luke goes on to argue, we need to move towards a more flexible and sociologically contingent version of language and power based on the work of Bourdieu, which brings us back, once again, to a notion of practice. A theory of practice, therefore, may allow us to move away from the static nature of theories of genre. The question is whether we see the regularities of social and linguistic behaviour as emergent from the practices we engage in or whether we assume either an over-regulated sense of social structure (that determines texts) or an over-regulated version of textual structure (that exists almost independent of social activity), overlooking in both cases the dynamics of textual construction.

Although there are clear affinities between a notion of genre and the idea of language practices, evident in the emphasis on repeated sociolinguistic activity, language practices are differently oriented. Writing a postcard can be understood as a language practice, a social practice (something people do) with a language component. Postcards are less likely, however, to be thought of in terms of genres, since the relation between the doing and the textual form is far more complex and open. Genres may be glossed as how we get things done through language, but the focus is almost invariably on the textual products of different doings. Writing a postcard is a language practice, postcards are texts, and neither is a genre. Postcards may be quite complex intertexts, with their references to the picture on the front ('We visited the castle yesterday'; 'Our hotel is marked with a cross'; 'Une petite vue du terrain de jeu de Gozo, ça ne vaut pas la baie de Sydney' – a little view of Gozo's (boat name) playground. Not quite up to Sydney Harbour; 'Yes, this is where we actually are as we write … And in glorious sunshine in a pleasant pub garden in the middle of Chagford'), to meals and drinks and places visited ('yummy food'; 'Been drinking local wine every night'; 'This church is in the village we visited yesterday'; 'Wonderful frescos'; 'Well cared for and pampered with music.'), to family and acquaintances ('Spent yesterday with my cousin, Rachel'; 'Ran into the same couple we met last year'; 'Finally got to meet your old friend'; 'Thanks so much for taking me flying … It was a wonderful experience that … brought back memories of flying with my father'), to other connections and contexts ('C'est dommage nous nous sommes loopé au Vietnam' – it's a shame we didn't meet up in Vietnam). Reading a postcard is a relocalized language practice, with many complex connections to the writing. Reading collections of postcards when one knows nothing of the context of original reading and writing is relocalized again.

The connection between the practice of reading, the text and image of the card, and the practice of writing may be distant, and the card may have been written elsewhere (the 'here' of the text relates to the picture, not necessarily the here of the writing). And in any case, the text may not matter much anyway: how often do people put postcards on fridge doors and shelves and noticeboards with the text facing the audience? It's the picture that matters, and the receiving, and the knowledge that it was sent. Writing a postcard, then, is a particular language practice. People often do follow certain conventions and styles (chatty, happy, located in the here and now, wishing you were here, sending good wishes – as Anne Frank wrote in a postcard to a friend in 1937 – "viel Glück im neuen Jahr" – good luck for the new year[2]). There may be certain regularities and generic possibilities, but unlike those highly regulated genres, such as aircraft safety announcements, or the more open but nevertheless regularized mission statement, writing a postcard is not usually an institutionalized practice. Writing a postcard is always local (in this place, here, now), the relocalization of other activities.

Literacy practices as concrete human activity

The applied linguistic domain that has most readily embraced a broader conception of practice is literacy studies, so much so that in certain domains at least it is now almost impossible to talk in terms of literacy in general rather than of specific literacy practices. In his book *Literacy practices* Baynham (1995, p. 1) explains that "investigating literacy as practice involves investigating literacy as 'concrete human activity', not just what people do with literacy, but also what they make of what they do, the values they place on it and the ideologies that surround it. Practice provides a way of linking the cognitive with the social, opening up the possibility of an integrated approach to the study of literacy in use." This way of thinking about literacy goes back at least as far as Scribner and Cole's (1981, p. 237) work in which they argued for the need to "consider the specific characteristics of specific practices" as these are embedded within larger social systems.

Gee (1990, p. 49) argues that instead of viewing literacy in abstract cognitive terms, it is more important to view "literacies as a plural set of practices". Literacy should no longer be considered an abstract capacity, no longer even tied to reading and writing, but rather should be seen as a set of contextualized, regulated things people do. For those associated with this approach to literacies – always plural, always situated – talking in terms of practices has become the *sine qua non* of literacy studies. As Barton and Hamilton (2000, p. 7) explain, their research starts with "the assertion that literacy is a social practice ... The notion of literacy practices offers a powerful way of conceptualising the link between the activities of reading and writing and the social structures in which they are embedded and which they help shape." Indeed they go on to suggest that the use of the term practices is "not just the superficial choice of a word but the possibilities that this perspective offers for new theoretical understandings about literacy".

This view has now become more or less the accepted way of looking at literacy within what are sometimes termed the 'New Literacy Studies'. Gemma Moss (2007) explains, for example, in her book on gender and literacy, that "literacy as social practice perspectives study literacy not as a finite set of mental skills but as a social practice which is defined and shaped through use in culturally specific contexts" (p. 39). The literacy event – "any occasion where a piece of written text plays an integral part in what is going on" (p. 40) – becomes the unit of analysis, while literacy practices are those broader categories into which events fall. Thus, from a literacy as social practices perspective, reading aloud in two different contexts – a primary school classroom and a Koranic school (see Baynham, 1995) – "is not the same thing, even though a psychological approach to literacy might well regard them as demonstrations of the same processing skills" (p. 41). This question of what constitutes the 'same thing' has been discussed in depth in Chapter 3, where it was argued that repeated activity could also be different activity.

As noted in Chapter 2, however, once this 'social practice' view of language, literacy, discourse or genre becomes the end point of the study, we are left with a form of analysis that simply describes language activity. To be sure, this avoids the black hole of asocial versions of language, literacy and cognition, but as Luke (2004) reminds us, this needs to be the starting point rather than the end point of the analysis. The next question is, what are the material or political consequences of different literacy practices? There is, then, a tendency in language and literacy studies to employ the term practices to suggest both the active and the social dimensions of language. When we read out loud, ask for directions, write a postcard, read a mission statement, or half attend to an airline safety announcement, we are doing something with language that is inevitably social as well as cognitive. In the same way that phrases such as 'socially constructed' have come to mean little other than a nod towards the obviously social nature of human life and thought, however, the idea of language and literacy as a social practice may fail to engage with the deeper political potential of a notion of practices.

Discourse, genre, style

Critical discourse analysis, it might be argued, takes up this challenge not only by making language as a social practice a *sine qua non* of its analysis, but also by seeking broader explanations for how and why language is being used in particular ways. For Fairclough (2003), practices are a middle, mediating level between social structures and social events, or between language structure and language events (from Fairclough's materialist orientation, language maps onto society fairly neatly). So things we do, such as teaching, or preaching, are practices that organize the more local event while reproducing the larger social structure. And discourse practices – a "network of social practices in its language aspect" (p. 24) – mirror this by forming the ground between texts (language events) and language structures. These orders of discourse are therefore social practices of language responsible for the "social organization and control of linguistic variation" (p. 24). For Fairclough, then, discourse practices operate at a level between the macro-social domains of language and society on the one hand, and the micro-social domains of texts, discourses[3] and genres.

Discourse, Fairclough goes on to explain, is an aspect of social practice in three main ways, as 'part of the action' (ways of acting, or genres); as discourses (ways of representing); and as styles (ways of being). This tripartite distinction works better, he suggests, than the Hallidayan (1978) interpersonal, ideational and textual division, since, at the very least, the textual has never sat comfortably with the other two. With some modifications, this gives us a useful way forward. Fairclough takes a Foucauldian notion of discourse (the pluralized form, or Gee's Big D discourse) to be tied to modes of representation. For Foucault, however, the issue was precisely not one of representation, but rather one of the discursive practice of creating the world. Foucault's (1972) concern in *The archaeology of knowledge* was to show, among other things, that discourses are not "a mere intersection of things and words", nor "a slender surface of contact, or confrontation, between a reality and a language (*langue*)" (p. 48); rather, he set out "to show with precise examples that in analysing discourses themselves, one sees the loosening of the embrace, apparently so tight, of words and things, and the emergence of a group of rules proper to discursive practice. These rules define not the dumb existence of a reality, nor the canonical use of a vocabulary, but the ordering of objects" (p. 49). This means

> no longer treating discourses as groups of signs (signifying elements referring to contents or representations) but as practices that system- atically form the objects of which they speak. Of course, discourses are composed of signs; but what they do is more than use these signs to des- ignate things. It is this more that renders them irreducible to the language (langue) and to speech.
>
> (Foucault, 1972, p. 49)

From this point of view, then, discourse practices are the things we do with languages that produce our ways of thinking about the world. Discourses are not merely systems of representation – as they are taken to be in more abstract versions of discourse – but things we do in language that bring about the ways in which we see and engage with the world. This takes us beyond Fairclough's (2003) view of discourses (pluralized) as ways of representing the world, and suggests instead that if discourse is about the production of knowledge through language, discursive practices are those types of social practices involved in the linguistic construction of knowledge. Discursive practices are one set of practices that are regularized ways in which language is used to make sense of the world. Although Green (2009) makes a case that representation can be incorporated into a theory of practice in terms of a resource, as an aspect of knowledge linked to experience and reflection, Thrift's (2007) non-representational theory, as part of a consideration of lan- guage practices, gives us a way of looking at language or discourse beyond representationality.[4] From this point of view, discourse is about movement and the making of the world, rather than its representation.

Van Leeuwen (2005) suggests that while for some, discourse is used to refer to an extended stretch of connected text, he prefers to see discourses as "socially constructed knowledges of some aspect of reality" (p. 94). Else- where, as discussed in previous chapters, van Leeuwen (2008) explains that discourse can best be understood as "recontextualized social practice" (p. 1). That is to say, the things we do socially are recontextualized as discourse when we do them in language, or more broadly as part of a social semiotics. These apparently divergent views on discourse – discourse as socially con- structed knowledge and discourse as recontextualized social practice – come together in the following way:[5] we engage in social practices (knitting, eating, getting money from a bank machine, taking the dog for a walk, going for a walk on a beach); when we turn them into language in order to describe, report, or complain to others about these practices ('you'll never guess who I saw while I was taking the dog for a walk'; 'two purl two plain for the ribbing'; 'too cold for swimming but went for a walk along this beach today') we have recontextualized the social practice as discourse. And this discourse is always about knowledge; it is always a socially constructed knowledge about some aspect of reality. As I have already discussed in previous chapters, I prefer to view this in terms of the relocalization of practice.

If, then, we take this sense of discursive practices – not as systems of representation, but as means of production – and link these to an active sense of genre, as ways of getting things done, we can think about discourse and genre as active processes of producing both texts and worlds. For Rampton (2006, p. 128), these temporary stabilizations that we call genres are "integrated, multi-level analyses that participants themselves implicitly formulate for their own practical activity". Genres are not therefore fixed textual categorizations so much as temporary ways of getting things done with language. This view also gives us insights into how genres and style are connected (Rampton, 2006; 2009). Style, as suggested by Fairclough, might be viewed as the third dimension of the tripartite discourse/genre/style relationship, where style is understood in terms of ways of being. Taking the notion of style a bit further, however, than Fairclough's (2003, p, 26) view of style as a "way of using language as a resource for self-identifying", we can see that "style (like language) is not a *thing* but a *practice*" (Eckert, 2004, p. 43). The focus here, then, is on "how people *use* or *enact* or *perform* social styles for a range of symbolic purposes" (Coupland, 2007, p. 3). As Coupland explains, rather than viewing language in structural sociolinguistic terms, an understanding of language style as "social practice" gives us "a better chance of articulating the lived social world of meaning-making through language" (p. 178). Putting these views together, we can see how discourse, genre and style, when viewed in terms of practices, direct our attention to different ways in which we achieve social life through language: we construct realities through discursive practices, form temporary regularities to get things done through generic practices, and perform social meanings with different effects though stylistic practices.

Turns, bundles and communities

As suggested earlier, Schatzki (2001) claims that the 'practices turn' in the social sciences may render practice the new discourse (where discourse is understood in the Foucauldian, Gee's Big D, or Fairclough's pluralized sense of discourses). If on one level Schatzki's comment appears to refer more closely to a Foucauldian notion of Discourse, we should also note that he views a practice turn as moving away from the abstractions of poststructuralism in favour of a more grounded, local level of discourse. To the extent that the practices turn signifies a major shift towards a less abstracted way of thinking about the social, a turn to Bourdieu rather than Foucault, an interest in how humans do the everyday rather than how frames of power/knowledge have come into being over time, we might view language as local practice as local language use, or discourse. But this won't do either, since this is to fall into the trap of over-contextualizing, or of making the local practice reducible only to real-time use. The important point about practice is that it sits between these levels, between Big-D discourse (the abstractions of worldview) and little-d discourse (everyday language use) and asks how they connect, how this meso-political level organizes local activity in relation to broader social, cultural or historical organization. If we view discourse as a practice, if we elide both senses of small d/Big D discourse, looking instead at discourse as the relocalization of social practices in language, then there is no need to replace discourse by practice. Rather than the term discourse practices being another of those half-empty terms – language practices, literacy practices, discourse practices – meaning simply the doing of discourse,[6] the notion of discourse practices can rejuvenate the notion of discourse by taking it seriously as a practice, and refocus the notion of practice by seeing it in terms of discourse. Discursive practices, from this point of view, carry considerable weight.

At the same time, we should be wary of claims to epistemological turns such as the linguistic, practice, postmodern and so forth. Discourse emerged in the late twentieth century as an all-encompassing idea that could account for how and why we did things. Discourse was what gave meaning to the world, the social semiotics of life, the organizing principle that formed our thoughts, desires and subjectivities. This view of discourse was always stronger in terms of meaning and interpretation than in its relation to social order, hence the attempt by more materialist discourse analysts such as Fairclough (2003) to map a direct relation between social orders and orders of discourse. Discourse became a key abstraction that influenced thinking in the social sciences for a considerable time. It was this focus on discourse that was meant by the so-called 'linguistic turn' in the social sciences (Pennycook, 2002). In many ways, the term 'linguistic turn' was something of a misnomer, since it was not so much an interest in language as a focus on the ways in which social life needed to be understood in terms of the meanings it was given through particular frames of thought and their articulations. With 'reality' under a cloud of postmodern suspicion, the poststructuralist response was to suggest that at least we could look at how reality was *constructed*, at the ways in which discourses provided interpretive lenses for understanding life. The linguistic turn was not really a linguistic turn but rather a cultural turn. While some of us wondered why the so-called linguistic turn had not affected language studies, we missed the point: as Eagleton (2004) suggests, postmodernist theorists "may simply have replaced one kind of anchoring with another. It is now culture, not God or Nature, which is the foundation of the world" (p. 59). We have never in fact had a linguistic turn.

Various other 'turns' have been announced alongside the linguistic (Poynton, 1993) and the practice (Schatzki, 2001), including the somatic (Shusterman,

2000), the postmodern (Cameron 2005), the ecological (Fettes, 2003), the spatial (Gulson and Symes, 2007a), and the decolonial (Maldonado-Torres, 2007), several of which we have encountered at various points in this book. Rather than seeing these turns as competing with each other, however, it may be more productive to look at the ways in which they in fact are similarly oriented (aside from their general interest in announcing something new to replace the old). Taken together, these turns all move the focus away from language as an autonomous system that pre-exists its use, and competence as an internal capacity that accounts for language production, towards an understanding of language as a product of the embodied (somatic), contextualized (ecological, spatial) and political (decolonial) social practices that bring it about. To that extent, they align themselves closely with the ideas emerging from a turn towards practices, and indeed it is common to talk in terms, for example, of 'spatial practices'. Rather than seeing language as an object in itself, all these emerging orientations locate language as something done in a particular time and space.

As we have seen throughout this book, a focus on language as local practice takes us away from abstract systems and competencies and focuses instead on language as a social activity. This activity, bundled together as practices, acts as a level of meso-political mediation between the larger social and linguistic worlds and local linguistic instantiations. It is interesting to look at the rather overused notion of communities of practice (another case might be made for a communities of practice turn) from this perspective. As proposed by Lave and Wenger (1991), communities of practice give us a way of thinking about social groups in terms of the activities they come together to perform. Learning and identity, from this point of view, are tied to the ways in which we participate in shared activities. As Wenger (1998) explains, a community of practice is not merely a community that shares certain interests but rather a group who develop a shared repertoire of resources, a set of shared practices through sustained interaction. In sociolinguistics, and particularly studies of language and gender (e.g. Holmes and Meyerhoff, 1999), the notion has been usefully mobilized to avoid the pitfalls of other ways of thinking about language-using communities. Although, as Davies (2005) points out, the sense of practice here often remains at the level of micro-sociolinguistic analysis, and thus fails to develop a wider sense of social action, gender from this point of view can, as Cameron (2005, p. 488) explains, be understood "as something that emerges from practice".

Here we see again that crucial reorganization of social relations that is so much part of thinking in terms of practices: rather than viewing gender as the prior identity which gives rise to gendered language use, gendered language practices from this point of view give rise to identities. Communities of practice are not therefore just groups of people who happen to be doing the same thing, but rather people whose communities are constituted by the language practices they engage in. Working with a view of language based not so much on prior assumptions about commonalities of users of particular language codes but rather on the shared practices language users are engaged in "moves the focus away from a-contextual language systems and toward communicative activities comprising particular communities of practice" (Hall et al., p. 2006, p. 232). From this point of view, individual language knowledge is defined "not in terms of abstract system components but as communicative repertoires – conventionalized constellations of semiotic resources for taking action – that are shaped by the particular practices in which individuals engage" (p. 232). Language knowledge is therefore "grounded in and emergent from language use in concrete social activity for specific purposes that are tied to specific communities of practice" (p. 235).

From this point of view, it is communicative acts, bundled together as a form of social practice, that become the primary focus of our attention, while language and identity are seen as products of these social performances. As Becker (1995) suggests, if we talk in terms of 'languaging' – a term that can be traced back to John Dewey's work – rather than language, we can think in terms of time and memory rather than system and structure. Rather than viewing grammar as a system of rules that maps abstract relations onto textual relations, we can view grammar in terms of time and memory, in terms of textual relations that accumulate over life. For Hopper (1998), as we saw in Chapter 3, grammar is *emergent*: "structure, or regularity, comes out of discourse and is shaped by discourse in an ongoing process. Grammar is, in this view, simply the name for certain categories of observed repetitions in discourse" (p. 156). Language, then, is not so much a "circumscribed object" as "a confederation of available and overlapping social experiences." (p. 171). Drawing on this view, Thorne and Lantolf (2007, p. 189) explain that a 'linguistics of communicative activity' is "based on a view of language as a historically contingent emergent system, one that provides a repertoire of semiotic devices that people can use to realize their communicative intentions". The challenge, then, for "progressive language theorists" is to understand language less in terms of an abstract system, and rather in terms of the "semiotic inscription of communicative practice".

This sense of practice provides the key element in an explanation of how we 'do things with words,' of the performativity of language. As Cameron (2005) explains, "masculinities and femininities are produced in specific contexts or 'communities of practice', in relation to local social arrangements" (p. 484). From this point of view, identities are not fixed and stable attributes of individuals, but are produced through language (and other) practices. Hence, "the relationship of language to gender is conceived in terms of the local practices women and men participate in and the terms on which they participate" (p. 489). As both Butler (1999) and Hopper (1998) explain, this is a process of sedimentation, the ways in which people repeatedly draw on resources that gradually over time build up an appearance of fixed identities or linguistic structures. Language and identity, therefore, are the products rather than the precursors of our language practices. If practices prefigure activities, however, it is the ways in which language practices are moulded by social, cultural, discursive and historical precedents and concurrent contexts that become central to any understanding of language use. Language practices from this perspective, therefore, become the central concern of applied linguistics.

Conclusions: language and human activity

While various approaches to discourse, genre or conversation analysis share a number of features with a notion of language as a local practice, there are several reasons why the addition of a strong version of language practices can bring us a better understanding of language. A difficulty with all these categories – discourse, genre, practice – is how we can account for their continuity through repeated performance while avoiding giving them too much solidity. There is always a move towards static accounts of language use. While this is in some senses inevitable – it's a bit like suggesting that the failing of photography is that it gives us static images of the world – it is also part of a broader epistemology that not only creates a linguistic snapshot but also starts to relate this to linguistic, conversational, generic, discursive or social rules. The problem with the notion of genre is that it is so often pulled in the direction of similarity – it is inherent, we might argue, in the term – and even more so once it falls into the clutches of enthusiasts for linguistic description.

This is a common problem across many socially oriented theories of language: while commendably arguing that the social cannot be left out of any useful theory of language, the tendency all too often, in both sociolinguistic and functional versions of language description, is that it is then assumed that language use – text, genre, discourse – reflects society and that a description of language use is therefore a description of society. But this framing of language and society misses several points: language is constitutive of social relations and thus language use is also part of change rather than stasis; once we start to describe, and even worse prescribe, fixed genres, we have misconstrued the priority of the social in favour of an apparent fixity of the textual; and repetition – apparently doing the same thing again – cannot so evidently be thought of in terms only of similarity. If, however, we can develop a view of discursive, generic and stylistic practices as the mobile ways in which language and locality are always under construction, we can move towards a more flexible sociolinguistic vision.

I have been arguing in this chapter for the importance of looking at language as a social practice, 'thinking small' as Fabian (2007; see Chapter 2) put it. And yet, as Thrift (2007) reminds us, all such notions of scale should be treated with suspicion. By thinking small I am also thinking big. It is important to consider what we might gain and lose by doing so: theories of the world are always partial. While looking at practices might be 'thinking small' as far as an anthropologist is concerned, for those in language studies, it might still look fairly big (language studies has a remarkable capacity to think very small indeed). By focusing on language practices we might potentially lose both the level of particularity carried out in close studies of discourse, genre and conversation, as well as the insights of broad visions of discourse and ideology. The notion of language as a local practice, however, allows us to avoid this split by taking an interest in the mediating level, the middle ground, the meso-political, between broad social categories and micro events. Practice as the meso-political allows us to move beyond the dichotom- ization of discourse (Big D/little d) brought about by the structuralist/ poststructuralist divide, and to focus instead on the meso-political practice between words (little d) and worldviews (Big D). Just as a focus on literacy practices has been able to embrace the social while eschewing neither a focus on reading as an activity nor the sociology of reading, so a focus on language practices more broadly can enable a move from trying to understand lan- guage on either too small or too grand a scale.

By focusing on language as a local practice, therefore, we are not confined by contextuality. The local is something that happens in particular places, but place, as we saw in Chapter 4, is itself both deeply perspectival and part of a larger space. Language practices are bundles of repeated language acts, but as we saw in Chapter 3, such repetition of the same does not imply the absence of difference. Lurking behind repeated language use are not fixed laws and rules of either competence or performance; rather it is these semblances of regularity that are produced by language use. Whenever we practice language – writing a postcard, ordering a pizza, describing a fish, instructing a boat crew, reading a text message, offering a prayer – we are engaged in a local language practice. If our analysis stops at this point however, if we are content to point out that this is social, we are in danger of ignoring the deeper poli- tical potential of language practices, for which we need a flexible and socio- logically contingent version of language and power. The move, in a sense, is one from discourse analysis to ethnography: "a perspective on language as intrinsically tied to context and to human activity" (Blommaert, 2005: 233), which is why, in the end, we cannot account for how the mission statements of the St Isidore The Farmer Catholic School in Lazi got there. We can cer- tainly point to their generic construction, to the intertextual relations, and to the discourses of neoliberalism, education and Christianity that inform them. We can also account for the presence of English rather than other languages. It is one type of local language practice for me to read them, but to under- stand how they are read locally, and how they were constructed, we need to fill in the ethnographic background, find out how they were put together, by whom, and with what relations between the makers of the first and second texts. Local language practices cannot be reconstructed as the assumed ori- gins of a text.

8 Conclusion
Language as a local practice

Thinking about language locally

Everything happens locally. However global a practice may be, it still always happens locally.[1] The notion of the local is not therefore confined to the non-global, as seems to be the case in various ways of thinking about the global and the local. When we talk of the global, we are referring to the apparent co-occurrence in different times and places of local practices. At one level, the local is just here and now, acknowledging that language always happens in relation to space and time. And yet, it is also far more than this: being local is not only about physical and temporal locality; it is also about the perspectives, the language ideologies, the local ways of knowing, through which language is viewed. The local should not be confused with the small, the traditional, the immutable, since it is also about change, movement and the production of space, the ways in which language practices, such as graffiti writing or talking in the city, create the space in which they happen. Locality is thus far more than context, and language as a local practice is very different from language use in context, which rests on the questionable assumption that languages are akin to tools employed in predefined spaces. Looking at language as a local practice implies that language is part of social and local activity, that both locality and language emerge from the activities engaged in.

As David Scott (1999) suggests, there ought by now to be a number of broad epistemological stances we can take more or less for granted across the social sciences: "positions are to be read as contingent, histories as local, subjects as constructed, and knowledge as enmeshed in power" (p. 4). For Scott, it is time to move on from debates about the modern and postmodern, the colonial and postcolonial. That we speak from particular, embedded social, cultural and political positions is surely now something we can accept without battling claims that there are positions outside discourse or ideology from which we can speak. This does not by any means suggest a hopeless relativism but rather a profound perspectivalism. We need to acknowledge this and move on. Likewise, and in a similar vein, we should now be able to take for granted that sweeping historical, or social, or anthropological, or educational perspectives without adequate attention to the local simply do not reveal much. To claim that subjects somehow exist outside the forces that construct them, as some kind of preformed psychological entity with set characteristics and evolutionary orientations, is also to avoid the necessity to understand locality. Subjects are always a work in progress, a way of being in struggle. And finally, knowledge can never be abstracted from questions of power. These interlinked understandings have surely by now become fairly obvious statements about human life.

Canagarajah (2008, p. ix) offers us a parallel set of assumptions that we ought now to be able to accept about language: in the same way that positions may be read as contingent, so too language: grammars and structures of language, from this point of view, are always emergent rather predefined. Once we accept that language is a social practice, it becomes clear that it is not language form that governs the speakers of the language but rather the speakers that negotiate what possible language forms they want to use for what purpose. From this point of view, Canagarajah (2008) suggests, if we want to retain a notion such as competence, it refers not so much to the mastery of a grammar or sociolinguistic system, as to the strategic capacity to use diverse semiotic items across integrated media and modalities. Lastly, the notion of discrete, bounded languages becomes very dubious, since languages are always mixed, hybrid and drawing on multiple resources. We might therefore suggest that languages, like subjects, are always a work in progress (indeed subjects and languages are mutually constitutive), and that we cannot therefore understand language without taking particular language practices in particular locations into account.

Thus, when Heryanto (2007) speaks of 'language-free communities' or when, from an integrational linguistic perspective, Harris (1990) tells us that linguistics does not need to posit the existence of languages as separate and autonomous objects, or when linguistic anthropology draws our attention to the imperative of understanding local ideologies of language, we have clearly embarked on a different trajectory from many linguistic and applied linguistic frameworks, with their belief in the existence and describability of discrete languages, their positing of languages as systems that exist outside and beyond communicative acts, their location of language within the heads of people, and their use of disembodied texts to represent language use. Worth questioning, then, is this very focus on separate and distinguishable languages. When I talk of language as a local practice, I am talking of language, not of languages. Languages, as described by linguistics and applied linguistics, are inventions of the disciplines that make them (Makoni and Pennycook, 2007). So how can we go about exploring language diversity without positing the existence of languages?

Ideas such as language ecology give us one way of looking at locality and diversity of languages by placing languages within complex social, political and cultural environments. And yet, as I argued in Chapter 6, we should be wary of the political implications of the metaphors we use: the enumeration, objectification and biologization of languages within some versions of language ecology render them natural objects rather than cultural artefacts. It may well be the case that linguistic diversity is crucial to humanity, but a diversity of language entities may not be its most important measure. At the very least, following Halliday (2002), we might want to take *semiodiversity* as seriously as *glossodiversity*, the possibility of a multiplicity of meanings within a language as seriously as a multiplicity of languages (Pennycook, 2004). We also need to think carefully about any idea that languages somehow adapt to the world, since, as I have been arguing, we need a more dynamic and active sense of language practices as part of human endeavours to create new worlds.

This perspective takes into account the historical construction of languages, both in terms of their political construction in relation to nations and in terms of their epistemological construction as autonomous objects. It no longer therefore postulates the existence, enumerability or separability of languages as part of its theoretical apparatus. An ecology of local language practices perspective would mean not that languages as entities exist in relation to each other, nor that languages adapt to physical environments, nor that languages are causally related to diversity; rather, it would mean that local language practices are a set of activities dynamically integrated across physical, social, mental and moral worlds. From this perspective, therefore, we are not trying to find a relationship between language and the world, language and mind, language and society, language and morality, language and the environment, but rather asking how it is they were ever separated (cf. Latour, 1999). An understanding of ecologies of local language practices gives us a way forward here, so that we are not tied to images of bounded languages and instead can see how language is used locally, in multiple ways, to do many things.

In many ways, then, an understanding of the locality of languages has been constrained by the particular emphases of language studies. The most common way in which language locality, or language in context, is conceived in linguistics operates more or less along the following lines: languages are lexicogrammatical systems held in place by a core which defines what they are. Languages are defined by their coherence as a system rather than by locality or by their speakers. Locality comes into play on the one hand in very broad geographic terms as part of the naming of languages (where locality is a mappable construct). Different social, cultural and geographical contexts, on the other hand, lead to variations from that core, which may be accorded the status of varieties in their own right (dialects, sociolects and so forth). It is this way of thinking that allows us to think of the global spread of English, for example, in terms of an entity called English – defined by its grammar and lexicon – that spreads and changes in different contexts. And yet, as I argued in earlier chapters, if we take seriously the idea that we can never step twice into the same river, if we start to rethink what it means to talk about things being 'the same' – the same language, the same text, the same discourse – then we can start to see that languages in general, and global Englishes in particular, do not have one point of origin but rather multiple, co-present, global origins. Global Englishes are not what they are because English has spread and been adapted but because they share different histories. English has always been local.

Viewing languages in terms of local practices, therefore, has major implications for how we think about languages in general. The historical and contemporary interests behind the long construction of things called languages oblige us to ask in whose interests we continue to divide language into these named entities. Significant here too are the ways in which the narrow purview of linguistics limits what we can say about language-related issues. As Blommaert (2005) remarks, "linguists have no monopoly over theories of language" (p. 35). For Blommaert, in order to overcome the ways in which an area of investigation such as Critical Discourse Analysis (CDA) is hamstrung by its reliance on a particular version of linguistics (in this case systemic functional linguistics), we need to use a much broader frame of analysis incorporating at the very least ethnographic perspectives on language use. This means a shift, for example, from discourse analysis to ethnography in order to gain "a perspective on language as intrinsically tied to context and to human activity" (Blommaert, 2005, p. 233). Or, as he might have put it, this implies a shift from looking at languages and texts as bounded entities and focusing instead on language as a local practice.

This view has many implications for applied linguistic domains such as language testing (for a critical exploration, see Shohamy, 2001; 2006): Why is it, we might ask, that language tests such as the TOEFL (Test of English as a Foreign Language) remain so desperately monolingual, so tied to a view that to test people who engage in complex ecologies of language practices, we can ask reductive questions in one language? At first glance, this question may seem bizarre: it is a test of English, after all. Yet the linguistics of communicative activity developed by Thorne and Lantolf (2007), which opens up ways for us to see how languages may be mediational tools to develop each other, as well as a broader questioning of languages as separable objects, suggests that a multilingual TOEFL may be a far more appropriate test (to the extent that testing can be appropriate) than a monolingual one. The point here is not of course that TOEFL should be offered in separate but discrete languages (Test of French, German, Japanese, Tsonga or Tagalog as foreign languages) but rather that to test language users in one narrow element of their linguistic repertoire while admitting of no leakage across the tight linguistic boundaries echoes a history of strange linguistic inventions. When we talk of 'washback' in testing, it is more common to think in terms of the curricular effects of evaluation, but more broadly we might consider washback in terms of the 'collateral damage' for language users, policy makers, citizens and educators of the strange notion that languages exist in separation from the world and each other and can be tested in isolation.

Language education suffers similarly from such peculiar linguistic inventions. For a start, the enumerative strategies based on the notions of *second* language acquisition, or English as a *second* language become highly questionable. This is not, it should be said, merely to reiterate the point that 'second' may in fact refer to 'third' or 'fourth' but to ask instead what such arithmetical views of language development achieve in the first place. From the point of view outlined here, there is no good reason to separate and count languages in this way. The question to ask is what language education might look like if we no longer posited the existence of separate languages. As Busch and Schick (2007) show, it is quite possible to develop educational materials that challenge these language separations. Language policy can become a very different project from its current orientation towards choosing between languages to be used in particular domains, or debating whether one language threatens another. If language policy could focus on translingual language practices rather than language entities, far more progress might be made in domains such as language education. An understanding of English as a global language, not so much in terms of an entity that has spread but in terms of local language practices, offers important insights into the ways in which English is locally mobilized (Pennycook 2007a; 2007b).

While bilingual education has often successfully challenged its monolingual nemesis, it has also frequently operated with a vision of bilingualism that is little more than a pluralization of monolingualisms, that is to say, it takes as a given the epistemology of the 'bi', the separability and duality of two languages. "What would language education look like", however, asks García (2007, p. xiii), "if we no longer posited the existence of separate languages? How would we teach bilingually in ways that reflect people's use of language and not simply people as language users?" As she goes on to argue, "Translation of instructional material, offering the tests in the child's language, bilingual teachers, bilingual pedagogy is not enough, for it is based on an invention and it rarely reflects the ways in which children communicate" (p. xiv). A problem in much of applied and sociolinguistics is that monolingualism has been decried as the great aberration, the foe against which we need to struggle, while bi- or multilingualism are the cornerstones of our preferred world. Now it is all very well to critique the blinkered monolingual lenses through which language may be viewed, but such critiques all too often fail to take into account the ways in which the emphasis on multilingualism reflects a pluralization of monolingualism. As Sonntag (2003), Canagarajah (2007), Heller and Duchêne (2007) and others remind us, it is no good campaigning for a more equitable world of languages if we fail to question the underlying linguistic epistemologies on which our arguments are based. Viewed, therefore, from a perspective of language as a local practice, the point is no longer to decry monolingualism and eulogize bi- and multilingualism, but rather to question the language epistemologies that allow for such divisions, singularisms and pluralizations.

One way forward here lies in starting to understand language and language education in terms of majority world local knowledge, in looking, as García suggests, at how children actually communicate, rather than regulating a form of pre-categorized bilingualism. If we start to reconsider language learning not so much in terms of an arithmetic progression (learning an additional, a second language, becoming bilingual) but rather in terms of a much more dynamic conceptualization of transidiomatic practice (Jacquemet, 2005), we can see how language learning may involve communicative practices across different codes, channels and resources. Jørgensen's (2008a) and Møller's (2008) analysis of 'polylingual languaging' among children and adolescents in Denmark suggests that rather than asking if something is in one, two or more languages, it is more useful to consider mixed language resources or features that people draw on (see Chapter 5). Makoni and Makoni's (2010) "plur-ilanguaging approach" similarly aims to "capture the dynamic and evolving relationship between English, other indigenous African languages and multi-ple open semiotic systems, from the point of view of the language users themselves" (p. 258). The concept of *metrolingualism* (Otsuji and Pennycook, 2010) addresses related issues with its focus on modern, urban interaction and the ways in which people of mixed backgrounds use, play with and negotiate identities through language. The translingual language practices of metro-lingualism, polylingual languaging, or plurilanguaging are not the occasional language uses of exceptional communities but rather the everyday language practices of the majority world.

We therefore need a way of taking into account the point that not only does everything happen locally, but so too does its understanding: all local hap-penings are interpreted locally (though not of course through the same prism of locality). While we may be able to make some useful generalizations about languages, we also need to appreciate that local language practices are inter-preted locally and thus have particular meanings related to other local prac-tices. We also need to appreciate that language is a result of local interaction, not a prerequisite for it. That is to say, language emerges from social practice rather than being mobilized in order for social practices to happen. Language does not therefore happen outside the realm of practice; languages are not tools that are used in contexts; languages are not pre-given entities but the results of practice. To understand this we need ways of thinking about ecologies of local language practices, the ways in which different language resources are drawn on for different effects.

Practising language

We do things as bundled sets of activities – practices – that are repeated, learned, changed and relocalized. As I pointed out in Chapter 2, applied lin-guistics has been hampered by its division between practice and theory, which contributes to condescending relations on the one hand between linguists and applied linguists (the former develop the theory, the latter apply it) and on the other between applied linguists and those they advise (the former apply theory to contexts of practice, the latter adopt the advice). Amongst much that is unsatisfactory in these relations, the undermining of practice as a space of theory and of politics is perhaps the most pernicious. One of the arguments of this book has been towards a reconsideration of these relations, a reconfiguration of epistemological concerns in relation to practice. If language is a practice, what does applied linguistics, which often defines itself in terms of an engagement with practice, have to say about language?

The tendency to add the term 'practices' to words such as literacy, language and discourse may be as much part of the problem as of the solution. In some cases, such as literacy or critical discourse analysis, the use of the term may be the result of a more considered development of the notion of literacy or discourse practices, yet even here it has now become such an automatic concatenation that it is not always clear what weight it carries. 'Practices' turns up in the indexes of work on literacy, though not usually, it must be said, as a category in itself. Hence Moss (2007), for example, indexes 'literacy as a social practice' and connects this to gender, literacy events and so forth (p. 215). In social theories of language and discourse, similarly, there may be reference to discursive practices, but often no further explanation of what this means. Fairclough (2003) points to a relation between social and discursive practices, explaining that social practices mediate between social structures, which define what is possible, and social events, which define what is actual. From this point of view "orders of discourse are elements of (networks of) social practices" (p. 223). In other domains, however, the term appears to be little more than a filler, or at best an attempt to turn the static vocabulary of language studies into something more active, a term used to overcome the lexical gap in English concerning the doing of language, culture, discourse and literacy. But why, we still need to ask, has it become increasingly common to think of language, literacy or discourse as activities? Is there not, perhaps, a connection between the growing use of terms such as 'languaging', which writers such as Shohamy (2006) now use to capture a far more dynamic sense of language than is usually the case in applied linguistics, and the growth of this use of the notion of practices? What does this shift towards viewing language rather than language teaching as the central practice in applied linguistics imply?

To suggest that applied linguistics has never really engaged with practice is not to denigrate the important work that has been done in relation to domains such as language teaching, language in the workplace, languages and institutions; nor is it to ignore the work in literacy studies, sociolinguistics or linguistic anthropology that has come to embrace notions of 'language practices' or 'literacy practices' as the central focus of their work. Rather, it is to argue that within applied linguistics a particular set of conceptualizations that has framed theory against practice and the interior workings of language against their social realization has led to practice itself being under-theorized. It is this that allows us to see that the applied linguistic positioning of practice as the other of theory, while appearing at one level to acknowledge the importance of the real world, of an accountability to doing, at another level has never acknowledged the equality of practice. For applied linguistics to deal seriously with 'real-world' problems, it needs to shift from theory–practice relations and engage instead with the implications of understanding practices as prefigured meso-political activity. From this perspective, language is not a system, but an effect of language practices, which are socially, discursively, historically and politically constituted acts of language. Theory, therefore, is not a domain that applied linguists need to make accountable to practice, nor is it a series of generalizations from practice; rather, theory is what we need to use to understand language practices. By taking practice seriously rather than rendering it a domain to which our theories should apply or from which they should derive, applied linguistics might be better equipped to gain more respect both from practitioners (which would include not only teachers, but also language users, doctors, lawyers, translators and ourselves) and from other areas of the social sciences, since our theories would not be aimed at informing practice but would be theories of practice, theories that could account for the role of language in the social world.

These questions go much further than challenging narrow linguistic and applied linguistic orthodoxies. The old issues of description versus prescription, linguistics applied versus applied linguistics simply fade from view as irrelevant. It might seem at first glance that the arguments I have made in this book are just another version of the language-in-use side of language studies. The formalist approach, which over the last century has staked out strong territory in the work of de Saussure, Chomsky and the slew of formal grammars that have followed in the wake of this work, can be seen as part of an intellectual tradition that goes back through Kant, Descartes, Port Royal grammarians and ultimately to Platonic conceptualizations of ideal form. Here language exists as an abstraction outside its use; it is rational, organized and cognitive. The other tradition, which can be traced back via Bourdieu, Vološinov and Vico to Aristotelian notions of practical reason, stresses practice, use, empiricism and language as a social activity; language is social, habitual, performative and variable. This tradition has had its expression in functional grammars, linguistic anthropology, sociolinguistics and pragmatics. Certainly the arguments I have made here sit much closer to this latter line of thinking than the former.

While I have indeed drawn on ideas from the second tradition, and critiqued aspects of the first tradition, I also want to suggest ways in which the arguments in this book are far more than a restatement of the empirical, use-based tradition of language studies. The arguments here would, first of all, oppose such two-sides-of-the coin dichotomous thinking, not in favour, as are many arguments from both sides of this divide, only of their own position, but rather as part of a larger rethinking of how language operates. Many of the assumptions of more socially oriented approaches to language study also need to come under critical scrutiny. The givens of sociolinguistics, such as bilingualism and multilingualism, notions such as language rights, or the idea of language pragmatics, are also questionable from this perspective, since they are in a sense the by-products of the invented languages and metadiscursive regimes that linguistics has produced: if languages hadn't been invented as isolated, enumerable objects separated from their environment in the first place, we wouldn't need these add-on frameworks, and thus to talk of socio-linguistics or pragmatics is to uphold metalinguistic inventions.

The goal of this discussion of language as a local practice, therefore, is not another attempt at alternative system building but rather an exercise, in Hoy's (2004) terms, following Foucault, of thinking otherwise. The integration of these ideas with theories of critical resistance and non-representational theory (Thrift, 2007) brings language into a new relationship with space, thought and movement. Viewing language in terms of a *geography of linguistic happenings*, draws attention to locality (a geography of social space) and language practices (what happens through language) in a way that enables us to question those things we have left in the background as context, system or use. Such a view suggests that when we talk of linguistic landscaping, we are looking at ways in which language produces the world around it. Such work, which is "both anti-cognitivist and, by extension, anti-elitist" aims to "counter the still-pre-valent tendency to consider life from the point of view of individual agents who generate action by instead weaving a poetic of the common practices and skills which produce people, selves, and worlds" (Thrift, 2007, p. 112). By drawing on philosophical positions outside those of the dominant themes of Western philosophy, furthermore, I have attempted here to go beyond the reproduction of another Western philosophical debate. The work of Heraclitus, for example, discussed in Chapter 3, fits neither with Plato nor with Aristotle; indeed as we saw, it may tie better with philosophy outside the Western tradition altogether. So finally, and most importantly, by emphasizing a perspectival worldliness, an understanding of the local that is not only about place but also about the understandings that emerge from place, this view of language insists that language cannot be understood according to these broad traditions, systems and dichotomies but rather must always be locally conceived.

What, then, does it mean to take seriously the idea that language as a practice might be the central concern of applied linguistics rather than a focus on applying theories of language to domains of practice such as language teaching? If we view language practices as a set of social activities that are always bound up with other practices, as mediating between the activity of language and the larger social sphere, we can see how social practices are relocalized in language and language practices are relocalized as other forms of doing. This view accords with Schatzki's (2002, p. 73) account of a practice as "a set of doings and sayings" that is always involved in more than just the doings/sayings themselves. Practices are "the contexture in which social orders are established" (p. 89). If, furthermore, we take seriously Kramsch's (2005) injunction to develop a 'theory of practice' in order for applied lin-guistics to engage with 'real-world' issues, it becomes evident that a notion of language as a local practice needs to lie at the heart of applied linguistics. Rather than borrowing inapplicable frameworks from linguistics, a notion of language practices can help applied linguistics on the one hand to avoid its own precarious and patronizing position between theories of language and language practitioners, and on the other to become a domain of theory about language that has far more to say about the practices of language than other approaches to language.

Sedimented pathways and relocalization

As I suggested above, the global may be conceived in terms of the co-occurrence of the local in time and space. Yet, such co-occurrences should not be taken to be transparently of the same thing, since to do something again may be to do something different (Chapter 3). An argument in this book has been that language as a local practice is not only repeated social activity involving language, but is also, through its relocalization in space and time, a process of change. In Tan Twan Eng's (2007) novel *The Gift of Rain* a constantly returning theme is that of (pre)destiny and free will. How much are our lives laid out according to pre-given pathways (which may be god-given, fate-driven, or in less metaphysical terms, the result of social norms and structures) and how much can we decide and change for ourselves? Such questions go to the heart of much of the human predicament: is what we do the result of decisions we make or is it the acting out of predestiny, whether laid out by gods, the stars, history, culture, ideology, discourse, Oedipal complexes or social structures? Towards the end of the novel (and the end of the lives of two main characters) a discussion returns to the question again (p. 474). Phillip Kok-Hutton muses on whether he ever had a choice in his life: "Everything had already been planned for me, long before I was born." Michiko replies that he should see this as a blessing, since it gives meaning to his life. Everything has a meaning because it is predestined. But Phillip is unhappy with this: there must, he insists, be free will to choose. "Do you know the poem about the two roads and the one not taken?" he asks.

The reference of course is to Robert Frost's (1916) well-known poem, 'The Road not Taken', about choice and different paths: "Two roads diverged in a yellow wood,/and sorry I could not travel both/ And be one traveler, long I stood ... Two roads diverged in a wood, and I –/ I took the one less traveled by,/ and that has made all the difference." "Yes," replies Michiko. "That poem has always amused me, because who created the two roads in the first place?" In response, Tan Twan Eng suggests this was apparently a question Phillip had never considered (p. 474). In a common reading of the poem, the question has to do with the decisions we make, and how, once we have made them, we cannot go back, though it can also be interpreted in terms of the ways in which we believe we made choices in retrospect. But let us pursue Michiko's question for a moment. How *do* paths get created? By endless walking along the same track. One person walks a certain way, making choices about whether to go this way or that. If another person follows, and finds this route suitable, eventually a path is formed.

Animals do this too: across the slopes of mountains in Bhutan, there are clear yak paths; in the Australian bush, you may find pademelon paths. They don't seem to traverse terrain that is much different from adjacent ground, but clearly yaks and pademelons make and follow paths. And in fact human paths are sometimes formed by following animal paths. Major highways may once have been sheep trails. There is choice here – the first walker's route was a range of choices, probably practical ones rather than random zigzags, staying clear of the wet ground, going in a fairly straight direction, avoiding high and low areas. A path becomes a path because people followed, perhaps just out of habit, but probably again for practical reasons, and increasingly so: once there is a path, it often pays to stick to it. Sometimes people diverge, or a change in the environment – floods, fire, a fallen tree, a slippery rock – cause diversions, but once a path is formed, we often adhere to it. So we do not need to posit a universal path maker or predestiny, nor do we need to insist that everything is a matter of choice. We may at times have to choose between paths, but when we ask how the paths got there, we only need to look at iterative human activity: we do them in the doing.

Paths are sedimented walks. And local language practices are sedimented language acts. As we saw in Chapter 3, just as Butler (1999) argues that identities are a product of ritualized social performatives calling the subject into being and sedimented through time, so for Hopper (1998) languages do not have fixed structures and rules but rather are the product of the sedimentation of frequently used forms, borrowed from previous experiences. This view of language and identity may from some perspectives appear a very open-ended one: without language rules, it's pretty much open to do what you like. A misunderstanding of the notion of performativity has also led at times to an interpretation of this view of language or identity as a voluntary performance. Both arguments miss the point that these are socially regulated acts. Like pathways, we tend to follow them. Others have focused precisely on this notion of regulation, seeing it as far more constraining than a preferred vision of regulated language structures from which we pick and choose. The point to grasp, however, is that it is in the small acts of repetition, of 'fertile mimesis' (Thrift 2007) that difference occurs. It is the constant relocalization of language and images, of headless vicars on ponds, that brings about change. Repetition is also about difference.

This is also why I prefer a notion of relocalization rather than recontextualization, since the latter may infer little more than doing something again somewhere else. Relocalization invokes a more dynamic sense of locality and landscaping. A renewed understanding of repetition and relocalization has important implications for language learning. When we threw out the behaviourist bathwater, with its reductive emphasis on memorization and replication, we also threw out the mimetic baby and the possibilities it presents for seeing language learning in terms of repetition. Aside from the more practical observation that repetition and rote memorization are actually very useful for learning aspects of a language, several broader concerns are worth considering. Looking at the importance of language play for language learning, Cook (2000, p. 162) points out that "Language play is often characterized by repetition of other people's meanings ('regurgitation' if one wants to be pejorative), by display, by conformity (though also by creativity), by practice, and by choices based on specific linguistic structures." The creative use of language play in language learning may involve repetition of language just as much as it may involve discernible difference. Language learning also profoundly involves mimicry, and once we are open to a view of mimicry as an act that changes the original, then the concern that language imitation is stultifying is no longer credible. Branson and Miller (2007, p. 122) point out that the rejection of mime as an aspect of language has led to the rejection of sign languages as real languages: since "mimesis is integral to sign language, sign language has frequently been defined as not really language, but 'gesture', lacking the arbitrariness intrinsic to the concept of language". As they argue, however, the problem here has not been so much the common assumption that sign languages are 'mere gesture' but rather that linguistics has been unable to incorporate a notion of mimesis into its theoretical landscape.

Mimicry can be a 'weapon of the weak' (Scott, 1985; Canagarajah, 2000), and in the face of the hegemony of global English, it is by imitating that those obliged to learn this language around the world unsettle relations of power. Language repetitions, imitations and relocalizations as creative acts may be at least as significant for language learning as acts of creative construction or individual difference. Viewed from this perspective, many acts of apparent repetition or mimesis – such as the use of African American language in hip-hop in Malawi, where English use is "radically recontextualised" as terms borrowed from African American English "take on new sets of meanings" based on Malawian interpretations of American inner-city gang life and "contemporary social experiences of Malawian youth" (Perullo and Fenn, 2003, p. 41) – can also be seen as relocalizations of language practices. Like Shonibare's headless vicar (see Chapter 3 and cover image), these repetitions and acts of mimesis are always relocalized. Once this mimetic use of English is seen in terms of relocalization rather than imitation, it is possible to start thinking of localization not necessarily in terms of the introduction of new lexis and grammar but rather in terms of the re-enactment of the same in a different context. We can never utter the same word twice.

For studies of writing, a notion of relocalization raises questions for the ways in which a cult of quasi-creativity – 'say it in your own words' – pervades our confusions over originality and repetition. We ask students to be critical, to paraphrase, to show overt signs of difference in their writing so that we are able to judge their understanding of texts. Haunted by the spectre of plagiarism, we insist on observable forms of difference (Pennycook, 1996). If we start from the premise that all writing is intertextual, however, we can consider writing not in terms of a product of creative language competencies, but rather as inevitably drawing on the texts of others (Chandrasoma, Thompson and Pennycook, 2004; Thompson and Pennycook, 2008). An understanding of relocalization allows us to appreciate that to copy, repeat and reproduce may reflect alternative ways of approaching creativity. We may therefore need to look at student writing practices not as merely deviant or overly respectful, but rather as embedded in alternative ways of under-standing difference: to repeat a text in another context is an inexorable act of relocalization and it is only a particular ideology of textual originality that renders such a view invisible. Specifically connecting writing pedagogy to the hip-hop world of sampling, Rice (2003, p. 453) talks of "a writing practice that models itself after digital sampling's rhetorical strategy of juxtaposition". This hip-hop writing pedagogy focuses on "the way hip-hop constructs dis-course, the way it produces rhetorical meaning through its complex method of digital sampling, and how such a rhetoric functions within the scope of argumentation" (p. 454). By connecting writing practices with digital sam-pling and Barthes' (1977) understanding of intertextuality, Rice opens up ways here for an engagement with alternative ways of thinking about writing and creativity in terms of relocalization.

Space, time and movement

The notion of time that gives a different dynamic to the idea of repetition also brings new understandings of space, place and movement. Language practices, I have been arguing, are always local and thus always occur in a particular place. And place, or locality, is far from a neutral backdrop against which social processes are enacted: space is an interactive and mediating element that is part of the social. Soja's (1996) observation that spatiality, historicity and sociality need to be understood in conjunction suggests that when we invoke the local, we are talking not just about place but also about space, history and society. If locality brings in space, history and the social, practice too invokes history (repeated action), the social (social activity) and space (situatedness). Language practices are thus always social, historical and loca-ted. But more than this, the locatedness of language is not just about being in a place at a time, but also about producing that place. Thrift's (2007) focus on movement helps us understand space and language not only in terms of location but also in terms of emergence, subjects in process – performed rather than preformed – and thus becoming. The notion of the local as dynamic, about movement and fluidity, helps us get beyond a vision of the local as static, traditional, immobile.

Hadi-Tabassum's (2006) use of spatial theory to better understand bilingual classrooms shows how the basic divisions we may make – scheduling different languages at different times of the day, or creating spatial boundaries around languages in classrooms – may have major implications for the development and use of languages. Where a dual-immersion class divides English and Spanish into equal halves in the curriculum, for example, this dichotomy "produces a linguistic differentiation through its border-making design in which each language is separated and segregated into its own discrete space and time and is not allowed to mix with the other" (p. 5). Spatial practices, time practices and language practices all inform each other. According to

Appleby (in press), a focus on time and space can help us understand gender and English language teaching (ELT) in development contexts. There is a particular temporal and spatial logic to ELT in relationship to developmentalism, she argues, in which development is seen as change in a specified modernist direction, with expertise imported from elsewhere to effect this change. Time, with its particular links to progress, curriculum and masculinity, is favoured over space and a far more localized understanding of gender, difference and teaching practices. Unless we understand the ways in which the social, the political and the spatial are mutually constituted, we will fail to establish a more complex understanding of space, gender and ELT.

Into this picture we also need to bring questions of movement, of writing and talking in the city not as activities against a blank urban backdrop, but rather as spatial and language practices that give the city meaning (Chapter 4). Human life is categorized by movement, whether through time or through space: we are always in motion. As a result, nothing is ever the same. Once we look at graffiti-writing or talking in the city in terms of a dynamic account of space, text and interaction, we can also see that speakers, listeners, writers, readers produce meaning as they move, write, read and travel through urban semiotic spaces. The locality of language practices is not then a stage back-cloth against which language is used, but is a space that is imagined and created. The landscape is not a canvas or a context but an integrative and invented environment. Thus, when we talk of linguistic landscaping, we are talking not so much of signs against backdrops but of signing – or perhaps even singing – the city into being. When we think of language in relation to our educational landscapes, the linguistic landscaping of local language practices becomes highly significant in relation to the movement of people and languages.

This is also why we need metaphors of movement rather than, say, ecology as part of the way we think about language. "When you translate," asserts Dasgupta (2005, p. 42) "you are part of the traffic." And this traffic, this constant coming and going of people, bikes, rickshaws, cars, trucks, ferries, tuktuks, ships, planes, trains, is a traffic in meaning, a passing to and fro of ideas, concepts, symbols, discourses. For Kramsch (2006, p. 103) this 'traffic in meaning' is precisely what language teaching should be about, so that language competence should be measured not as the capacity to perform in one language in a specific domain, but rather as "the ability to translate, transpose and critically reflect on social, cultural and historical meanings conveyed by the grammar and lexicon". The role of the language teacher from this perspective, therefore, is "to diversify meanings, point to the meanings not chosen, and bring to light other possible meanings that have been forgotten by history or covered up by politics". Language teaching is indelibly tied to translation and the diversity of meanings. When we learn a language, we enter the traffic, and if English language teaching can escape its narrow vision of itself as a monolingual enterprise, as a place where English is taught only in its own presence, it might be able to take up a more dynamic, mobile role in the world as a form of translingual activism (Pennycook, 2008), as an activity tied not so much to the provision of the linguistic wherewithal for the movement of people but to the linguistic movement of meanings.

Local language practices and conditions of possibility

Although, as we saw in Chapter 7, Schatzki (2001) has suggested that practice may be the new discourse (the use of the concept of practice in social sciences may be replacing other broad concepts such as discourse as ways of thinking about social organization), a focus on language as a local practice does not necessarily push aside other concepts such as discourse or genre. It is quite possible to see how discourse, genre and style, when viewed in terms of practices, direct our attention to different ways in which we achieve social life through language: we construct realities through discursive practices, form temporary regularities to get things done through generic practices, and perform social meanings with different effects though stylistic practices. At the same time, however, if we want to understand how texts happen regularly – why the same language and textual forms continue to be repeated – it is not enough to describe such forms on the basis that this will also therefore account for their production. A focus on language practices demands that we move beyond a focus only on text.

This is akin, in some ways, to Hacking's (2004) discussion of the need to find a space between discourse in the abstract, as described by Foucault, and face-to-face interaction, as discussed by Goffman: Foucault, as Hacking explains, "gave us ways in which to understand what is said, can be said, what is possible, what is meaningful", yet he did not give us ways of thinking about "how, in everyday life, one comes to incorporate these possibilities and impossibilities as part of oneself. We have to go to Goffman to begin to think about that" (Hacking 2004, p. 300). This is not of course to suggest that we all need to go back to Goffman, but rather that we need to be able to work with an understanding of language that incorporates both text and society. What Hacking is suggesting more generally here is that we need a way of looking at language that not only looks at society or institutions, that not only includes an understanding of the interactions of the everyday, but that also seeks an understanding of how such interactions are institutionally framed and such institutions are interactionally realized. What Hacking seeks to address through a mixture of Foucault and Goffman, I have been trying to articulate through an exploration of the meso-political space of language practices.

I have elsewhere (Pennycook, 2007a) suggested, following Scott (1999), that Fanon and Foucault in combination provide us with a way to remain both political and sceptical by acknowledging the reality of struggle and the particularity of knowledge. As Scott (1999) suggests, we need to work both with the postcolonial politics of Frantz Fanon – "the revolutionary architect par excellence of anticolonial liberation" (p. 200) – and also with the epistemological scepticism of Michel Foucault – to warn us that "politics must never be allowed to rest on the satisfaction of its own self-conception, on the identities it affirms as the constituents of its community" (p. 207). On the one hand, the urgency and realities of political struggle, on the other hand the need to always question our own and others' assumptions, a combination that comes together in the 'decolonial turn' that seeks to undo and to rethink the 'coloniality of being' (Maldonado-Torres, 2007). This, then, brings us to a three-way reconciliation between Fanon, Foucault and Goffman, or rather the broad epistemological positions they represent: the centrality of politics, history and political struggle and the need to continue to undo the coloniality of being; the discursive production of ways of thinking and acting, and the imperative to never allow ourselves to settle easily on our own terminologies; the implications of talk within institutions, and the conditions of possibility for what can be said.

The relation between the three should not be considered as simply a local/non-local one, or an attempt to reconcile micro and macro, text and society, 'small d' discourse and 'big D' Discourse, or other such dialectics. Analysis of everyday language – as represented in the work of Goffman or other textual analysts – is not so much a focus only on the local as it is an acknowledgement that everything happens locally while also participating in a wider field of action. While Foucault's analyses may seem broad in the extreme, his understanding of the intellectual and of discourse is also precisely in opposition to the universal. It is therefore local in a different sense: when Foucault (1980) asks what forms of knowledge have been discounted by prevailing discourses, what forms of subjugated knowledge might mount an insurrection when we show the ways in which discursive formations have taken particular forms, he is asking local questions. And discourses, it is worth reminding ourselves, are constituted by discursive practices, which always happen somewhere, at some time, in a particular way. Fanon's postcolonial struggle, moreover, while set against the broad history of colonial encounter, always takes us back to the locality of power and resistance. To take these three epistemologies, therefore, is not to juxtapose local analysis and macro-politics but rather to frame the need for an understanding of language as a local practice as always requiring political, historical, epistemological, spatial, social and textual considerations.

Notes

1 Introduction

1 It is of course possible to make more of the notion of context, as does Blommaert (2005), arguing that context is crucial but needs to be a 'higher-level situatedness' (p. 67) than is common in many accounts of language and context. More generally, Blommaert's (2005) arguments for the need for context to be understood ethnographically rather than read textually have strong affinities with the position I am taking here.

2 'Press 1 for English'

1 Researchers in second language acquisition, for example, have refuted such claims, insisting that theory development may be a goal in itself without having to address or be accountable to practice (see for example, Long, 2006, or the debates in Seidlhofer, 2003).

2 This is based on an extensive survey of all articles in the 2005 issues of the journal *Applied Linguistics*. My thanks to Astrid Lorange for some long and tedious hours mapping every use of the term practice.

3 By analogy with acro-, meso- and basilectal terminology, I am using the term meso-political to capture that need for something in between the acro/macro and the basi/micro levels of analysis

4 This is a gloss of a more complex formulation whose opacity need not concern us here.

5 Arguably, this is one of the problems of approaches to language study such as systemic functional grammar and critical discourse analysis which, by constituting themselves as already social, allow for the study of texts to substitute for the study of the social (see Blommaert, 2005).

6 "We are what we repeatedly do; excellence, then, is not an act but a habit." This is apparently a misquote from Aristotle, drawn from a text about him by Durant (1926) (see Wikiquote.org). As a gloss on his work rather than a direct quotation, it nevertheless captures this central line of thought: we are what we do.

7 Marx's Theses on Feuerbach were first written in 1845 but only published in 1888 as part of Engel's work on Feuerbach.

3 The *Reverend on Ice* again

1 This is the point that Widdowson (2008), drawing on Jakobson's poetics, and his own mixture of structuralism and stylistics, apparently fails to grasp in his suggestion that there is nothing very new here, that stylistics has always acknowledged that repetition is part of creativity.

2 As Huggan (1997) suggests, the two terms can be distinguished by viewing mimicry as usually mischievous imitation of others, and mimesis as imitation across different symbolic or cultural systems. Since the two terms are often used interchangeably in the sources cited here, however, I shall not adhere to this distinction further in this chapter.

3 Creationists, or those that believe in some version of 'Intelligent Design' may not agree on this point, but then there are interesting connections between views of evolution that depend on a supreme being to get everything going and views of language that depend on a supreme structure to keep everything in place.

4 Talking in the city

1 Barcelona, Bologna, New York, Paris and São Paulo are among the great graffiti cities of the world. Thanks to Emi Otsuji for bringing this exhibition to my attention.

2 Jørgensen (2008b) suggests this is an English word, though it is also widely used in Quebec French and its characterization is difficult.

3 A well-known street in Melbourne.

4 Held every four years, the Commonwealth Games is an international Olympics-type sporting event for the fifty-three member nations of the Commonwealth of Nations (formerly the British Commonwealth).

5 Also known as *Yamakasi,* the name of one well-known group of practitioners, *l'art du déplacement* (the art of movement) or free running. See www.le-parkour.com/.

6 It is a shame that the English translation elides the original – "l'énonciation (le speech act)" – as only 'speech act'. While de Certeau's gloss of enunciation as a speech act is itself problematic, the English translation misses the significance of enunciation.

7 See, for example, the global graffiti on sites such as graffiti.com. Although graffiti can also be found in rural settings, they remain a largely urban phenomenon.

5 Kerala tuskers

1 These interviews were part of the Local Noise project at UTS. See Localnoise.net.au.

6 *Alibangbang* and ecologies of local language practices

1 Volunteer work for the Coastal Conservation and Education Foundation, based in Cebu, and its specific Saving Philippines Reefs (SPR) projects. See www.coast.ph.

2 There are also numerous debates and arguments about the status of ecology as 'real', 'metaphorical' and so forth (see Steffensen, 2007) This is not my focus here.

3 I am not of course arguing here for a voluntaristic version of language shift and death. The reasons for such change are far more complex than any argument that suggests merely that people choose to speak another language. Rather, my emphasis on human agency here has to do with the relation between human action and language adaptability.

4 It might also be argued, in light of the rapacious practices of pharmaceutical companies in copyrighting local medicines, that it is the semiodiversity of Latin and pharmaceutical nomenclatures that is increasing at the expense of both local semiodiversity and glossodiversity.

5 While Japanese use kanji names (characters) for commonly eaten fish – tuna, mackerel and so forth – it seems more commmon to use katakana for these fish, even though the words are Japanese. Since these names are in katakana it is not always easy to tell if this is the preferred reading of the word. My thanks to Emi Otsuji and Keiko Yasukawa for help with these names.

6 Visayan is not generally taken to refer to a language but rather to an ethnolinguistic group that lives in the Visayas, the central region of the Philippines, where,

according to Ethnologue (2009), around 50 of the Philippines' 170 languages are spoken. Rappa and Wee (2006) suggest there are between 80 and 120 languages and dialects. I use the term Visayan here, however, since it is one often used by Filipinos, including Cebuano speakers, to talk about the region linguistically. According to my informants, whose business is fish-naming, there is not in fact much variation in fish names across the region. Once again, here we confront the fraught areas of language counting and what it means to say that something is in a particular language.

7 The Tagalog term *paru-paro*, meaning butterfly, may also be used. *Alibangbang* means butterfly but can also be used to refer to a 'flirtatious woman' (thanks to Beatriz Lorente for pointing this out). I am grateful to members of the SPR team for help in understanding the issues around fish names in the Philippines.

7 'Molding hearts ... Leading minds ... Touching lives'

1 Other forms of analysis that also take an interest in language use, such as systemic functional grammar, for example, may start with a premise that ostensibly puts use or function before system, suggesting that grammar is a function of the uses to which it is put, yet in many of its instantiations it ultimately focuses logocentrically on structural choices in a pre-given network of language items (Luke, 1996).

2 There are a number of postcards in the Anne Frank museum in Amsterdam, sent by Anne Frank as a young girl before she and her family went into hiding.

3 Fairclough distinguishes between countable and non-countable discourse(s) in an attempt to capture a distinction similar to Gee's between Big-D and little-d discourse.

4 This is of course a complex question on which much more could be said. Part of the difference between Fairclough, Green and Thrift depends on different interpretations of the idea of representation (which in itself raises questions of representation).

5 This is my relocalization of a discussion I had with Theo van Leeuwen about this. The social practice of going for a drink after work to discuss the notion of discourse is here relocalized as an explanation of the ways in which discourse can be understood. Generically, of course, I might have written this as: "Theo van Leeuwen (personal communication)" but genres are flexible, and I would prefer: A relocalized afterwork drink with Theo.

6 The notion of discourse practices might in any case be a bit strange to some applied linguists for whom discourse is more or less defined as the doing of language, thus rendering discourse practices the doing of the doing of language.

8 Conclusion

1 This is akin to S Fuchs' (2001) point that "everything that happens happens locally, at a certain place and time. All that exists exists empirically, and only until further notice" (p. 337). I have also partially drawn here on Fuchs' practice of listing key theoretical positions, though I have chosen to embed them within the more general discussion.

Bibliography

Abrams, D and Strogatz, S (2003) Modelling the dynamics of language death. *Nature*, 424, 21 August, p. 900.

Aitchison, J (2003) *Words in the mind. An introduction to the mental lexicon* (3rd edition). Oxford: Blackwell.

Alexander, R (2009) *Framing discourse on the environment. A critical discourse approach*. London: Routledge.

Alim, H S (2006) *Roc the Mic Right: The language of Hip Hop culture*. New York: Routledge.

Alim, H S and Pennycook, A (2007) Glocal linguistic flows: Hip-hop culture(s), identities, and the politics of language education. *Journal of Language, Identity and Education*, 6(2), 89–100.

Alim, S, Ibrahim, A, and Pennycook, A (2009) *Global linguistic flows: Hip Hop cultures, youth identities and the politics of language*. New York: Routledge.

Alter, S (1999) *Darwin and the linguistic image: Language, race and natural theology in the nineteenth century*. Baltimore: Johns Hopkins University Press.

Appadurai, A (1996) *Modernity at large: Cultural dimensions of globalization*. Minneapolis: University of Minnesota Press.

—— (2001) Grassroots globalization and the research imagination. In A. Appadurai (ed.) *Globalization*. Durham: Duke University Press, pp. 1–21.

Appleby, R (in press) *Time and space in English language teaching, gender and development*. Bristol: Multilingual Matters.

Ashcroft, B and Ahluwalia, P (1999) *Edward Said: The paradox of identity*. London: Routledge.

Austin, J L (1962) *How to do things with words: The William James Lectures delivered at Harvard University in 1955*. Oxford: Clarendon Press.

Bakhtin, M (1981) *The dialogic imagination: Four essays*. (Trans Caryl Emerson and Michael Holquist). Austin: University of Texas.

—— (1986) *Speech genres and other late essays*. Austin: University of Texas Press.

Barbour, J (2006) Referential coherence: Some observations on the Neverver language of north-central Malakula (Vanuatu). Terry Crowley Memorial Workshop on Vanuatu Languages. Victoria University of Wellington, NZ, 13–14 Nov 2006.

Barthes, R (1977) *Image, music and text*. London: Fontana Press.

Barton, D and Hamilton, M (2000) Literacy practices. In D Barton, M Hamilton, and R Ivanic (eds) *Situated literacies: Reading and writing in context*. London: Routledge.

Batibo, H (2009) Poverty as a crucial factor in language maintenance and language death: Case studies from Africa. In W Harbert, S McConnell-Ginet, A Miller and J Whitman (eds) *Language and poverty*. Bristol: Multilingual Matters.

Bauman, R (2004) *A world of others' words: Cross-cultural perspectives on inter-textuality*. Oxford: Blackwell.

Bauman, R and Briggs, C (2003) *Voices of modernity: Language ideologies and the politics of inequality*. Cambridge: Cambridge University Press.

Baynham M (1995) *Literacy practices: Investigating literacy in social contexts*. London: Longman.

Bearn, G (2000) Differentiating Derrida and Deleuze. *Continental Philosophy Review*, 33, 441–65.

Becker, A (1995) *Beyond translation: Essays towards a modern philology*. Ann Arbor: University of Michigan Press.

Beckett, D and Hager, P (2002) *Life, work and learning: Practice in postmodernity*. London: Routledge.

Benton, T (2002) Wittgenstein, Winch and Marx. In G Kitching and N Pleasants (eds) *Marx and Wittgenstein: Knowledge, morality and politics*. London: Routledge, pp. 147–59.

Bernstein, B (1990) *The structuring of pedagogic discourse*. London: Routledge.

Bhabha, H (1985) Of mimicry and man: The ambivalence of colonial discourse. *October*, 34, 126–33.

Block, D (2008) On the appropriateness of the metaphor of LOSS. In K W Tan and R Rubdy (eds) *Language as commodity: Global structures, local marketplaces*. London: Continuum, pp. 187–203.

Blommaert, J (2005) *Discourse: A critical introduction*. Cambridge: Cambridge University Press.

—— (2008) *Grassroots literacy: Writing, identity and voice in central Africa*. London: Routledge.

Bloor, D (2001) Wittgenstein and the priority of practice. In T Schatzki, K Knorr Cetina and E von Savigny (eds) *The practice turn in contemporary theory*. London, Routledge, pp. 95–106.

Bolton, K (2005) Symposium on World Englishes today (part II). Where WE stands: approaches, issues, and debate in world Englishes. *World Englishes*, 25(1), 69–83.

Bosire, M (2006) Hybrid languages: The case of Sheng. In Olaoba F. Arasanyin and Michael A. Pemberton (eds) *Selected Proceedings of the 36th Annual Conference on African Linguistics*. Somerville, MA: Cascadilla Proceedings Project, pp. 185–93.

Bourdieu, P (1977) *Outline of a theory of practice*. Cambridge: Cambridge University Press.

Bourne, J (1988) 'Natural acquisition' and a 'masked pedagogy'. *Applied Linguistics*, 9(1), 83–99.

Branson, J and Miller, D (2000) Maintaining, developing and sharing the knowledge and potential embedded in all our languages and cultures: On linguists as agents of epistemic violence. In R Phillipson (ed.) *Rights to language: Equity, power and education*. Mahwah, NJ: Lawrence Erlbaum, pp. 28–32.

——and — (2007) Beyond 'language': Linguistic imperialism, sign languages and linguistic anthropology. In S Makoni and A Pennycook (eds) *Disinventing and reconstituting languages*. Clevedon: Multilingual Matters, pp. 116–34.

Brumfit, C (1995) Teacher professionalism and research. In G Cook and B Seidlhofer (eds) *Principle and practice in Applied Linguistics*. Oxford: Oxford University Press, pp. 27–41.

Bruthiaux, P (2003) Squaring the circles: Issues in modeling English worldwide. *International Journal of Applied Linguistics*, 13(2), 159–77.

Brutt-Griffler, J (2002) *World English: A study of its development*. Clevedon: Multilingual Matters.

Busch, B and Schick, J (2007) Educational materials reflecting heteroglossia: Disinventing ethnolinguistic differences in Bosnia-Herzegovina. In S Makoni and S Pennycook (eds) *Disinventing and reconstituting languages*. Clevedon: Multilingual Matters, 216–32.

Butler, J (1990) *Gender trouble: Feminism and the subversion of identity*. London: Routledge.

—— (1997) *Excitable speech: A politics of the performative*. London: Routledge.

—— (1999) Performativity's social magic. In Richard Shusterman (ed.) *Bourdieu: A critical reader*. Oxford: Blackwell Publishers, pp. 113–28.

Bybee, J and Hopper, P (2001) Introduction to frequency and the emergence of linguistic structure. In J Bybee and P Hopper (eds) *Frequency and the emergence of linguistic structure*. Amsterdam: John Benjamins, pp. 1–26.

Cameron, D (2003) Globalizing 'communication'. In J Aitchison and D Lewis (eds) *New media language*. London: Routledge, pp. 27–35.

—— (2005) Language, gender, and sexuality: Current issues and new directions. *Applied Linguistics*, 26 (4), 482–502.

—— (2007) Language endangerment and verbal hygiene: History, morality and politics. In A Duchêne and M Heller (eds) *Discourses of endangerment: Ideology and interest in the defence of languages*. London: Continuum, pp. 268–85.

Canagarajah, S (1999) *Resisting linguistic imperialism in English teaching*. Oxford: Oxford University Press.

—— (2000) Negotiating ideologies through English: Strategies from the periphery. In T Ricento (ed.) *Ideology, politics, and language policies: Focus on English*. Amsterdam: John Benjamins, pp. 121–32.

—— (2005a) Introduction. In S Canagarajah (ed.) *Reclaiming the local in language policy and practice*. Mahwah, NJ: Lawrence Erlbaum, pp. xiii–xxx.

—— (2005b) Reconstructing local knowledge, reconfiguring language studies. In S Canagarajah (ed.) *Reclaiming the local in language policy and practice*. Mahwah, NJ: Lawrence Erlbaum, pp. 3–24.

—— (2007) The ecology of global English. *International Multilingual Research Journal*, 1(2), 89–100.

—— (2008) Foreword in A Clemente and M Higgins *Performing English with a postcolonial accent: Ethnographic narratives from Mexico*. London: The Tufnell Press, pp. ix–xiii.

Cannadine, D (2000) *Class in Britain*. London: Penguin.

Capra, F (1985) *The Tao of physics: An exploration of the parallels between modern physics and eastern mysticism* (2nd edition). Boston, MA: New Science Library.

Carter, R (2004) *Language and creativity. The art of common talk*. London: Routledge.

Castleman, C (2004) The politics of graffiti. In M. Forman and M A Neal (eds) *That's the joint: The hip-hop studies reader*. New York: Routledge, 21–29.

Chandrasoma, R, Thompson, C and Pennycook, A (2004) Beyond plagiarism – transgressive and non-transgressive intertextuality. *Journal of Language, Identity and Education*, 3 (3), 171–93.

Chomsky, N (1971) *Problems of Knowledge and Freedom*. Bungay: Fontana.

Chouliaraki, L and Fairclough, N (1999) *Discourse in late modernity: Rethinking critical discourse analysis*. Edinburgh: Edinburgh University Press.

Christen, R S (2003) Hip hop learning: Graffiti as an educator of urban teenagers. *Educational Foundations*, 17(4), 57–82.

City of Melbourne (2007) Graffiti Management www.melbourne.vic.gov.au/info.cfm? top = 145& pg = 1150.

Colebrook, C (2002) *Gilles Deleuze*. London: Routledge.

Compass (2006) *The mistery of Hip Hop* (TV documentary) 6 August, Australia: ABC.

Connell, J and Gibson, C (2003) *Sound tracks: Popular music, identity and place*. London: Routledge.

Conquergood, D (1997) Street Literacy. In J Floord, S Brice Heath and D Lapp (eds) *Handbook of research on teaching literacy through the communicative and visual arts*. New York, Simon & Schuster, pp. 354–75.

Cook, G (2000) *Language play, language learning*. Oxford: Oxford University Press.

Cook, V (1999) Going beyond the native speaker in language teaching. *TESOL Quarterly*, 33/2, 185–209.

Cope, B and Kalantzis, M (1993) Introduction: How a genre approach to literacy can transform the way writing is taught. In B Cope and M Kalantzis (eds) *The powers of literacy: A genre approach to teaching writing*. London: The Falmer Press, pp. 1–21.

—— and — (eds) (2000) *Multiliteracies: Literacy learning and the design of social futures*. London: Routledge.

Coslovich, G (2005) Our colourful underbelly. *The Age*, 4 December, np.

Coulmas, F (2009) Linguistic landscaping and the seed of the public sphere. In E Shohamy and D Gorter (eds) *Linguistic landscape: Expanding the scenery*. London: Routledge, pp. 13–24.

Coupland, N (2007) *Style: Language variation and identity*. Cambridge: Cambridge University Press.

Cowen, P (2005) *The rose window*. London: Thames and Hudson.

Crang, M (2001) Rhythms of the city: Temporalised space and motion. In J May and N Thrift (eds) *Timespace: Geographies of temporality*. London: Routledge, pp. 187–207.

Crang, M and Thrift, N (eds) (2000) Introduction. In M Crang and N Thrift (eds) *Thinking space*. London: Routledge, pp. 1–30.

—— (2000) *Thinking Space*. London: Routledge.

Crawford, J (1998) Endangered native American languages: What is to be done, and why? In Thomas Ricento and Barbara Burnaby (eds) *Language and politics in the United States and Canada: Myths and realities*, Mahwah, NJ: Lawrence Erlbaum, pp. 151–66.

Cresswell, T (1996) *In place/out of place: Geography, ideology and transgression*. Minneapolis: University of Minnesota Press.

Croft, W (2001) *Radical construction grammar*. Oxford: Oxford University Press.

Crystal, D (1998) *Language play*. Harmondsworth: Penguin.

Daara J (2004) *Boomerang*. Wrasse Records (CD).

Dasgupta, P (2005) Trafficking in words: Languages, missionaries and translators. In P St-Pierre and P Kar (eds), *In translation: Reflections, refractions, transformations*. Delhi: Pencraft International, pp. 42–56.

Davies, A (1999) *An introduction to applied linguistics: From practice to theory*. Edinburgh: Edinburgh University Press.

Davies, B (2005) Communities of practice: Legitimacy not choice. *Journal of Sociolinguistics*, 9/4, 557–81.

De Beaugrande, R (1997) Theory and practice in applied linguistics: Disconnection, conflict or dialectical? *Applied Linguistics*, 18(3), 279–313.

De Certeau, M (1984) *The practice of everyday life.* (Trans Steven Rendall *L'invention du quotidien, 1. Arts de faire.* Paris: Gallimard). Berkeley: University of California Press.

DeKeyser, R (2007) Introduction: Situating the concept of practice. In R DeKeyser (ed.) *Practice in a second language: Perspectives from applied linguistics and cognitive psychology.* Cambridge: Cambridge University Press, pp. 1–18.

Deleuze, G (2004) *Difference and repetition.* (Trans Paul Patton *Différence et Répétition* [1968]). London: Continuum.

Deleuze, G and Guattari F (1987) *A Thousand plateaus: Capitalism and schizophrenia.* London: Continuum. (Trans B. Massumi; original 1980).

De Meija, A-M (2002) *Power, prestige, and bilingualism: International perspectives on elite bilingualism.* Clevedon: Multilingual Matters.

Derrida, J (1976) *Of grammatology.* (Trans G C Spivak). Baltimore: Johns Hopkins University Press.

Derrida, J (1982) *Margins of philosophy.* Chicago: University of Chicago Press.

De Souza, L M and Andreotti, V (2009) Culturalism, difference and pedagogy: Lessons from indigenous education in Brazil. In J Lavia and M Moore (eds) *Cross-cultural perspectives on policy and practice: Decolonizing community contexts.* London: Routledge.

Dixon, R (1997) *The rise and fall of languages.* Cambridge: Cambridge University Press.

Drew, P and Curl, T (2008) Conversation analysis: Overview and new directions. In V K Bhatia, J Flowerdew and R Jones (eds) *Advances in discourse studies.* London: Routledge, pp. 22–35.

Duchêne, A (2008) *Ideologies across nations: The construction of linguistic minorities at the United Nations.* Berlin: Mouton de Gruyter.

Dulay, H, Burt, M and Krashen, S (1982) *Language two.* New York: Oxford University Press.

Durant, W (1926) *The story of philosophy: The lives and opinions of the world's greatest philosophers.* New York: Simon & Schuster.

Eagleton, T (2004) *After theory.* London: Penguin.

Eckert, P (2004) The meaning of style. *Texas Linguistic Forum,* 47, 41–53.

Edwards, J (2004) Language minorities. In A Davies and C Elder (eds) *The handbook of applied linguistics.* Oxford: Blackwell, pp. 451–75.

Edwards, L (2006a) Graffiti blitz gives city a quick facelift. *The Age,* 2 March.

—— (2006b) Stencil art on the run thwarts graffiti crackdown. *The Age,* 16 March, np.

Edwards, R and Usher, R (2008) *Globalisation and pedagogy: Space, place and identity* (2nd edition). London: Routledge.

Emirbayer, M and Mische, A (1998) What is agency? *The American Journal of Sociology,* 103 (4), 962–1023.

Eng, T T (2007) *The gift of rain.* Newcastle Upon Tyne: Myrmidon Books.

Errington, J (2001) Colonial linguistics. *Annual Review of Anthropology,* 30, 19–39.

—— (2008) *Linguistics in a colonial world: A story of language, meaning and power.* Oxford: Blackwell.

Ethnologue (2009) www.ethnologue.com. Accessed 31 March 2009.

Evans, N (2010) *Dying words: Endangered languages and what they have to tell us.* Chichester: Wiley-Blackwell.

Fabian, J (1986) *Language and colonial power: The appropriation of Swahili in the former Belgian Congo 1880–1938.* Berkeley: University of California Press.

—— (1990) *History from below* Amsterdam: John Benjamins.

—— (2007) *Memory against culture: Arguments and reminders.* London: Duke University Press.

Fairclough, N (1995) *Critical discourse analysis.* London: Longman.

—— (2001) Critical discourse analysis as a method in social scientific research. In R Wodak and M Meyer (eds) *Methods of critical discourse analysis.* London: Sage, pp. 121–38.

—— (2003) *Analysing discourse: Textual analysis for social research.* London: Routledge.

—— (2005) Critical discourse analysis in transdisciplinary research. In R Wodak and P Chilton (eds) *A new agenda in (critical) discourse analysis.* Amsterdam: John Benjamins, pp. 53–70.

Fettes, M (2003) Critical realism, ecological psychology, and imagined communities. In Jonathan Leather and Jet van Dam (eds) *Ecology of Language Acquisition,* Dordrecht: Kluwer Academic Publishers, pp. 31–47.

Fill, A (2001) Ecolinguistics: State of the art 1998. In Alwin Fill and Peter Mühlhäusler (eds) *The ecolinguistics reader: Language, ecology and environment.* London: Continuum, pp. 43–56.

Fill, A and Mühlhäusler, P (eds) (2001) *The ecolinguistics reader: Language, ecology and environment.* London: Continuum.

Flewelling, C (2005) *The social relevance of philosophy: The debate over the applicability of philosophy to citizenship.* Lanham, MD: Lexington Books.

Foucault, M (1972) *The archaeology of knowledge.* (Trans A M Sheridan Smith *L'Archéologie du Savoir,* 1969). London: Routledge.

—— (1980) *Power/Knowledge: Selected interviews and other writings, 1972–1977.* New York: Pantheon Books.

Frost, R (1916/ 1962) The road not taken. In O Williams and E Honig (eds) *The mentor book of major American poets.* New York: The New American Library, p. 250.

Fuchs, B (2001) *Mimesis and empire: The New World, Islam and European identities.* Cambridge: Cambridge University Press.

Fuchs, S (2001) *Against essentialism: A theory of culture and society.* Cambridge, MA: Harvard University Press.

García, O (2007) Intervening discourses, representations and conceptualizations of language. Foreword in S Makoni and A Pennycook (eds) *Disinventing and reconstituting languages.* Clevedon: Multilingual Matters, pp. xi–xv.

Garfinkel, H (1967) *Studies in ethnomethodology.* Cambridge: Polity Press.

Gee, J (1990) *Social linguistics and literacies: Ideology in discourses.* London: Falmer.

—— (1999) *An introduction to discourse analysis. Theory and methods.* New York: Routledge.

Ghosh, D and Muecke, S (2007) Introduction: Oceanic cultural studies. In D Ghosh and S Muecke (eds) *Cultures of trade: Indian Ocean exchanges.* Newcastle: Cambridge Scholars Publishing, pp. 1–8.

Gibson, C, and Connell, J (2005) *Music and tourism: On the road again.* Clevedon, UK: Channel View Publications.

Giddens, A (1979) *Central problems in social theory: Action, structure and contradiction in social analysis.* Berkeley: University of California Press.

Gilroy, P (1993) *The Black Atlantic: Modernity and double consciousness.* London: Verso.

Gluck, M (2003) Wine language: Useful idiom or idiot-speak? In J Aitchison and D Lewis (eds) *New media language.* London: Routledge, pp. 107–15.

Goffman, E (1969) *Strategic interaction.* Philadelphia, PA: University of Pennsylvania Press.

Grabe, W and Kaplan, B (1996) *Theory and practice of writing: An applied linguistic perspective.* London: Longman.

Graham, P, Luke, C and Luke, A (2007) Globalization, corporatism, and critical language education. *International Multilingual Research Journal*, 1 (1).

Green, B (2009) The primacy of practice and the problem of representation. In B Green (ed.) *Understanding and researching professional practice*. Rotterdam: Sense Publishers, pp. 39–54.

Grierson, G (1907) Languages. In W W Hunter (ed.) *The imperial gazetteer of India, vol. 1: The Indian Empire – descriptive* (new edition). Oxford: Clarendon Press, pp. 349–401.

Gulson, K and Symes, C (2007a) Knowing one's place: space, theory, education. *Critical Studies in Education*, 48(1), 97–110.

—— and — (2007b) *Spatial theories of education: Policy and geography matters*. New York: Routledge.

Hacking, I (2004) Between Michel Foucault and Erving Goffman: between discourse in the abstract and face-to-face interaction. *Economy and Society*, 33(3), 277–302.

Hadi-Tabassum, S (2006) *Language, space and power: A critical look at bilingual education*. Clevedon: Multilingual Matters.

Hall, J K, Cheng, An and Carlson, M (2006) Reconceptualizing multicompetence as a theory of language knowledge. *Applied Linguistics*, 27(2), 220–40.

Halliday, M A K (1978) *Language as social semiotic: The social interpretation of language and meaning*. London: Edward Arnold.

—— (2001) New ways of meaning: The challenge to applied linguistics. In A Fill and P Mühlhäusler (eds) *The ecolinguistics reader: Language, ecology and environment*. London: Continuum, pp. 175–202.

—— (2002) *Applied linguistics as an evolving theme*. Plenary address to the International Association of Applied Linguistics. Singapore, December.

Handsfield, L (2002) Teacher agency and double agents: Reconceptualizing linguistic genocide in education. Essay review of T Skutnabb-Kangas (2000) *Linguistic genocide in education – or worldwide diversity and human rights?* Mahwah, NJ: Lawrence Erlbaum, *Harvard Educational Review*, 72(4), 542–60.

Hansen, N (2005) *Rash*. Melbourne: Mutiny Media (DVD).

Hardt, M and Negri, A (2000) *Empire*. Cambridge, MA: Harvard University Press.

Harris, R (1988) *Language, Saussure and Wittgenstein: How to play games with words*. London: Routledge.

—— (1990) On redefining linguistics. In H Davis and T Taylor (eds) *Redefining linguistics*. London: Routledge, pp. 18–52.

—— (1998) *Introduction to integrational linguistics*. Oxford: Pergamon.

Haugen, E (1972) *The ecology of language: Essays by Einar Haugen* (Edited by A S Dil). Stanford, CA: Stanford University Press.

Heath, S B (1983) *Ways with words: Language, life, and work on communities and classrooms*. Cambridge: Cambridge University Press.

Heidegger, M and Fink, E (1993) *Heraclitus seminar* (Trans Charles Seibert). Evanston, IL: Northwestern University Press.

Heller, M and Duchêne, A (2007) Discourses of endangerment: Sociolinguistics, globalization and social order. In A Duchêne and M Heller (eds) *Discourses of endangerment: Ideology and interest in the defence of languages*. London: Continuum, pp. 1–13.

Heryanto, A (2007) Then there were languages: Bahasa Indonesia was one among many. In S Makoni and A Pennycook (eds) *Disinventing and reconstituting languages*. Clevedon: Multilingual Matters, pp. 42–61.

Higgins, C (2009) *English as a local language: Post-colonial identities and multilingual practices.* Bristol: Multilingual Matters.

Hogan, P (2003) Teaching and learning as a way of life. *Journal of Philosophy of Education,* 37(2), 207–23.

Holborow, M (1999) *The politics of English: A Marxist view of language.* London: Sage.

Holmes, J and Meyerhoff, M (1999) The community of practice: Theories and methodologies in language and gender research. *Language in Society,* 28, 173–83.

Hopper, P (1998) Emergent grammar. In M. Tomasello (ed.) *The new psychology of language.* Mahwah, NJ: Lawrence Erlbaum, pp.155–75.

Hoy, D C (2004) *Critical resistance: From poststructuralism to post-critique.* Cambridge, MA: The MIT Press.

Huggan, G (1997) (Post)Colonialism, anthropology, and the magic of mimesis. *Cultural Critique,* 38 (Winter), 91–106.

Hutton, C (1999) *Linguistics and the Third Reich: Mother-tongue fascism, race and the science of language.* London: Routledge.

Inoue, M (2004) Introduction: Temporality and historicity in and through linguistic ideology. *Journal of Linguistic Anthropology,* 14(1), 1–5.

Irvine, J (1989) When talk isn't cheap: Language and political economy. *American Ethnologist,* 16, 248–67.

Irvine, J and Gal, S (2000) Language ideology and linguistic differentiation. In Paul V Kroskrity (ed.) *Regimes of language: Ideologies, politics and identities.* Santa Fe, NM: School of American Research Press, pp. 35–85.

Iyer, L (2005) Logos and difference: Blanchot, Heidegger, Heraclitus. *Parallax* 11(2), 14–24.

Jacquemet, M (2005) Transidiomatic practices: Language and power in the age of globalization. *Language and Communication,* 25, 257–77.

Jenkins, J (2000) *The phonology of English as an international language.* Oxford: Oxford University Press.

—— (2003) *World Englishes: A resource book for students.* London: Routledge.

Jinman, R (2007) Street art moves to a posh new hang-out. *Sydney Morning Herald,* 9 April, p. 11.

Jørgensen, J N (2008a) Polylingual languaging around and among children and adolescents. *International Journal of Multilingualism,* 5(3), 161–76.

—— (2008b) Urban wall writing. *International Journal of Multilingualism,* 5(3), 237–52.

Kachru, B (2005) *Asian Englishes: Beyond the canon.* Hong Kong: Hong Kong University Press.

Kachru, Y and Nelson, C (2006) *World Englishes in Asian contexts.* Hong Kong: Hong Kong University Press.

Kahn, C (1979) *The art and thought of Heraclitus: Fragments with translation and commentary.* Cambridge: Cambridge University Press.

Kandiah, T (1998) Epiphanies of the deathless native users' manifold avatars: A post-colonial perspective on the native-speaker. In Rajendra Singh (ed.) *The native speaker: Multilingual perspectives.* New Delhi: Sage Publications, pp. 79–110.

Kaya, Ayhan (2001) *'Sicher in Kreuzberg': Constructing diasporas: Turkish hip-hop youth in Berlin.* Bielefeld: Transcript Verlag.

Kearney, R (1988) *The wake of imagination.* Minneapolis: University of Minnesota Press.

Kelly, J (2006) 24-hour attack on graffiti. *Herald Sun,* 15 March.

Kemmis, S (2009) Understanding professional practice: A synoptic framework. In B Green (ed.) *Understanding and researching professional practice.* Rotterdam: Sense Publishers, pp. 19–38.

Kibbee, D (2003) Language policy and linguistic theory. In J Maurais and M Morris (eds) *Languages in a globalizing world.* Cambridge: Cambridge University Press, pp. 47–57.

Kramsch, C (2005) Post 9/11: Foreign languages between knowledge and power. *Applied Linguistics,* 26 (2), 545–67.

—— (2006) The traffic in meaning. *Asia Pacific Journal of Education,* 26(1), 99–104.

Kress, G (2003) *Literacy in the new media age.* London: Routledge.

Kress, G and Van Leeuwen, T (2001) *Multimodal discourse: The modes and media of contemporary communication.* London: Arnold.

Krishnaswamy, N and Burde, A (1998) *The politics of Indians' English: Linguistic colonialism and the expanding English empire.* Delhi: Oxford University Press.

Kroskrity (2000) Regimenting languages: Language ideological perspectives. In Paul V Kroskrity (ed.) *Regimes of language: Ideologies, politics and identities,* Santa Fe, NM: School of American Research Press, pp. 1–34.

Kulick, D and Stroud, C (1993) Conceptions and uses of literacy in a Papua New Guinean village. In B Street (ed.) *Cross-cultural approaches to literacy.* Cambridge: Cambridge University Press, pp. 30–61.

Latour, B (1999) *Pandora's hope: Essays on the reality of science studies.* Cambridge, MA: Harvard University Press.

—— (2005) *Reassembling the social: An introduction to actor-network theory.* Oxford: Oxford University Press.

Lave, J and Wenger, E (1991) *Situated learning: Legitimate peripheral participation.* Cambridge: Cambridge University Press.

Leather, J and van Dam, J (2003) Towards an ecology of language acquisition. In J Leather and J van Dam (eds) *Ecology of language acquisition,* Dordrecht: Kluwer Academic Publishers, pp. 1–29.

Lee, L, Seddon, G and Stephens, F (1976) *Stained glass.* London: Mitchell Beasley.

Lefebvre, H (1991) *The production of space.* (Trans D. Nicholson-Smith *La production de l'espace,* 1974). Oxford: Blackwell.

Liddicoat, A (2007) *An introduction to conversation analysis.* London: Continuum.

Liddicoat, A and Baldauf, R (2008) Language planning in local contexts: Agents, contexts and interactions. In A Liddicoat and R Baldauf (eds) *Language planning and policy: Language planning in local contexts.* Clevedon: Multilingual Matters, pp. 3–17.

Lin, A (2000) Lively children trapped in an island of disadvantage: Verbal play of Cantonese working-class schoolboys in Hong Kong. *International Journal of the Sociology of Language,* 143, 63–83.

—— (2009) 'Respect for Da Chopstick Hip Hop': The politics, poetics, and pedagogy of Cantonese verbal art in Hong Kong. In H S Alim, A Ibrahim and A Pennycook (eds) *Global linguistic flows: Hip Hop cultures, youth identities, and the politics of language.* New York: Routledge, pp. 159–77.

Lin, A, Wang, W, Akamatsu, N and Riazi, A M (2002) Appropriating English, expanding identities, and re-visioning the field: from TESOL to teaching English for glocalized communication (TEGCOM). *Journal of Language, Identity, and Education,* 1(4), 295–316.

Lobkowicz, N (1967) *Theory and practice: History of a concept from Aristotle to Marx.* Notre Dame, IN: University of Notre Dame Press.

Local Noise *Localnoise.net.au* (last accessed 01 June 2009).

Long, M H (2006) *Problems in SLA*. Mahwah, NJ: Lawrence Erlbaum.

Luk, J (2005) Voicing the 'self' through an 'other' language: Exploring communicative language teaching for global communication. In S Canagarajah (ed.) *Reclaiming the local in language policy and practice*. Mahwah, NJ: Lawrence Erlbaum, pp. 247–68.

Luke, A (1996) Genres of power? Literacy education and the production of capital. In R. Hassan and G. Williams (eds), *Literacy in society*. London: Longman, pp. 308–38.

—— (2004) On the material consequences of literacy. *Language and Education*, 18(4), 331–35.

Lynch, B (1996) *Language program evaluation: Theory and practice*. Cambridge: Cambridge University Press.

Ma, E K W (2002) Translocal spatiality. *International Journal of Cultural Studies*, 5(2), 131–52.

MacIntyre, A (2007 [1981]) *After virtue: A study in moral theory* (3rd edition) (first edition 1981). London: Duckworth.

MacIntyre, A and Dunne, J (2002) Alasdair MacIntyre on education: in dialogue with Joseph Dunne. *Journal of Philosophy of Education*, 36(1), 1–19.

Maffi, L (2000) Linguistic and biological diversity: The inextricable link. In R Phillipson (ed.) *Rights to language: Equity, power and education*, Mahwah, NJ: Lawrence Erlbaum, pp. 17–22.

Maher, J (2005) Metroethnicity, language, and the principle of cool. *International Journal of the Sociology of Language*, 175/176, 83–102.

Makoni, S and Makoni, B (2010) Multilingual discourses on wheels and public English in Africa: A case for 'vague linguistique'. In J Maybin and J Swann (eds) *The Routledge companion to English language studies*. London: Routledge, pp. 258–70.

Makoni, S and Pennycook, A (2005) Disinventing and (re)constituting languages. *Critical Inquiry in Language Studies*, 2(2), 137–56.

—— (2007) Disinventing and reconstituting languages. In S Makoni and A Pennycook (eds) *Disinventing and reconstituting languages*. Clevedon: Multilingual Matters, 1–41.

Malcolm, I G (2000) Aboriginal English: From contact variety to social dialect. In Jeff Siegel (ed.) *Processes of language contact: Studies from Australia and the South Pacific*, Montreal: Fides, pp. 123–44.

Maldonado-Torres, N (2007) On the coloniality of being. *Cultural Studies*, 21(2), 240–70.

Malinowski, D (2009) Authorship in the linguistic landscape: A multimodal-performative view. In E Shohamy and D Gorter (eds) (2009) *Linguistic landscape: Expanding the scenery*. London: Routledge, pp. 107–25.

Martin, J (1993) A contextual theory of language. In B Cope and M Kalantzis (eds) *The powers of literacy: A genre approach to teaching writing*. London: The Falmer Press, pp. 116–36.

Martin, L (1986) 'Eskimo words for snow': A case study in the genesis and decay of an anthropological example, *American Anthropologist*, 88(2), 418–23.

Marx, K (2000 [1845]) *Selected Writings* (Edited by David McLellan, 2nd edition). [Oxford: Oxford University Press.

Massey, D (1992) Politics and space/time. *New Left Review*, 196, 65–84.

—— (1994) *Space, place and gender*. Cambridge: Polity Press.

May, J and Thrift, N (2001) Introduction. In J May and N Thrift (eds) *Timespace: Geographies of temporality*. London: Routledge, pp. 1–46.

May, S (2001) *Language and minority rights: Ethnicity, nationalism and the politics of language*. Harlow: Longman.

Metcalf, T (1995) *Ideologies of the Raj.* Cambridge: Cambridge University Press.

Mignolo, W (2000) *Local histories/global designs: Coloniality, subaltern knowledges and border thinking,* Princeton, NJ: Princeton University Press.

Miller, C L (2008) *The French Atlantic Triangle: Literature and culture of the slave trade.* Durham, NC: Duke University Press.

Miller, P (DJ Spooky (aka That Subliminal Kid)) 2004. *Rhythm science.* Cambridge, MA: MIT Press.

Milon, A (2002) Tags and murals in France: A city's face or a natural landscape? In A-P Durand (ed.), *Black, Blanc, Beur: Rap music and hip-hop culture in the Francophone world.* Lanham, MD: The Scarecrow Press, pp. 87–98.

Minister for Police and Emergency Services (2005) Media release. Last accessed 10 May 2007 www.legislation.vic.gov.au/domino/Web_Notes/newmedia.nsf/b0222c68 d27626e2ca256c8c001a3d2d/0e47076ab0768debca2570bf007f8989!OpenDocument.

Modan, G (2007) *Turf wars: Discourse, diversity and the politics of place.* Oxford: Blackwell.

Møller, J S (2008) Polylingual performance among Turkish-Danes in late-modern Copenhagen. *International Journal of Multilingualism,* 5(3), 217–36.

Morgan, M (2001) 'Nuthin' but a G thang': Grammar and ideology in Hip Hop identity. In S Lanehart (ed.) *Sociocultural and historical contexts of African American English.* Philadelphia, PA: John Benjamins,pp. 187–209.

Moss, G (2007) *Literacy and gender: Researching texts, contexts and readers.* London: Routledge.

Mufwene, S (2001) *The ecology of language evolution.* Cambridge: Cambridge University Press.

—— (2004) Language birth and death. *Annual Review of Anthropology,* 33, 201–22.

Muehlmann, S (2007) Defending diversity: Staking out a common global interest? In A Duchêne and M Heller (eds) *Discourses of endangerment: Ideology and interest in the defence of languages.* London: Continuum, pp. 14–34.

Mühlhäusler, P (1996) *Linguistic ecology: Language change and linguistic imperialism in the Pacific region.* London: Routledge.

—— (2000) Language planning and language ecology. *Current Issues in Language Planning,* 1(3), 306–67.

—— (2001) Babel revisited. In Alwin Fill and Peter Mühlhäusler (eds) *The ecolinguistics reader: Language, ecology and environment.* London: Continuum, pp. 159–64.

—— (2003) English as an exotic language. In Christian Mair (ed.) *The politics of English as a world language: New horizons in postcolonial cultural studies,* Amsterdam: Rodopi, pp. 67–86.

Munro, I (2008) Down Mexico way. *Sydney Morning Herald,* weekend edition, 27–28 September, p. 27.

Myers, G (2005) Applied linguists and institutions of opinion. *Applied Linguistics,* 26(4), 527–44.

Nagai, Y and Lister, R (2003) What is our culture? What is our language? Dialogue towards the maintenance of indigenous culture and language in Papua New Guinea. *Language and Education,* 17(2), 87–104.

Nakata, M (1999) History, cultural diversity and English language teaching. In Peter Wignell (ed.) *Double power: English literacy and indigenous education,* Canberra: NLLIA, pp. 5–22.

—— (2007) *Disciplining the savages: Savaging the disciplines.* Canberra: Aboriginal Studies Press.

Nettle, D and Romaine, S (2000) *Vanishing voices: The extinction of the world's languages.* Oxford: Oxford University Press.

Nevile, M (2008) Overlapping talk as evidence of trouble in airline pilots' work. In V K Bhatia, J Flowerdew and R Jones (eds) *Advances in discourse studies.* London: Routledge, pp. 36–50.

Noddings, N (2003) Is teaching a practice? *Journal of Philosophy of Education,* 37(2), 241–51.

North, S (2005) Disciplinary variation in the use of theme in undergraduate essays. *Applied Linguistics,* 26(3), 431–52.

Nyhan, B (2006) Collective reflection for excellence in work organizations: An ethical 'community of practice' perspective on reflection. In D Boud, P Cressey, and P Docherty (eds) *Productive reflection: Learning for changing organizations.* London: Routledge, pp. 133–45.

Omoniyi, T (2009) 'So I choose to do Am Naija style': Hip-Hop, language, and postcolonial identities. In H S Alim, A Ibrahim and A Pennycook (eds) *Global linguistic flows: Hip Hop cultures, youth identities, and the politics of language.* New York: Routledge, pp. 113–35.

Otsuji, E and Pennycook, A (2010) Metrolingualism: Fixity, fluidity and language in flux. *International Journal of Multilingualism,* 7.

Paltridge, B (2006) *Discourse analysis: An introduction.* London: Continuum.

Parakrama, A (1995) *De-hegemonizing language standards: Learning from (post)colonial Englishes about 'English'.* Basingstoke: Macmillan.

Pardue, D (2004) 'Writing in the margins': Brazilian hip-hop as an educational project. *Anthropology and Education,* 35(4), 411–32.

Pennycook, A (1994) *The cultural politics of English as an international language.* Harlow: Longman.

—— (1996) Borrowing others' words: Text, ownership, memory and plagiarism. *TESOL Quarterly,* 30(2), 201–30.

—— (2001) *Critical applied linguistics: A critical introduction.* Mahwah, NJ: Lawrence Erlbaum.

—— (2002) Language and linguistics/ Discourse and disciplinarity. In C Barron, N Bruce and D Nunan (eds) (2002) *Knowledge and discourse: Towards an ecology of language.* London: Longman/Pearson, pp. 13–27.

—— (2004) Language policy and the ecological turn. *Language Policy,* 3, 213–39.

—— (2006) Language policy and postmodernism. In T Ricento (ed.) *An introduction to language policy: Theory and method.* London: Blackwell, 60–76.

—— (2007a) *Global Englishes and transcultural flows.* London: Routledge.

—— (2007b) The myth of English as an international language. In S Makoni and A Pennycook (eds) *Disinventing and reconstituting languages.* Clevedon: Multilingual Matters, pp. 90–115.

—— (2007c) Language, localization and the real: Hip-hop and the global spread of authenticity. *Journal of Language, Identity and Education,* 6(2) 101–16.

—— (2008) English as a language always in translation. *European Journal of English Studies,* 12(1), 33–47.

—— (2009a) Plurilithic Englishes: Towards a 3D model. In K Murata and J Jenkins (eds) *Global Englishes in Asian contexts: Current and future debates.* Palgrave-Macmillan, pp. 194–207.

—— (2009b) Linguistic landscapes and the transgressive semiotics of graffiti. In E Shohamy and D Gorter (eds) *Linguistic Landscape: Expanding the scenery*. London: Routledge, pp. 302–312.

—— (in press a) Spatial narrations: Graffscapes and city souls. In A Jaworski and C Thurlow (eds) *Semiotic Landscapes: Language, Image, Space*. London: Continuum.

—— (in press b) Rethinking origins and localization in global englishes. In T Omoniyi and M Saxena (eds) *Contending with globalization in World Englishes*. Bristol: Multilingual Matters.

Pennycook, A and Makoni, S (2005) The modern mission: the language effects of Christianity. *Journal of Language, Identity and Education*, 4(2), 137–55.

Pennycook, A and Mitchell, T (2009) Hip hop as dusty foot philosophy. Engaging locality. In S Alim, A Ibrahim and A Pennycook (2009) *Global linguistic flows: Hip Hop cultures, youth identities and the politics of language*. New York: Routledge, pp. 25–42.

Perry, I (2004) *Prophets of the hood: Politics and poetics in hip hop*. Durham, NC: Duke University Press.

Perullo, A and Fenn, J (2003) Language ideologies, choices, and practices in East African hip hop. In H Berger and M Carroll (eds) *Global pop, local language*. Jackson: University Press of Mississippi, pp. 19–51.

Phillipson, R (1992) *Linguistic imperialism*. Oxford: Oxford University Press.

—— (2008) The linguistic imperialism of neoliberal empire. *Critical Inquiry in Language Studies*, 5(1), 1–43.

Piller, I and Takahashi, K (2006) A passion for English: Desire and the language market. In A Pavlenko (ed.) *Bilingual minds: Emotional experience, expression and representation*, Clevedon: Multilingual Matters, pp. 59–83.

Potter, R (1995) *Spectacular vernaculars: Hip-hop and the politics of postmodernism*. Albany, NY: State University of New York Press.

Poynton, C (1993) Grammar, language and the social: poststructuralism and systemic-functional linguistics. *Social Semiotics*, 3(1), 1–21.

Pullum, G K (1989) The great Eskimo vocabulary hoax, *Natural Language and Linguistic Theory*, 7, 275–81.

Radhakrishnan, R (2007) Globality is not worldliness. In R Radhakrishnan, Kishori Nayak, R Shashidhar, Ravishankar Rao Parinitha, and D R Shashidhara (eds) *Theory as variation*. New Delhi: Pencraft International, pp. 313–28.

Rahn, J (2002) *Painting without permission: Hip-hop graffiti subculture*. Westport, CT: Bergin and Garvey.

Rajagopalan, K (1999) Of EFL teachers, conscience and cowardice. *ELT Journal*, 53/3, 200–206.

—— (2004) The concept of 'World English' and its implications for ELT. *ELT Journal*, 58(2), 111–17.

Ramanathan, V (2002) *The politics of TESOL education*. New York: Routledge.

Rampton, B (1995) *Crossing: Language and ethnicity among adolescents*. London: Longman.

—— (2006) *Language in late modernity: Interaction in an urban school*. Cambridge: Cambridge University Press.

—— (2009) Interaction ritual and not just artful performance in crossing and stylization. *Language in Society*, 38, 149–76.

Rappa, A and Wee, L (2006) *Language policy and modernity in Southeast Asia: Malaysia, the Philippines, Singapore and Thailand*. Springer.

Reckwitz, A (2002) Towards a theory of social practices: A development in culturalist theorizing. *European Journal of Social Theory*, 5(2), 243–63.

Rice, J (2003) The 1963 hip-hop machine: Hip-hop pedagogy as composition. *College Composition and Communication*, 54(3), 453–71.

Ricento, T (2000) Historical and theoretical perspectives in language policy and planning. In Thomas Ricento (ed.) *Ideology, politics and language policies: Focus on English*, Amsterdam: John Benjamins, pp. 9–24.

Robbins, J (2001) God is nothing but talk: Modernity, language, and prayer in a Papua New Guinea Society. *American Anthropologist*, 103(4), 901–12.

Romaine, S (1994) *Language in society: An introduction to sociolinguistics*. Oxford: Oxford University Press.

Rouse, J (2001) Two concepts of practices. In T Schatzki, K Knorr Cetina and E von Savigny (eds) *The practice turn in contemporary theory*. London, Routledge, pp. 189–98.

Rubdy, R and Saraceni, M (2006) Introduction. In Rubdy, R and M Saraceni (eds) *English in the world: Global rules, global roles*. London: Continuum, pp. 5–16.

—— and — (eds) 2006. *English in the world: Global rules, global roles*. London: Continuum.

Sacks, H, Schegloff, E A and Jefferson, G (1974) A simplest systematics for the organization of turn-taking for conversation. *Language*, 50, 696–735.

Said, E (1983) *The world, the text and the critic*. Cambridge, MA: Harvard University Press.

—— (2004) *Power, politics and culture: Interviews with Edward Said*. (Edited and with an Introduction by Gauri Viswanathan). London: Bloomsbury.

Schama, S (1995) *Landscape and memory*. New York: Alfred Knopf.

Schatzki, T (1996) *Social practices: A Wittgensteinian approach to human activity and the social*. Cambridge: Cambridge University Press.

—— (2001) Introduction: practice theory. In T Schatzki, K Knorr Cetina and E von Savigny (eds) *The practice turn in contemporary theory*. London, Routledge, 1–14.

—— (2002) *The site of the social: A philosophical account of the constitution of social life and change*. University Park, PA: Pennsylvania State University Press.

Schegloff, M (1992) Repair after next turn: The last structurally provided defense of intersubjectivity in conversation. *American Journal of Sociology*, 97(5), 1295–1345.

Schieffelin, B (2000) Introducing Kaluli literacy: A chronology of influences. In P Kroskrity (ed.) *Regimes of language: Ideologies, politics and identities*. Santa Fe, NM: School of American Research Press, pp. 293–327.

Schleppergrell, M (2001) What makes a grammar green? A reply to Goatly. In Alwin Fill and Peter Mühlhäusler (eds) *The ecolinguistics reader: Language, ecology and environment*. London: Continuum, pp. 226–28.

Scollon, R and Scollon, S W (2003) *Discourses in place: Language in the material world*. London: Routledge.

Scott, D (1999) *Refashioning futures: Criticism after postcoloniality*. Princeton, NJ: Princeton University Press.

Scott, J (1985) *Weapons of the weak: Everyday forms of peasant resistance*. New Haven: Yale University Press.

—— (1990) *Domination and the arts of resistance: Hidden transcripts*. New Haven: Yale University Press.

Scribner, S and Cole, M (1981) *The psychology of literacy*. Cambridge, MA: Harvard University Press.

Seargeant, P (2009) *The idea of English in Japan: Ideology and the evolution of a global language*. Bristol: Multilingual Matters.

Seidlhofer, B (2001) Closing a conceptual gap: The case for a description of English as a lingua franca. *International Review of Applied Linguistics*, 11(2), 133–58.

—— (ed.) (2003) *Controversies in applied linguistics*. Oxford: Oxford University Press.

Shohamy, E (2001) *The power of tests: A critical perspective on the uses of language tests*. London: Longman.

—— (2006) *Language policy: Hidden agendas and new approaches*. London: Routledge.

Shohamy, E and Gorter, D (2009) Introduction. In E Shohamy and D Gorter (eds) (2009) *Linguistic landscape: Expanding the scenery*. London: Routledge, pp. 1–10.

—— and —— (eds) (2009) *Linguistic landscape: Expanding the scenery*. London: Routledge.

Shonibare, Yinka (2008) MBE interview www.ngv.vic.gov.au/crossingborders/interview/yinka_interview.html.

Shusterman, R (2000) *Performing live: Aesthetic alternatives for the ends of art*. Ithaca, NY: Cornell University Press.

Silverstein, M (2003) Indexical order and the dialectics of sociolinguistic life. *Language and Communication*, 23, 193–229.

Simon, R (1992) *Teaching against the grain: Essays towards a pedagogy of possibility*. Boston: Bergin & Garvey.

Simpson, P (2004) *Stylistics*. London: Routledge.

Skutnabb-Kangas, T (2000) *Linguistic genocide in education – or worldwide diversity and human rights*? Mahwah, NJ: Lawrence Erlbaum.

—— (2003) Linguistic diversity and biodiversity: The threat from killer languages. In Christian Mair (ed.) *The politics of English as a world language: New horizons in postcolonial cultural studies*, Amsterdam: Rodopi, pp. 31–52.

Smallman, J and Nyman, C (2005) *Stencil graffiti capital: Melbourne*. New York: Mark Batty.

Soja, E (1989) *Postmodern geographies: The reassertion of space in critical social theory*. London: Verso.

—— (1996) *Thirdspace: Journeys to Los Angeles and real-and-imagined places*. Oxford: Blackwell.

Sonntag, S (2003) *The local politics of global English: Case studies in linguistic globalization*. Lanham, MD: Lexington Books.

SSHRC (2009) Social Sciences and Humanities Research Council of Canada (SSHRC)/ Conseil de recherches en sciences humaines du Canada (CRSH), www.SSHRC.ca. Accessed 01 June 2009.

Steffensen, S V (2007) Language, ecology and society: An introduction to dialectical linguistics. In J C Bang, J Døør, S V Steffensen and J Nash (eds) *Language, ecology and society: A dialectical approach*. London: Continuum, pp. 3–31.

Steiner, G (1975) *After Babel*. Oxford: Oxford University Press.

Sutherland, W (2003) Parallel extinction risk and global distribution of languages. *Nature*, 423, 15 May, 276–79.

Swales, J (2000) Languages for specific purposes. *Annual Review of Applied Linguistics*, 20, 59–76.

Swan, M (2005) Legislation by hypothesis: The case of task-based instruction. *Applied Linguistics*, 26(3), 276–301.

Swedenburg, T (2001) Islamic hip-hop vs Islamophobia. In T Mitchell (ed.) *Global noise: Rap and hip-hop outside the USA*. Middletown, CT: Wesleyan University Press, pp. 57–85.

Swidler, A (2001) What anchors cultural practices. In T Schatzki, K Knorr Cetina and E von Savigny (eds) *The practice turn in contemporary theory.* London, Routledge, pp. 74–92.

Tan, P and Rubdy, R (2008) *Language as commodity: Global structures, local market-places.* New York: Continuum.

Tannen, D (1989) *Talking Voices: Repetition, dialogue and imagery in conversational discourse.* Cambridge: Cambridge University Press.

Taussig, M (1993) *Mimesis and alterity: A particular history of the senses.* New York: Routledge.

Thompson, C and Pennycook, A (2008) Intertextuality in the transcultural contact zone. In R M Howard and A Robillard (eds) *Pluralizing plagiarism: Identities, contexts, pedagogies.* Boynton/Cook.

Thorne, S and Lantolf, J (2007) A linguistics of communicative activity. In S Makoni and A Pennycook (eds) *Disinventing and reconstituting languages.* Clevedon: Multilingual Matters, pp. 170–95.

Thrift, N (2007) *Non-representational theory: Space|politics|affect.* London: Routledge.

Thurlow, C and Aiello, G (2007) National pride, global capital: A social semiotic analysis of transnational visual branding in the airline industry. *Visual Communication*, 6(3), 305–44.

Toolan, M (2003) An integrational linguistic view of coming into language. In J Leather and J van Dam (eds) *Ecology of Language Acquisition*, Dordrecht: Kluwer Academic Publishers, pp. 123–39.

Toulmin, S (1999) Knowledge as shared procedures. In Y Engestrom, R Miettinen and R Punamaki (eds) *Perspectives on action theory.* Cambridge: Cambridge University Press.

Tupas, R (2006) Standard Englishes, pedagogical paradigms and conditions of (im) possibility. In R Rubdy and M Saraceni (eds) *English in the world: Global rules, global roles.* London: Continuum, pp. 169–85.

Unesco – Terralingua – World Wide Fund for Nature (Principal authors: Tove Skutnabb-Kangas, Luisa Maffi, David Harmon) (2003) *Sharing a world of difference: The earth's linguistic, cultural, and biological diversity.* Paris: UNESCO.

Urla, J (2001) 'We are all Malcolm X!' Negu Gorriak, Hip-Hop, and the Basque political imaginary. In Tony Mitchell (ed.) *Global noise: Rap and hip-hop outside the USA.* Middletown, CT: Wesleyan University Press, pp. 171–93.

Urry, J (1995) *Consuming places.* London: Routledge.

—— (2002) *The tourist gaze* (2nd edition). London: Sage.

—— (2005) The 'consuming' of place. In A Jaworski and A Pritchard (eds) *Discourse, communication and tourism.* Clevedon: Channel View Publications, pp. 19–27.

Van Leer, L (2004) *The ecology and semiotics of language learning: A sociocultural perspective.* Dordrecht: Kluwer Academic Publishers.

Van Leeuwen, T (2005) *Introducing social semiotics.* London :Routledge.

—— (2008) *Discourse as practice: New tools for critical discourse analysis.* Oxford: Oxford University Press.

Van Treeck, B (2003) Styles – Typografie als Mittel zur Identitätsbildung. In J Androutsopoulos (ed.) *HipHop: Globale Kultur – Lokale Praktiken.* Bielefeld: Transcript Verlag, pp. 102–10.

Varma, Sivadas (2006) Jumbos driving Tripunithuraites crazy. *New Indian Express,* 22 December, p. 3.

Venn, C (2000) *Occidentalism: Modernity and subjectivity.* London: Sage.

Vintage Cellars (2009) *Cellar Press,* 98, 18 May–14 June.

Vološinov, V N (1973/1929) *Marxism and the philosophy of language.* (Trans Ladislav Matejka) Cambridge, MA: Harvard University Press.

Wajnryb, R (2009) To boldly venture into an adverbial quagmire. *Sydney Morning Herald Spectrum,* 18–19 April, p. 28.

Walcott, R (1997) *Black like who?* Toronto: Insomniac Press.

Wee, L (2005) Intra-language discrimination and linguistic human rights: The case of singlish. *Applied Linguistics,* 26(1), 48–69.

Wenger, E (1998) *Communities of practice: Learning, meaning, and identity.* Cambridge: Cambridge University Press.

White, A (2001) *Philippine coral reefs: A natural history guide,* 2nd edition. Manila: Bookmark Inc. and Sulu Fund for Marine Conservation Foundation.

Widdowson, H G (1984) *Explorations in applied linguistics 2.* Oxford: Oxford University Press.

—— (2008) Language creativity and the poetic function. A response to Swann and Maybin (2007) *Applied Linguistics,* 29(3), 503–9.

Williams, G (1992) *Sociolinguistics: A sociological critique.* London: Routledge.

Wittgenstein, (1963) *Philosophical investigations* (Trans G Anscombe *Philosophische Untersuchungen*). Oxford: Blackwell & Mott.

Woolard, K (2004) Is the past a foreign country? Time, language origins, and the nation in early modern Spain. *Journal of Linguistic Anthropology,* 14(1), 57–80.

Xie, P F, Osumare, H and Ibrahim, A (2007) Gazing the hood: Hip-Hop as tourism attraction. *Tourism Management,* 28(2), 452–60.

Young, R (1995) *Colonial desire: Hybridity in theory, culture and race.* London: Routledge.

Index